HEROES FROM THE ATTIC

A History of the 48th Surgical Hospital /
128th Evacuation Hospital
1941 - 1945

Photo by Kathleen Flynn

G. JESSE FLYNN

BUTLER BOOKS

LOUISVILLE

Author Jesse Flynn in 1999 retraced the steps of his parents and other members of the 48th/128th along Utah Beach. (Photo by Kathleen Flynn)

The reunion of the 48th/128th, September 1999, Louisville, KY. In the front row, left to right, are Doris "Britt" Simion, Gladys Flynn, Maurice Halverson, Marcus Duxbury, Gerhardt Herbolsheimer, and Edna Browning. Back row, left to right, are George Howe, Walter Larson, Agatha Griebel, Loren Butts, Martha Cameron, James Dick, George Willett, Gilbert Smith, Alvin Burrack, Fritz Griebel, and Lawrence Inderrieden. *(Photo courtesy G. Jesse Flynn)*

DEDICATION

Utah Beach, Normandy, France was wide and empty that cool day in May, 1999. Walking along, I recounted the many stories and documents that I'd reviewed in the previous year about the 48th/128th Evacuation Hospital. Boutteville, the first staging area for the 128th after D-Day, was five miles inland. What was it like to be there on the night of June 10, 1944? A few miles further west were St. Lo and Falaise, sites of epic battles yet to be fought. What had happened to the French baby, Aime Consfnufeory Biene, born in the MASH tent June 22, 1944? He now must be almost sixty years old. Where is the captured 18 year-old German patient who worried about his family home in Hamburg? Had his home been bombed and his family killed, as he feared?

The medical unit of some three hundred personnel had previously served near the front lines in the campaigns in Algeria, Tunisia and Sicily. They had been the first and only hospital unit in American Army history to land with invasion troops on D-Day in North Africa. By the time the war in Europe ended less than a year later, they had treated almost 70,000 American casualties. The total United States Armed Forces wounded from Pearl Harbor to the end of the war was 670, 846. This statistic is a tribute to the magnitude of the effort required from this small group of soldiers.

I had traveled to Cefalu, Sicily, Aachen, Germany and many other small towns in the European Theatre of World War II that had been temporary homes to the 48th/128th. My travels represented my quest to understand, to some small degree, the scope of the work and sacrifice my parents and their comrades had undertaken six decades before. George Howe, Doris Simion, Marcus Duxbury and many others slept on the beaches and cow pastures of these towns, some five to six years before my birth. The history in these places was fading just as surely as the photos I had discovered in an attic trunk.

In September 1999, at my invitation, veterans of the 48th/128th came to Louisville, Kentucky for a reunion, moving slowly, some in wheelchairs. It was apparent that their story was not only incomplete, it was becoming a dim memory. During that reunion I became committed to chronicling their experiences during the war years. This book is my humble attempt to do just that.

I dedicate this effort to my parents—1st Lt. Gladys Martin and 1st Lt. John Flynn—and the rest of the soldiers, doctors and nurses who served with the 48th/128th from 1941 to 1945.

This group did not request a champion, nor did they need one. Their record stands for itself. They were unique in a generation of unique people. I salute them.

—G. Jesse Flynn

TABLE OF CONTENTS

INTRODUCTION

Unsettled is the best word to describe the world in the mid 1930s. Political and economic turmoil extended from Moscow to Tokyo. In Berlin, Adolph Hitler and the Nazis had seized leadership and were seeking to avenge the alleged crime of the Treaty of Versailles. That document, signed by the defeated Germans in 1919, granted large portions of Germany to France, Belgium, Denmark, and newly created states of Poland, Czechoslovakia, and Lithuania. It also provided for the forfeiture of all German colonies in Africa and the Pacific, plus reparation to the victors of most German domestic production for many years.

Russia was in the middle of a violent consolidation of power by the fanatical communist leader Joseph Stalin. Benito Mussolini, a renowned fascist, was firmly in control in Italy. General Francisco Franco was busy in Spain building an army that would eventually (with the assistance of Adolph Hitler) establish fascist control in Spain.

Japan had gained size in its empire in 1919 by claiming former German colonies in the Pacific. The warlords in control of the government were convinced that they would have little opposition in claiming parts of Manchuria, China, Korea and other territories in the Far East.

France, still exhausted from a titanic effort in World War I, was in the final stages of building a fortress extending from the Swiss border to Belgium. The "Maginot Line" was a series of defensive armored fixed positions connected by underground railroads along the border with Germany.

England was rebuilding its navy and trying to control its vast and restless colonies. She had no appetite for another conflict of the magnitude of The Great War.

The United States was in its third year of the "New Deal." Government spending on roads, dams, schools, tunnels and bridges provided work for the millions left jobless in the depression. The problems of countries separated from the United States by thousands of miles of water were of no concern to the average American.

By the late thirties, general peace and prosperity had returned to the world. The autobahns were being built in Germany, the Spanish civil war was almost over and it seemed the great nations had learned to talk as an alternative to war.

The year 1938 was a time of great hope and expectation in America. The Great Depression was over and the young people born between 1912 and 1920 were looking forward to a life of peace and prosperity. The war clouds in Europe had parted with the declaration of "Peace in our Time" made by British Prime Minister Neville Chamberlain following the signing of the Munich Accord. This long-term pact had been struck with Germany to secure "permanent" political boundaries in Europe and the threat of world war seemed to have passed.

Ed Rosenbaum had just completed medical school at the University of Nebraska and was accepted to a residency at the Mayo Clinic. Nineteen-year-old Gladys Martin was in her second year of nursing school in Kentucky. Walt Larson and Mayme Goky were planning to be married in Minnesota. James Dick of Los Angeles was in the eighth grade, enjoying his childhood in the southern California sun. Charles Thorsen, Oliver Sorlye, Gilbert Smith and Arnum Sorlie were working on farms in eastern South Dakota. Jodie Harmon was a twenty-year-old West Texan clearing brush on the family ranch near Robert Lee.

These Americans were typical of the youth in a country that had lived through the post World War I prosperity of the "roaring twenties" and the subsequent economic crash that led to the depression of the 1930s. They were optimistically looking forward to a life of freedom and opportunity, unaware that fate would bind them as comrades traveling the war-ravaged continents of Africa and Europe for a good portion of the next decade.

Within a year the climate in Europe had changed. Adolph Hitler had decided to press his claim on lands to the East that had been lost in World War I. The British and French responded with an ultimatum, and on September 1, 1939, World War II began as German forces invaded Poland. The Russians joined Germany in erasing the country of Poland from the map. By June of 1941 Germany had control of all of Western Europe with the exception of the British Isles. Hitler then turned his armies east again and attacked his former ally, Russia. One and a half million German soldiers advanced on three fronts. By December 6, 1941 Nazi troops were in the suburbs of Moscow.

The young Americans viewed these disturbing events through the prism of American politics. The vast Atlantic Ocean and the election of 1940 gave them assurances that whatever conflict occurred in far off Europe would not include the United States. Franklin Roosevelt had proclaimed, "Your boys are not going to be sent to foreign wars."

Something gone unnoticed by the average American was the expansion of the empire of Japan. The Japanese Empire had been expanding since the early 1930s. Manchuria, Korea and China were falling like dominos to the territorial needs of the emperor. In an effort to stem Japan's aggressive moves in the Far East, President Franklin Roosevelt embargoed all oil shipments to Japan beginning in the summer of 1941. The desperate reaction of the Japanese to this move was to plan an attack on American and British bases in Hawaii, Singapore and the Philippine Islands, all within a 24-hour period.

On December 7, 1941, hundreds of Japanese aircraft launched from aircraft carriers, bombed and destroyed a large part of the American Pacific Fleet at Pearl Harbor. War the young Americans had been avoiding was upon them. Initially it appeared not to be a European war but an isolated battle in the Pacific against a small island country. Events occurring several days later in Berlin dramatically changed the dynamics. On December 11, 1941, Nazi Germany declared war on the United States.

Within a four day period, America faced a two-front war and the requirement of a total national commitment of its youth and treasure.

The United States began from a "standing start." Its military ranked fourteenth in the world in numbers, behind Romania. New training facilities, war production factories and shipyards were established at a tremendous pace.

The need to strike back immediately contrasted with the woeful level of trained personnel. Nonetheless, the decision to attack in the European Theatre was made, and reserve units, cannibalized regular army units and a makeshift naval fleet were assembled in 1942 to attack and occupy French Colonial North Africa. The purpose of this action was to secure the southern coast of the Mediterranean Sea, protect the Suez Canal and take the pressure off our new Russian allies who were in a fight to the finish with the overwhelming bulk of the German Army.

In the spring and summer of 1942 young nurses and doctors with little or no military training were "fleshing out" American support units. Newly inducted enlisted men and draftees, some with no medical experience, were attached to the mobile hospitals. By August elements of the 48th Surgical Hospital were en route to England where they would form into one unit, then divide to support the Central Task Force of the North African Invasion landing on both sides of Oran, Algeria, on November 8, 1942.

I had the opportunity to meet and interview many of the personnel who were former members of the 48th/128th. This interaction occurred 54 years from the time they returned home. Ironically, I had spent my childhood with parents who were veterans of the 48th and had never discussed this most fascinating story.

This book will attempt to introduce you to the "old soldiers" as I met them and take you through the tears, laughter, horror and triumph that bonded them in their youth to a lifetime of comradeship.

—by G. Jesse Flynn

Cpl. Marcus Duxbury

Left to right: Gilbert Smith, Marcus Duxbury, Oliver Sorlye, and Floreine Duxbury, June 2001 at the Duxbury home, Salem, South Dakota. (Photo courtesy of G. Jesse Flynn)

CHAPTER ONE
THE OLD SOLDIERS

G. Jesse Flynn

HOWLING WIND AND SNOW came across the black plain and tossed our small rental car around like a toy. The drive from Sioux Falls to Salem, South Dakota (population 1,208) is only forty-five miles, but as we traveled that lonely road on the night of February 2, 2003, it seemed much further. Eighty-three-year-old "Gib" Smith and I were going to the Salem Funeral Home to pay our respects to Marcus Duxbury, who had died two days before. We had made a similar trek in 2001 to Canton, South Dakota for the funeral of Charlie Thorson.

As we drove, Gib and I talked about times that he, Charlie and Dux shared more than sixty years ago during the North African Campaign of WWII. A surreal feeling came over me as the radio in the background spoke of the imminent invasion of Iraq. Dux, Gib and Charlie were three of the many veterans that I had come to know, love and respect over the past five years. They had served with my mother and father in an Army MASH unit from 1942 through 1945.

Marcus Duxbury had welcomed me gladly to this special circle of friends. Dux had been tireless, in the years since the war, in his devotion to the veterans with whom he had served. He was the "Radar O'Reilly," the glue that kept stability in their outfit. He was there February 10, 1941, at Fort Francis E. Warren, Wyoming when the 48th Surgical Hospital was formed, and although he was quite ill, he was there August 13, 2001 at the last unit reunion in Louisville, Kentucky.

I had come late to the realization that my parents and the other World War II veterans of the 48th/128th MASH had lived out an extraordinary story. At the cusp of the new millennium they had become, for me, an obsession. This led to me initiating my own investigation into that story, having finally recognized the remarkable simplicity and humility with which they viewed their service to our nation. I nudged my way into their midst by convincing my mother to attend a Unit reunion for the first time in the fall of 1998. I escorted her on that trip to Sioux Falls, South Dakota and was forevermore a hanger-on. It was at the annual reunions that they gathered to once again revel in the bond of love and trust forged at a time when extraordinary sacrifice and selflessness was demanded and quickly given by a select few. I found myself at age 49 making a desperate effort to get to know them and learn from them. I wanted so much to stop the clock and begin telling the story of the "greatest generation" to my generation and others who had tuned out the history our parents had lived. Time was not on my side; the nation was losing a thousand WWII veterans a day, and their personal stories were passing with them.

We arrived at the funeral home about 8:30 PM, an hour late for the wake. There were no cars on the lot but we could see lights through the swirling snow and frosted windows of the white frame building. Gib, a retired meatpacker who had been an army surgical technician, remained in the car as I walked up the icy ramp and entered an empty lobby. Slowly moving down a short hallway, I entered a small chapel where I found Dux at rest just beyond two rows of wooden pews. Near his flag-draped casket sat a small wooden basket containing an American Legion cap, playing cards, a pocket knife, fishing gear, photos and other personal items all giving homage to the life of an American patriot.

St. Mary's Church, Salem, South Dakota. (Photo courtesy of G. Jesse Flynn)

Conflicting feelings of desperation and peacefulness were cascading over me. The last few grains of sand in the hourglass were falling. Time was running out for the WWII veterans. The comfort I felt was in the knowledge that I had gotten to know them and could pass their story on to others. We would be the better for their legacy.

I walked up to the casket and we "talked." Dux had a slight smile on his lips as if saying life had been good and he had lived it fully. I had come to know a man comfortable with himself. Calloused hands reflected the years spent in the concrete business. He was short in stature but big in heart. Marcus was one of millions of ordinary, hard-working family men who had grown up during the Depression, given his twenties to his country, came home, married, raised a family and served his community.

The morning of the funeral was cold, overcast and windy. Gib and I arrived at the beautiful stone church early for a change. The elderly twelve-man American Legion Honor Guard stood at attention by the street in the numbing cold awaiting Dux. We seated ourselves next to Gib's lifelong friend and fellow soldier, 85-year-old Oliver Sorlye. Saint Mary's was an immigrant-built church with three beautiful,

St. Mary's exterior. (Photo courtesy of G. Jesse Flynn)

The Legion Honor Guard at Duxbury's funeral awaiting their fallen comrade. (Photo courtesy of G. Jesse Flynn)

Dr. Leonard Schwade, Africa 1943. (Photo courtesy of Sandy Schmidt)

Dr. George Howe, Louisville 2001. (Photo courtesy of G. Jesse Flynn)

ornate wood carved altars. The wooden pews were filled with people of all ages.

Floreine Duxbury, her sons, daughters-in-law and grandchildren followed the white cloth-draped casket to the front of the church. After the funeral Mass we drove to the cemetery on a hill outside of town where Dux would be laid to rest. I shivered from the cold and emotion as the Legion Honor Guard fired the twenty-one-gun salute. Some shots were fired late, due, I'm sure, to fingers that were numb with cold.

Oliver, Gib and I headed back to Hudson, promising that we would see each other again before another funeral.

This routine had become too common for me over the past three years. Oscar Aasheim, Howard Bellrichard, Edna Browning, Max Lanning, Dr. Frank Burton, Rev. Samuel Grove, Alvin Griebel, Dr. George Howe, Joseph James, Edward Kaufmann, Helen (Moloney) Reichert, Dr. Leonard Schwade, Charlie Thorson, Vilma Vogler, Kenneth Willis and my mother had joined the growing list of "gone but not forgotten."

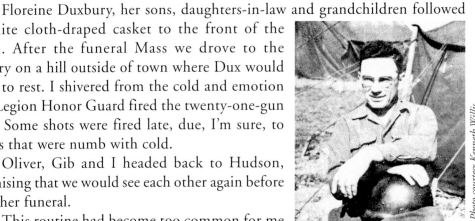

Kenneth Willis, 1943

Photo courtesy Kenneth Willis

They had generally grown up in poverty and had the common experience of hearing on the radio the events of December 7, 1941. The Japanese had attacked Pearl Harbor, declaring war on the United States. Germany joined them in a declaration five days later. The course of their lives changed with these events. They willingly donned the uniform of their country to oppose the Germans and Japanese aggressors in Europe and Asia. Ironically, in less than a year they would be on the continent of Africa, being shot at and receiving dead and wounded American soldiers who had been maimed and killed by the French army.

Photo courtesy G. Jesse Flynn

Max Lanning, 2001

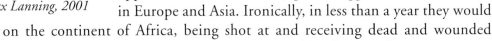

Helen (Moloney) Reichert, 2001

G. Jesse Flynn

This was truly a difficult time to live through, and even more difficult to explain. This was the generation that answered the call, paid the price and carried on in silence. They were an enigma to me. I was a middle-aged businessman when I finally decided to elbow my way into their space to see who they were.

WHO WERE THEY?

I take on this endeavor not as a writer but as a son of two of the participants of the largest military and social experience in the history of the world. They were First Lieutenant John J. Flynn, Army Medical Corps (MAC), from Boston, Massachusetts, and First Lieutenant Gladys Martin, Army Nurse Corps (ANC), from Mt. Eden, Kentucky.

I am humbled and honored by the most fascinating and extraordinary/ordinary people I have ever had the privilege of meeting and researching. I do not tell their story. I only compile their recollections, excerpts of letters home and expound on official records, artifacts and news accounts of events more than sixty years ago. I write out of respect for them in the hope that their accomplishments are never forgotten.

An interesting irony is that I never formally interviewed either of my parents who were junior officers in one of the first American Army MASH units. My quest for information about the outfit has taken me on visits to Arkansas, Florida, Georgia, Iowa, Kentucky, Oregon, South Dakota, Texas, Washington, West Virginia, Wisconsin, Belgium, England, France, Germany, and Sicily.

The 48th, which later became the 128th Evacuation Hospital, was the first American medical unit to see combat in the African/European theatre of World War II. The unit landed with the Army Rangers in Algeria November 8, 1942, in "Operation Torch." A hasty retreat of forty miles occurred in the middle of the night under the onslaught of German Field Marshall Erwin Rommel (The Desert Fox) at Kasserine Pass in Tunisia. The 128th went ashore at Licata Sicily in "Operation Husky", Normandy, France on D-Day plus four in "Operation Overlord", served at St. Lo in "Operation Cobra", the battle of the Falaise Pocket in France, Aachen in Germany, the Battle of the Bulge in Belgium and the Ruhr and Rhine Valleys of Germany. This unit of some three hundred consisted of about sixty female nurses and two hundred-forty men— doctors, medics, surgical assistants and logistical support personnel. They treated seventy thousand patients in thirty-one months of combat service. Their unit packed up and moved its 58-tent hospital dozens of times. They were involved in three of the largest amphibious landings in history. The wounded were treated, the dying comforted and even babies delivered. Their tents were the target of artillery, bombers, hurricanes and snipers. Living conditions in their nomad city varied from the one-hundred-ten degrees in the desert of Tunisia, to minus-ten degrees in Germany and Belgium. Life was celebrated in party and romance. Marriage resulted in at least ten relationships between the nurses and the men of the 48th / 128th.

The soldiers of this unit had an educational range from eighth grade to graduate resident of the Mayo Clinic. The average age during the formation was about twenty-eight and with replacements occurring throughout the war, the median moved up one year. The enlisted men and draftees ranged in age from 18 (James

Sgt. Walter Gacke, Dr. Frank Burton, and Nurse Gladys Martin in January, 1943 in Tunisia. (Photo courtesy of Nell Harwell)

Nurses of the 128th relax outside their home in the field. (Photo courtesy of Isabel Anthony)

Dick, from California) to 33 (Alvin Burrack, from Nebraska).

The junior officers were mostly doctors in their late 20s to mid-30s. The commanding officers were in their late thirties to mid forties. The nurses ranged from mostly early twenties to a few in their mid-thirties. There was a sprinkling of logistical junior officers in charge of motor pool, maintenance and supply that were non-medical personnel. My father was one of these.

Medical Specialist 4th Class Jesse Flynn, 1971.

I SUPPOSE I SHOULD TRY to explain where my interest in this research began. It was over thirty years ago and I was in my last day in the army serving as a medical specialist 4th class stationed at Fort Knox, Kentucky. The Vietnam "peace accord" had been signed some two months before and many of us were being released from duty ninety days early.

When the barrack lights came on at 5:30 a.m., I was already checking my Class "A" uniform in the latrine mirror. My out-processing would begin at eight and I didn't want anything to be amiss. The exit physical was routine. I was twenty-three years old, six feet four inches tall, one hundred eighty-five pounds, slightly farsighted; pretty much the same as my draft physical some two years before.

It was a warm, sun-bathed April morning in 1973 as I drove through the rolling hills of Central Kentucky. My teal-green 1966 Mustang had been quite

The John Flynn family, Lawrenceburg, Kentucky, 1960. Left to right are Anne, Jesse, Margaret, John, Jr., Joan, Nancy, Gladys, Ed, Patty, John, Mary, Dan, and Susan. (Photo courtesy of G. Jesse Flynn)

reliable transportation for my many cross-country trips while in the service. About three hours from Fort Knox, I pulled into the long gravel driveway just outside of Lawrenceburg.

The Flynn house in Lawrenceburg, Kentucky, 1959. (Photo courtesy of G. Jesse Flynn)

The farmhouse, built in the pre-Civil War era, was white, quite large and built from wood. It was a two-story house with twelve-foot ceilings, wraparound porch and a green metal roof. Our family had moved from Georgetown, Massachusetts in the fall of 1958, relocating in central Kentucky. For the sum of six thousand dollars, we took ownership of eleven acres and a ten-room house with no plumbing and primitive electrical service. Our clan at that time consisted of five girls and four boys ranging in age from one to thirteen years. Patty and Nancy would arrive in 1959 and 1960, respectively.

My father, a career civil service truck inspector, had suffered a severe stroke nine months before my return home. The stroke had left him unable to move his left side. There were six siblings in grade school, high school or college at that time. Five of us had earned degrees in education, business or nursing.

As I made the last turn in the drive between two large pine trees, I saw her on the roof. Mom was repairing and painting the ragged metal on the ancient roof. She was fifty-four years old, slightly over six feet tall and razor thin. I greeted her from the front yard and asked what I could do to help. She advised me that the yard needed mowing. As I retrieved the Sears push mower from the adjacent garage, which Mom and Dad had completed constructing November 22, 1963 (the day John F. Kennedy was killed), I found myself buried in deep thought as to who that woman was and what made her tick.

I checked the oil and filled the mower with gasoline as I had done dozens of times before. The front yard was two and a half acres of grass with large trees interspersed.

As I mowed I let my mind wander to what the future might hold for me. Having worked as a dental hygienist in the Army, I was set on attending dental school. However, my degree in Business Administration would not prove to be helpful in reaching this goal. I was being offered a construction job in Louisville at a company where my older brother, John, was a sales engineer. He had been a high school teacher and athletic coach for one year before discovering he could not survive on a teacher's salary.

John had always looked after me. He was fifteen months older and we had attended college in Louisville, Kentucky together. We had shared a fifty-dollar a month apartment above an antique store and had joint responsibility running the intramural sports program at Bellarmine College. We were also partners on the school tennis team. He had graduated in December 1970 with a degree in secondary education and I received my degree on May 9, 1971.

John Flynn and crew, 1952.

As I finished mowing the lower part of the yard, I could see the large barn with the chicken house on the side and the pigpen in the rear. The buildings were showing signs of neglect, which made me realize that it had been over six years since I had milked the cow and over eight years since I had sold my pigs. I experienced

Left to right: Jesse Flynn, Bessy (the cow), Mike Ryan (cousin), sister Patty (with chicken) and sister Nancy in Lawrenceburg, Kentucky, 1962. (Photo courtesy of G. Jesse Flynn)

Gladys Martin (right) in Mt. Eden, Kentucky, 1937. (Photo courtesy of G. Jesse Flynn)

a sense of growing old as I recalled an embarrassing memory of walking to the Lawrenceburg police station to retrieve Bessy, my cow, after she had taken a mile and a half "taste test" of the lawns along Main Street.

Task completed, I returned the mower to the garage and went into the kitchen, a large room with a fireplace at one end and sink and cook stove at the other. Mom was preparing the evening meal of soup beans, corn bread, pickle relish and hot dogs. She greeted me with a hug and welcomed me home. Dad was still in the early stages of rehabilitation from his stroke. He was seated near the fireplace with a sling attached to his left arm which was tied to a pulley. He could raise and lower his left arm by pulling a rope attached to the pulley and sling. Although he had just turned sixty, he looked much older. His face drooped to the left and his speech was slurred. I held his hand and he greeted me with a smile.

Nancy, Patty, Ed and Dan were respectively in the eighth, ninth, tenth and eleventh grades and were due home from school within the hour. Susan was attending Bellarmine College and Joan was at Kentucky State. Anne had just completed her degree at Eastern Kentucky and was teaching at the local high school where she also coached the girl's basketball team on which Patty and Nancy were players. Margaret and Mary were both Registered Nurses following in mom's chosen profession.

As I sat there with them, I realized what a rare experience this was. I could not recall another time in my almost twenty-four years when I was alone with my mother and father. I didn't know what to say. Who were they? How did they get here? Why did they do what they did? What was the glue that bound them?

My only view of them had been that of a child in the eye of the proverbial storm. Our crew was in constant motion. Our small farm was populated with chickens, ducks, turkeys, pigs, horses and cows. All of us had outside jobs, played school sports and participated in many extracurricular activities.

Our parents were a strange combination. My father was born November 17, 1912, in Boston, Massachusetts, a second-generation Irish-Catholic immigrant. His father was a carpenter. His mother took care of five children and the home. As I would discover after his death many years later, dad was a straight "A" student in grade school and high school. He graduated from Boston College in 1935 with a pre-dental degree. He was proficient as a violinist and excelled in the usual sports boys of his day enjoyed—baseball, hockey, tennis and football. After graduation he worked in a pharmacy filling prescriptions for a period of time and operated a small café with a partner for two years. He then sold electrical appliances and supplies to hotels and businesses along the eastern seaboard. He apparently couldn't afford to go to dental school. He had just become engaged to be married when his plans were interrupted in March of 1941 by the draft. He was called to serve for one year; when America declared war on Japan, it became an almost five-year tour.

An agreement was made between our parents to raise us in the Catholic Church even though Mom was, and remained, a staunch Southern Baptist. Dad

Senior Class, Mt. Eden High School, 1937. Gladys Martin is back row center. (Photo courtesy of G. Jesse Flynn)

was the person who mandated church attendance on Sundays, First Fridays and Holy Days. Sometimes it was difficult since there were only 78 Catholics in Anderson County, Kentucky at the time, and we were served by a "mission priest" who would travel in for services. Dad taught us work and sports skills such as carpentry and baseball. Although his work had him traveling quite often, he was involved in our scouting activities and sports teams.

My mother, the former Gladys Martin, was born October 4, 1918 on a farm outside of the small town of Mt. Eden, Kentucky to a Baptist family of German-English descent. She had one older and two younger brothers and a younger sister. Mom was five years old when her mother died after suffering severe burns in an accident involving a kerosene clothes iron. She worked on the farm with her siblings, rode a horse to a one-room school and became "mother" to the younger children. Her father later remarried and had an additional daughter and son. After high school, Mom attended nursing school at the Kentucky Baptist Hospital in Louisville and became a registered nurse in May of 1940.

Easter Sunday, 1955, in Georgetown, Massachusetts.

She was a person definitely in charge of her own fate, seldom showing shock or excitement in times of crisis. She would always go into "attack mode." Broken bones, bee stings, cancer, car wrecks, house fires, frozen pipes and many other events were met with her swift analysis and action. Mom would simply dissect the problem and fix it. She did not allow us to give up. No problem for Gladys Flynn was insurmountable.

As I sat alone with them that April afternoon in 1973, I knew very little about their pasts. I only knew that they had been in the Army together during World War II, had gotten married near the end of the war and raised eleven children.

They had never, to my knowledge, gone out for dinner, a movie, or anything that was not related to work or children. Their lives had revolved around us and each other. Our family was task-oriented and driven. We were simply instructed by example. Discipline was normally handled with a glance or gesture. On rare occasions when John or I would challenge authority, we were met with swift and certain corporal punishment.

The Flynns were always quite self-sufficient. We had a vegetable garden that provided potatoes, tomatoes, beans and corn. Mom made most of our clothes. We never had much money but we always had clothing on our backs and enough to eat.

I had been away from Lawrenceburg for almost six years—four at Bellarmine College, one at Fort Sam Houston, San Antonio, Texas and one at Fort Knox, Kentucky. During the last two years, in particular, I had a chance to take an overview of who I was. My conclusion was that I did not have a clue.

The only thing I knew that day was, for the first time in my recollection I had mom and dad in the same room, there was no one else in the house and all of the questions were coming from them! Did I have a job, girlfriend and a place to live?

The John Flynn family, Lawrenceburg, Kentucky, 1989. Left to right, starting in back row, are Anne, Jesse, Margaret, John, Jr., Joan, Mary, Gladys, Nancy, John, Patty, Dan, Ed, and Susan. (Photo courtesy of G. Jesse Flynn)

Why couldn't I find out something about them? After I explained that I had a job, a place to live, no girlfriend and I was planning to go back to school, Nancy and Patty walked into the house. School was out and I had missed my golden opportunity.

My ambition to attend the University of Kentucky Dental School was derailed in August of 1973 when I performed poorly on the science portion of the entrance exam. During the interim, I had partnered with my brother, John, to start a weekend business of patching potholes. I had also met a tall, dark-haired, good-looking girl who had a paying job as a

John and Gladys Flynn, 1989. (Photo courtesy of G. Jesse Flynn)

social worker. My new course was set. I would develop this new business and see if this relationship had potential.

The childhood advice given by mom to John and me—that "we would never make it on our looks"—played over in my head. This meant that we had to put our backs and brains to work and make a living. So we did. Dad recovered enough to come to work in our "office", a small rented house in southern Louisville, on a daily basis to answer the phone and check the newspaper for small jobs. We grew in volume from $30,000 in revenue in 1973 to over $400,000 in 1975. John was still in sales with another company and would send dad and me the small jobs that his company did not want. Our workload expanded until March 1977, when we began competing with John's employer and he soon was fired. We became true partners that month. Our father continued to work with us for the next twelve years and our company eventually grew to annual revenues exceeding forty million dollars.

In late 1989, dad was taking a walk in his neighborhood with the assistance of a cane when a sixteen-year-old girl backed out of her driveway and ran over him. He had a compound fracture of his left leg and other injuries. We reached a decision to place him in a nursing home.

This decision was terribly difficult and was made over the objection of mom. Dad would call me any day I didn't visit him and ask if I'd made a "million dollars" that day. I usually got the point and stopped by to see him. He died in 1990 just short of one year after the accident. He was gone and I still didn't know much about him.

John Flynn, sister Betty, and brother Vincent in Waltham, Massachusetts, 1920. (Photo courtesy of G. Jesse Flynn)

We simply were too busy as children and adults to find out who they were. School, athletics, work, marriage, children—there was always something more important. Then he was gone.

In April 1998 I took my 79 year-old mother to the funeral of an old Army friend, Margaret Hornback, whom I had never met. During this trip mom began to talk. Margaret, an ex-Army nurse, had been the bridesmaid in my parents' wedding. I found that John and Gladys had met in a mess tent in the middle of the cold North African desert after midnight, March 13, 1943. It was dad's first day with the unit and he was serving sandwiches to the night shift nurses. Although she had a strong southern accent and he an equally strong New England accent, they had instant chemistry. Mom demanded an immediate vote of the nurses that night. The voting procedure was simple; the new officer was married or not. The vote on Lt. John Flynn by the four pre-op nurses was three for married and one for single. Mom was the lone negative vote. I was fascinated by this.

I began to investigate their life on my own. Closets and attics revealed interesting artifacts. I found romantic notes, maps through the tents to clandestine meetings, a receipt for the Royal Hotel in Bristol England, New Years Eve 1943, with a pressed red rose. Many of these artifacts were tucked inside the aged pages of mom's army-issued New Testament. I learned mom had received a Bronze Star for actions above and beyond the call of duty. Her citation read:

"First Lieutenant Gladys Martin, N-728653, Army Nurse Corps, United States Army. For meritorious service in connection with military operations against the enemy as Ward Nurse, 128th Evacuation Hospital, from 11 June 1944 to 20 July 1944, in France. When the hospital received an unexpectedly large number of patients in shock, First Lieutenant Martin, in charge of the nursing staff of the preoperative shock ward, began resuscitative measures on her own initiative. Many patients whose wounds were very serious and who were dependent upon skillful medical and nursing care were saved by her prompt and energetic care. Disregarding routine hours of duty and ignoring the enemy's artillery fire and air attack, she performed so skillfully and exhibited such bravery and coolness that all around her were inspired by her actions."

I also found a rebuttal letter published in the September 25, 1944 edition of *Stars and Stripes* that was written by Dad. It seems several front-line wounded soldiers had written a letter complaining of decorations being awarded to "non-combat" troops. He defended the men in his charge as follows:

"...Remember, you men who took chances at every step, that your part in the ceremony of launching this invasion is not forgotten by any who partook in the activities. Medals mean a lot to every soldier's morale regardless of who gets them.

"In our case, there is a group of lowly truck drivers who worked 24 hours straight, unloading our hospital from a ship, driving the trucks to the assigned hospital area, helping setting up tents. And after the hospital was operating and receiving patients, they carried litters all night long so that you wounded front-line men might be as comfortable as possible, and as many of your lives saved as possible. None of these men received medals, but they do not complain, nor do they begrudge deserved awards to anyone else. Neither did they flinch under constant artillery fire while unloading the ship, nor were they stopped by constant enemy air activity in those first few days. Remember, too, that the Red Cross is very little protection at night.

"I wonder if the whole point of this thing isn't the fact that when we return home we will have a feeling way down deep of having done our part, regardless of medals and headlines.

"Good luck to everyone, front line or rear echelon, from a member of the masses, doing the job." — *Ist Lt. John J. Flynn, MAC*

After reading, rereading and consuming the weight of this and other material, I fought dueling emotions.

I was proud, elated and resigned. My pride came from the confirmation that they had done their part in the war and done it well. The elation came from the fact that I had gotten a glance into their youth and the genesis of the lifetime commitment to each other. But then I was fighting an embarrassing but real feeling of resignation. They had never told us what to do, where to go to school, what sport to play, or anything else. The imaginary bar of expectation my parents set was always placed in simple phrases such as, "Find something to do and do it well;" "You'll never make it on your looks;" "Don't quit when you hit a bump in the road;" "Take care of your family," etc.

All eleven of us had competed to achieve unspoken goals. Success was never defined in real words, so we just went. I recently paid more in annual income tax than my parents' combined lifetime earnings, but I had not come close to achieving their success. I had discovered that the bar was far too high for me to ever reach and had come to the realization that they had always known this fact.

THE MARTINS

I also uncovered through interviews and historical documents how the war had become a "family" crusade with the Martins (Mom's family), as was the case with thousands of other American households. The discussion as to the geographic location of Pearl Harbor between 19-year-old Matthew and his older sister, Gladys, on December 7, 1941 would be followed 1,092 days later December 4, 1944 at 10 AM with 1st Lt. Matthew Martin in a P-51 fighter escorting an American bomber group to Berlin 22,000 feet above 1st Lt. Gladys Martin's Surgical Hospital in Aachen, Germany. One hour later, "Math" would be parachuting to the ground near Hanover, Germany and spend the rest of the war in a POW camp. Ed Martin was serving with the army engineers in the Pacific and brother Greer was in the army in Texas. Capt. John Kelly, a future brother-in-law of the Martins (husband of younger sister,

1st Lt. Matthew Martin. (Photo courtesy of Math Martin)

Ed Martin. (Photo courtesy of G. Jesse Flynn)

Greer Martin. (Photo courtesy of Lucille Martin)

1st Lt. Gladys Martin and Capt. John Kelly in England, May 1944. (Photo courtesy of G. Jesse Flynn)

Maggie) was in command of the armor point company of General Patton's tanks. John was a local Kentucky boy who visited the Shelby County contingent of the MASH unit often in England and Belgium.

In the last few years of mom's life, I usually spent one afternoon a week taking her for a ride to see jobsites our company had under construction. On one particular September day in 1998 our weekly ride took us to the airport in Louisville, Kentucky, where we boarded a flight to Omaha, Nebraska. In Omaha we picked up our rental car for another ride to our final destination, Sioux Falls, South Dakota. The occasion that called for such elaborate travel plans was the annual reunion of the 48th Surgical/128th Evacuation Hospital Unit that served in the North African/

Oliver Sorlye, Jesse Flynn, and Charlie Thorson, Sioux Falls, 2000. (Photo courtesy of G. Jesse Flynn)

European Theater of WWII. As a young couple with a large family, mom and dad had never had the time nor money to attend the reunions. As the years progressed, their memories of WWII were consigned to boxes in the attic. Now, on her way to her first reunion, mom was nervous, but showed great anticipation. I had made travel arrangements and had given her only a twenty-four hour notice of our trip. In that time, she had her hair done and called my sister, Susan, for advice on what to wear. As she prepared for the trip, I recognized a woman I had not known before—a woman concerned with "frivolous things" like her appearance. Before my eyes, mom was returning to an earlier time, one that up until then I had known little about. I was seeing the unsure young woman I had never known.

When we entered the lobby of the Sioux Falls Holiday Inn late in the afternoon, we were met by Marcus Duxbury, Walter Larson, Alvin Burrack and several others. They hugged and smiled broadly at each other, then had dinner and talked for hours before turning in for the night.

Alone, I went to the hotel bar, ordered a beer and began reflecting. It wasn't

Reunion 1998, Sioux Falls, South Dakota. Left to right, front row: Gerhardt Herbolsheimer, Marcus Duxbury, Agatha (Duer) Griebel, Genevieve (Kruzic) Thompson, Edna Marie Browning, Gladys (Martin) Flynn, Oliver A. Sorlye, Maurice Halverson. Back row: James Dick, Alvin Burrack, Fritz Griebel, Walter Larson, Julian Sagan, Gilbert Smith, Charlie Thorson. (Photo courtesy of G. Jesse Flynn)

long before I noticed an old pickup truck pull into the parking lot. Two elderly gentlemen in heavy work jackets and baseball caps stepped out of the truck and walked into the lobby. Oliver Sorlye and Charles Thorson had made the fifty-mile trip south from their farms near Hudson, South Dakota.

Edna Marie Browning, 1944. (Photo courtesy of Linda Burrack)

Instantly I knew they were there for the reunion and I introduced myself and invited them to have a beer. We found a table in the rear of the bar. As we talked, I asked their permission to record the conversation and turned my tape recorder on and listened. Oliver and Charles had worked as ambulance drivers, truck drivers, maintenance men and general help around the MASH unit. Their section leader was 1st Lt. John Flynn, my father. They had driven a "deuce and a half" truck off a landing craft at Utah Beach into an eight-foot artillery shell hole and nearly drowned. After we talked for an hour, they decided to go home for the night. My efforts to get them to stay were in vain. They climbed into the 1967 International pickup and headed north with a promise to return the next day.

Alvin Burrack, 1942

I had returned to the bar and engaged the bartender in conversation when a five-foot-tall, peppy elderly woman hopped up on the stool next to me. We began a conversation and I learned that her name was Edna Browning. She was formerly 1st Lt. Edna Browning, a nurse in the 128th Evacuation Hospital. She was quite animated and we talked for several hours. I pressed her for specific stories of incidents in combat and one of her stories still stands out in my memory:

George and Lucille Willett, 2003. (Photo courtesy of George Willett)

"I was just a replacement nurse that joined the 128th in England. The unit had already been in combat in North Africa and Sicily. We had just begun operations in Normandy and were receiving quite a few wounded. I had been working steadily with your mother from 3:00 p.m. until almost 9:30 p.m. without a break. My eyeballs were capsizing as I ran out of the tent with a flashlight looking for the latrine. The sentry on duty jumped in front of me shouting "Halt! Turn out the light." I wet my pants! I returned to the pre-op tent, my head down with shame. Your mother simply looked up, pointed to my helmet and indicated that it had other uses!"

The next morning I got up early and was seated in the lobby waiting for someone to talk to when 93-year old Alvin Burrack sat down beside me. We chatted for a few minutes and I learned that he had been the oldest draftee in the unit. He had been drafted at age thirty-three and spent nearly four years with the 128th. His companion and close friend was Edna Browning, the nurse I had interviewed the night before. I concluded that she apparently was a late night person and he was early morning. Alvin had been drafted out of a thriving business that he had started and gave up to a 4-F (non-draftable) partner. He asked me to take him to a casino boat on the Missouri River in Sioux City and I complied. We got there at eight a.m. and I proceeded to engage in a poker game to Alvin's suggestion and delight. I won a thousand dollars before losing it back, plus a hundred dollars. By 10 a.m. we were back at the hotel where the balance of the reunion attendees, including my mother, were seated around tables talking old times.

After hours of sharing memories and swapping stories, someone read a list of names of members who had died. We toasted in their honor. Soon after, the subject of future reunions was raised and there were no volunteers as sponsors. It happened so fast, I cannot remember whether I volunteered or was appointed by Walt Larson to sponsor the next reunion in Louisville.

A display at the 1999 Louisville reunion. (Photo courtesy of G. Jesse Flynn)

Approximately one year later, we met in September 1999, at the Executive Inn in Louisville, Kentucky. About thirty-five members and relatives of members attended the reunion. Louisvillians George and Lucille Willett and mom were the official sponsors. Patricia Douglas, daughter of the late Sgt. Joseph Douglas and Lt. Ruth Wheeler also attended. I had the assistance of a good friend, Charlie Ricketts, a prominent local attorney, and a number of his associates in putting together a total MASH unit at a local convention center. We had trucks, jeeps, ambulances, tents, surgical facilities and a communication center erected with camouflage netting and stars on the ceiling. Music from the war years was piped in and a great nostalgic time was had by all.

Four months later on January 20, 2000, mom died. She had attended two reunions and I know that it had been a blessing for her to see her old comrades.

In September 2000 my wife, Elaine, and I attended the next reunion in Sioux Falls, South Dakota. I spent hours interviewing and recording the wartime recollections of the former members of the 128th. A number of their children and other adult relatives attended the event. Several of us, including Patricia Douglas, had met at the earlier reunion.

Elaine had regularly urged me to "take a sabbatical" from our construction firm in order to focus on chronicling the unit's story. The chance viewing of a particular scene from the movie "Dead Poets Society" while at the reunion led Elaine and Pat into a discussion of the need to seize the day—*carpe diem*. Patricia works with a production company in Burbank, California and she understands the value of my interviewing and cataloging of data and recollections pertinent to "their story." She, too, encouraged me to get on with it in order to acknowledge the service of the 48th/128th "while there were members still with us to accept the recognition and honor. Too many of the postwar generation have no idea what our mothers and fathers endured and accomplished."

I would take three more trips to South Dakota in the next three years. In early June 2001, Charlie Thorsons' wife called with the news of his death. I went to

Hudson to meet with Oliver, Gilbert Smith and the Thorson family. We went to the funeral home in Canton, South Dakota. I had the opportunity on this visit to see first-hand where the children of Norwegian immigrants were born, worked and lived out their lives. Charles Thorson was laid to rest June 11, 2001, fifty-seven years and one day from the time he came ashore at Utah Red Beach, Normandy, France where he and Oliver Sorlye had driven their "deuce and a half" truck off a landing craft into the eight-foot shell hole.

Gilbert Smith and Oliver Sorlye at the Norway Center, Hudson, South Dakota. (Photo courtesy of G. Jesse Flynn)

During that visit I convinced Oliver and Bill Thorson, Charlie's son, to attend the last reunion of the 128th in Louisville in August 2001. Oliver had previously ridden on a plane only once, returning home after the end of World War II in 1945. He had flown in a B-17 bomber from France to Africa to Brazil to Miami. He was reluctant to fly again. However, they arrived safely on a Boeing 737 in Louisville in August 2001. Oliver was amazed at the advance which aviation had made in the intervening six decades.

Our 2001 reunion was highly successful. We had over 100 in attendance. Among those attending was Col. Casey Jones, the chief medical officer of the Ireland Army Hospital at nearby Fort Knox. He acknowledged the contribution of the 48th/128th to America's victory in World War II. All ten of my brothers and sisters, several children and grandchildren of unit members and several surviving spouses also were there. We had tours of Fort Knox, a large picnic at our family farm with tractor rides and live folk music provided by my good and talented friend, John Gage.

Since many of the former members of the 48th/128th Evacuation Hospital could not travel to Louisville, Kentucky to attend the reunions and be interviewed, I traveled the country during the next two years in order to interview them.

The troubador of the 1999 reunion, singer John Gage. (Photo courtesy of G. Jesse Flynn)

During my conversations with Gilbert Smith in Hudson, South Dakota, I found that many of his photographs included a nurse from Pennsylvania by the name of Vaughn Fisher. They had become close friends in the three years they worked together in the surgery department of the 128th. Although they ended up

Genevieve (Kruzic) Thompson, of Moses Lake, Washington, September 6, 2002. (Photo courtesy of G. Jesse Flynn)

Oliver Sorlye, Max Lanning, and Charles Thorson, 2000. (Photo courtesy of G. Jesse Flynn)

Dee and Dr. Ed Rosenbaum of Portland, Oregon, January 2002. (Photo courtesy of G. Jesse Flynn)

marrying others, I felt there was a strong bond worth exploration. Vaughn was added to my travel agenda.

In my reading I found that Dr. Ed Rosenbaum, Dr. Frank Burton, Dr. Leonard Schwade, and Dr. Frederick Mackenbrock were referenced quite often. Dr. Rosenbaum was the only survivor of this group and I visited his home in Portland, Oregon twice. I also traveled to Milwaukee, Wisconsin to meet with Sandy Schmidt, Dr. Schwade's daughter and Hot Springs, Arkansas, to see Mrs. Burton, Dr. Frank Burton's widow.

Martha Cameron, Walter Larson and George Howe were interviewed in Tampa, Florida; Vaughn Fisher in Clarksburg, West Virginia; George Willett, in Louisville, Kentucky; Jodie Harmon, in Robert Lee, Texas; Genevieve Kruzic Thompson, in Moses Lake, Washington; and Margaret Reinier, in Cedar Rapids, Iowa (the wife of medical specialist Hugh Reinier) also made my travel agenda.

Rosie Orr (honorary veteran) and Dr. George Howe, 2001. (Photo courtesy of G. Jesse Flynn)

Martha Cameron and Evelyn (Kemer) Slotwinski, 2000. (Photo courtesy of G. Jesse Flynn)

Linda Wilhoit (daughter of Gilbert Smith), Gilbert Smith, and Maurice Halverson, 1998.(Photo courtesy of G. Jesse Flynn)

Gilbert Smith and Evelyn Vaughn Fisher, 1944. (Photo courtesy of Gilbert Smith)

Jodie Harmon. (Photo courtesy of G. Jesse Flynn)

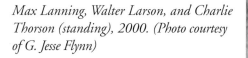

Max Lanning, Walter Larson, and Charlie Thorson (standing), 2000. (Photo courtesy of G. Jesse Flynn)

LaRue Burton, wife of the late Dr. Frank Burton, 2003. (Photo courtesy of G. Jesse Flynn)

Martha Cameron, Gerhardt Herbolsheimer and his wife, Bev, 2000. (Photo courtesy of G. Jesse Flynn)

Floreine and Marcus Duxbury, 2000. (Photo courtesy of G. Jesse Flynn)

CHAPTER TWO
ORGANIZATION TO ENGLAND

THE 48TH SURGICAL HOSPITAL had its origins at Fort Warren, Cheyenne, Wyoming in 1941. The male officers and logistic personnel were the nucleus.

The original group of enlisted men of the 48th received basic training at Fort Warren also, after which most received advanced training in surgical assistance, laboratory or x-ray work at various bases and hospitals across the midwest and Texas. At Indiantown Gap, Pennsylvania, while en route to their port of embarkation, New York City, they would be joined by more than twenty men from Fort Snelling, Minnesota. Their ranks would not be completed until their arrival in Great Britain, where a group of soldiers, originally assigned to the 77th Evacuation Hospital, were attached to the 48th instead, bringing the total personnel to approximately 300. That number included 60 nurses who came from Army bases all over the country, not learning of their assignment until after boarding the USS *Wakefield* under way to parts unknown in the summer of 1942.

As in any history written about an event or military unit, there are as many versions as there are participants. A viewpoint is simply a view from a point. In the case of the 48th/128th, I have chosen to tell the story through three main and divergent points of reference—three specific sets of eyes from which to view a common experience.

From the first window, the war is seen through the eyes of the nurses. The nurses, all female, were volunteers, numbered approximately sixty and were all officers. They were quartered separately, ate in the officers mess and traveled in staterooms on the ships.

The original group of women were civilian volunteers drawn from sixteen army posts in the south and east of the United States. Twenty percent of the total came from Fort Knox, Kentucky.

Letters written by Margaret Hornback, a nurse from Shelby County, Kentucky, stationed originally at Fort Knox, will provide the primary nurses' view of the war.

Dr. Edward Rosenbaum, a Mayo Clinic-trained doctor from Omaha, Nebraska in his mid-twenties, and the late Dr. Leonard Schwade, in his diary, will provide the view from the second window—that of medical and administrative officers.

The officers, who were a blend of draftees, reserve officers and volunteers, traveled in staterooms on the ships, had special dining areas, liquor rations, better clothing, billeting and better food than the enlisted men. They were mostly medical

Margaret Hornback. (Photo courtesy of Marnie Terhune)

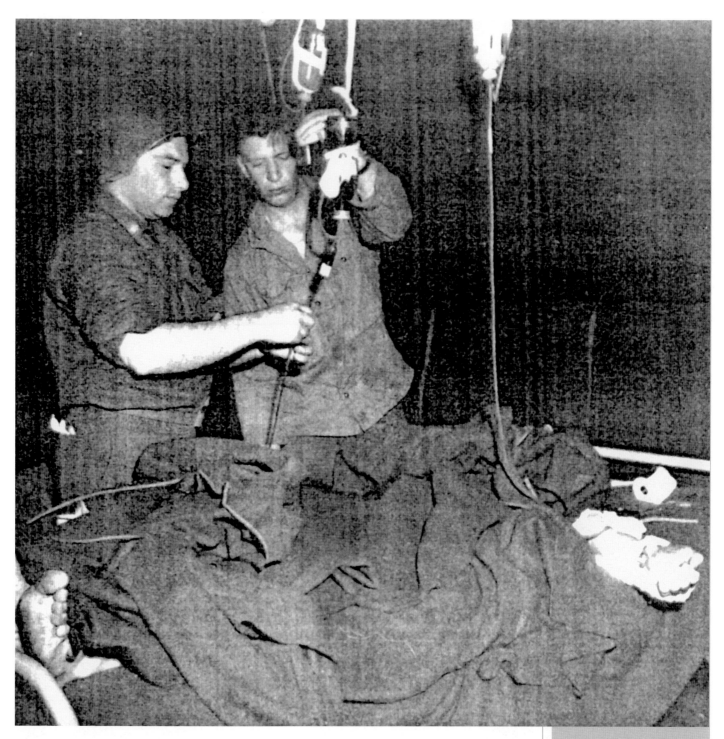

doctors with a few logistical and administrative officers who had been regular army before 1942.

Doctors were divided into two categories. The career Army doctors were generally higher ranking, older, and had administrative duties. Called up reservists, volunteers or draftees performed the bulk of the "hands on" work. Dr. Leonard Schwade was a volunteer from Wisconsin. Dr. Edward Rosenbaum was a reserve officer called up to active duty.

Maj. Edward Rosenbaum, M.D., administers whole blood plasma to a wounded GI at a field hospital in France, 1944. He is assisted by Pvt. Bruce Folks. (Photo courtesy of U.S. Army Signal Corps)

Jodie Harmon. (Photo courtesy of Jodie Harmon)

Below: The post main gate at Fort Warren. (Photo courtesy of George Willett)

From the third window, the war of the enlisted man is told in the person of Jodie Harmon, a young rancher from West Texas. Enlisted men in the 48th Surgical Hospital were comprised of a mixture of draftees and volunteers. I have also used details provided by enlisted men including Marcus Duxbury, Walt Larson, Oliver Sorlye, Charlie Thorson, Loren Butts, James Dick, Gilbert Smith, Max Lanning, Kenneth Willis, George Willett and several others. They endured the most difficult living conditions. They had to sleep in shifts in the holds of the ships, do the back-breaking labor of moving the tents and other equipment and usually had the crudest billeting. They were mostly young and had high school educations or less. The men performed work such as ward orderly, surgical assistant, medic, driver, stretcher-bearer, typist and truck driver.

This is the story of the young Americans who formed the first army MASH unit— who they were and what they accomplished.

THE NURSES

In order to properly describe the experiences of the volunteer nurses in the 48th/128th, I interviewed or had access to many interviews with veterans Martha Cameron, Edna Browning, Vaughn (Fisher) Pulice, Genevieve (Kruzic) Thompson,

Doris (Brittingham) Simion, Helen (Moloney) Reichert, Agatha (Duer) Griebel, and several others. I also received valuable information from Anna Clark of Mt. Washington, Kentucky, who is the niece of the late Lt. Ora White. Each interview was rewarding, inspiring and informative.

But the most contemporaneous and detailed chronology I obtained was contained in hundreds of letters written home by nurse Margaret Hornback to her mother and to Lillian Stout, a friend of the family. Margaret, from Shelbyville, Kentucky, worked as a civilian nurse at Fort Knox from late 1941 through August 1, 1942. Gladys Martin and Ora White, also from Shelby County, joined her in early 1942. Vaughn Fisher, Ella Ferree, Mildred Kaelin, Doris Friedlund, Margaret Madagan, Phyllis MacDonald, Carrie Smith, Beryl Karban, and Ursula Hall were also working on the wards at Ireland Army Hospital. This was the largest single contingent of nurses to be attached to the unit.

Photo courtesy Helen (Moloney) Reichert

Helen Moloney

Photo courtesy Marnie Terhune

Margaret Hornback, 1942

Although I had never interviewed Margaret, nor even recall meeting her, I feel that I know her very well. A chance phone call in the fall of 2002 led me to her niece, Marnie Terhune, who resides in Shelby County, Kentucky. She had in her possession a vintage army trunk filled with more than a thousand letters and military information from the war years.

Photo courtesy G. Jesse Flynn

Ora White and Gladys Martin.

The trunk was olive drab, scratched, dented and had seen much travel. The name stenciled on the top, faded and barely legible, was 1st Lt. John J. Flynn, Prentice Street, Waltham, Massachusetts. How my dad's trunk ended up in an attic near Simpsonville, Kentucky some fifty-seven years after leaving Germany, is probably a good story—but I will never know. Marnie graciously allowed me to read and use the remarkable letters and made me a gift of the trunk. I'm eternally grateful.

All of the sixty nurses that joined the 48th Surgical Hospital in the summer of 1942 had been stationed at military posts throughout the south and east. Margaret Hornback in several letters home in the spring of 1942 described typical experiences of nurses new to the military, working among thousands of sick and injured soldiers and the anxiety of going to war:

"I'm working in the operating room now. It's in the permanent part of the fort, is brick and is a lovely place compared with the other hospital. My window looks out on the parade grounds, where somebody is generally putting on a show, and outside the window on the other side, I can hear the band practicing for the

Photo courtesy Vaughn Pulice

Vaughn Fisher, 1942

*Ireland Army Hospital,
Fort Knox, Kentucky,
1942. (Photo courtesy of
Anna Clark)*

Fort Knox parade.

"We saw by the paper today that our first nurses reached Ireland. They, of course, had left here before I came. We were all so worried about them. They say you don't have to go unless you want. I hope to make myself quite efficient, so they won't want to send me for a while anyhow.

"I kinda hated to leave the wards after I got accustomed to them. The boys were cute old things, always around under your feet. They reminded me of Sneezie on a larger scale."

May, 1942: Fort Knox, Kentucky:

"The Post is so pretty now. I wish you could come to see it and me. This permanent part looks like anything else than preparation for war. Now since we have the windows open, we can hear the bugle blow revile etc. and taps ring out so clear on the still nite. It all rather seems like a movie, and after while it will be over, and there won't be any war. You hear much more about it on the outside than here.

"(Ora) White (her good friend from Shelby County) and I wore our uniforms to town yesterday and we really rated attention. One guy looking back at Orie, tripped over a doorstep and almost fell."

The rumors of "call up" had been circulating for weeks. Nine volunteers were selected for overseas duty. They did not include my mom, Gladys Martin. This letter of August first explains the circumstances surrounding the imminent departure for overseas duty. There was a last minute change due to one of the nurses assigned for travel having recently been married. Mom apparently volunteered to take her place.

*Gladys Martin and a
patient at Fort Knox,
1942. (Photo courtesy of
G. Jesse Flynn)*

August 1, 1942 (after seeing her family and being unable to tell them of her impending departure due to security measures), Margaret writes:)

"I couldn't bring myself to tell you, and was so thankful you didn't guess what my orders were yesterday. Guess you thought I acted rather funny but I couldn't think of any good excuses. Ora, Martin and I with thirteen others leave for a port

Photo courtesy Anna Clark

of embarkation somewhere on a 4:30 train this afternoon. We will be allowed to send an address when we arrive. I surely hated to leave, as you saw but we have to keep our chins up, don't we? You all just try not to worry about me for I know I'll be all right. Were it not for leaving you all, I would be most glad to go and do my small part and woe betide Hitler if I ever get a crack at him."

Margaret remarks on Gladys Martin's last-minute inclusion in the group:

"I was amazed at Martin. She had heard we were going before she left Saturday p.m., so she told Miss Dare [the nurse officer in charge] if there would be a vacancy, she'd be glad to go with us. But she didn't know she was going till she got back Sunday noon. Then she had to have her physical, sign all clearance papers, etc. etc. We thought we had awfully short notice but hers was worse. I feel sorry for Orie Lee [Ed. Another nurse from Shelby County, Kentucky, not to be confused with Ora White.] She'd worked so hard to get in to be with Martin and now she won't for she'll have limited service and those don't go to Foreign Service, at least not now. Try to console her if you can.

"It was awfully hard to leave the kids at Knox. My sons (patients) all came down to see me off. They gave me a most beautiful make-up case. I don't expect to ever find such a swell bunch again. I regret that I shed a few tears when I said goodbye to Lightnin' Larry. Such embarrassed me no end."

As the twelve volunteer nurses from Ft. Knox, Kentucky departed for the railway station to go to places unknown, nurses from military posts all over the

The civilian nurses were given commissions and a booklet that explained the expectations of the Army. The cover sheet explained the contents:

"The United States Army is preparing to defend the Western Hemisphere and the interests of the people of the United States. In order to accomplish this, we of the Army must be prepared for anything, anytime, anywhere!

"In accepting your commission as an Army Nurse you have accepted the responsibilities of a United States Army Officer and those responsibilities are many—and of a serious nature. Militarily speaking, the Army Nurse Corps *must* be ready the same as any other arm or branch of the service. It is to prepare YOU, whether you have been in the service years, months or days, that this booklet has been prepared. Read it! Failure to do so may cost you a lot both socially and professionally."

The nurses at Fort Knox, Kentucky display their new uniforms, early 1940s. (Photo courtesy of Anna Clark)

Amy Nickles. (Photo courtesy of Helen Reichert)

Margie Hart. (Photo courtesy of Helen Reichert)

Helen Moloney. (Photo courtesy of Helen Reichert)

country were also answering the call. Genevieve Kruzic [who I interviewed at her home in Moses Lake, Washington] was at Camp Shelby, Mississippi where she had met her future husband, Sgt. Murray Thompson, a patient on her ward. She packed her suitcase and headed north.

The nurses and posts where they were stationed are as follows:

FORT KNOX – KENTUCKY:
Ferree, Ella J.
Fisher, E. Vaughn
Friedlund, Doris
Hall, Ursula
Hornback, Margaret
Karban, Beryl
Kaelin, Mildred H.
MacDonald, Phyllis
Madigan, Margaret
Martin, Gladys
Smith, Carrie
White, Ora

FORT SLOCUM, NEW ROCHELLE, NY:
Brittingham, Doris
Hobson, Helen
Kelly, Marie
Molony, Helen
Nickerson, Emily

CAMP TYSON – TENNESSEE:
Atkins, Edna
Farabough, Frances
Francis, Mary
Stanfill, Margaret

FORT McCLELLAN – ALABAMA:
Vogler, Vilma

FORT TILDEN – NEW YORK:
Miller, Violet

CAMP WHEELER – GEORGIA:
Grier, Etoyl
Nickles, Amy
Sheridan, Vivian

CAMP FOREST – TENNESSEE:
Harris, Mildred
Hart, Margaret

CAMP LEE – VIRGINIA:
Hatcher, Mary

CAMP STEWART – GEORGIA:
English, Helen
Williams, Nell

Joined Army in England:
Self, Gladys
Sullivan, Mary Ann

FORT MONMOUTH – N.Y.:
Cunningham, Katharine
Miller, Margaret

FORT JAY – NEW YORK:
Hamaker, Mary

CAMP EDWARDS – MASS.:
Coates, Elizabeth

FORT DUPONT – DELAWARE:
Cameron, Martha

CAMP BLANDING – FLORIDA:
Parks, Ruth

CAMP SHELBY – MISSISSIPPI:
Kruzic, Genevieve

THE ADVENTURE OF A LIFETIME for the young women of Fort Knox began August 2, 1942.

These women would encounter in the next thirty-six months, highs and lows rarely experienced in people their age. Their names will always be associated with historical, well-known battles and many lesser known. Oran, Kasserine, Gafsa, Hill 609, Normandy, St. Lo, Aachen, Cefalu, and Falaise are a few, but there were many more.

They would witness humanity at its strongest and weakest. Most would encounter the loves of their lives during this period and in the case of Margaret Hornback, there were two men. Both died during the war and she never married.

Nurses Hobson, Nickerson, Brittingham and Moloney at Fort Slocum, New York. (Photo courtesy of Doris Simion)

Capt. Dare and Ora White, Fort Knox, Kentucky, 1942. (Photo courtesy of Anna Clark)

Genevieve Kruzic and patient, Murray Thompson, at Camp Shelby, Mississippi, 1942. They married in 1945. (Photo courtesy of Genevieve Thompson)

Gladys B. Self. (Photo courtesy of Walter L. Jones, Jr.)

Nurses marching at Fort Knox, 1942. (Newspaper photo courtesy of Anna Clark)

She died in 1996 after a long career that ended serving as a volunteer nurse in the Gaza Strip in Israel.

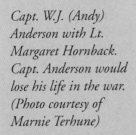

Lt. Hornback in her letters home described their deployment in brilliant detail:

"4:00 p.m. Arrived at railway station, Fort Knox. Train one hour late. Sat, as usual, on our suitcases. Arrived in Louisville 6:10. Took Yellow cab to Central Station. Left Louisville 7:30 p.m. We have an air-conditioned Pullman all to ourselves, and I keep thinking how you'd like being this ritzy. Being me, I don't suppose I'd ever have gotten around to taking a trip like this if Uncle Sam hadn't footed the bill. We spend a large part of our time eating it seems. We got this train out of Louisville at 7:30. Dinner was served soon. Our berths are ready when we finish. All crawl in exhausted. Orie and I sleep in together in an upper berth. We were to pick up one of our party in Dayton. She was on leave and didn't have time to get back. Guess she had a worse time than we. Anyhow, when we awakened, the porter was putting her into Orie's bed. So, we spent the nite together and if you've ever tried to share an upper berth —well. Guess we wouldn't have slept too much anyhow. The porter looked awfully surprised when he got two of us out of there this a.m.

Capt. W.J. (Andy) Anderson with Lt. Margaret Hornback. Capt. Anderson would lose his life in the war. (Photo courtesy of Marnie Terhune)

"We've made good time, I suppose. We're almost to Philadelphia now and are supposed to get to New York by five. We don't know, of course, how long we'll be there, and, I don't suppose we can announce our departure. But if I possibly can, I'll send the folks a cable when I arrive, and they'll whistle to you.

"2:25: "We're now getting into the outskirts of Philadelphia. Too bad we had to see America first from the uninspiring view of a railroad only."

Martha Cameron at the Louisville reunion, 2001. (Photo courtesy of G. Jesse Flynn)

August 3, 1942:

"Arrive in the big city, Penn Station. We are met by an open army truck. What a ride across town. Everyone calls us WACs. We go directly to N.Y.P.E. and who'd have thought there was so much work to be done. It's all finished after twelve and we get home about two. What a day."

Right: Lt. Martha Cameron, Fort DuPont, Delaware. (Photo courtesy of Martha Cameron)

August 4, 1942:

"Up and at it again today. We get our Field equipment and patiently (did I say patiently?) we wait all day for our lockers. They seem to have detoured by way of Tennessee. At last at 3:00 p.m. we hear that they are at the hotel. Madly, we dash across town and arrive with fifteen minutes to spare before the lockers must go to the pier. This is the maddest packing we've done yet. But we make it. Then back across town to make our bedrolls. They are at last assembled, and Orie discovers that she's carrying an empty file instead of her official papers. Our hearts are in our mouths. The chief says she'll be turned over to the FBI or it will take months worrying Miss Dare to get those copies. She can't decide which would be worse. But we find them lying safely at home on the bed."

<u>August 5, 1942:</u>

"6:30 a.m. We report at N.Y.P.E. bag and baggage which may be taken literally. We carry one handbag, one overcoat, one gas mask, one musette bag, helmet, and official papers. Aside from that our hands are empty. The ferry *General Harry Rodgers* takes us out to our ship, The USS *Wakefield*, formerly the liner *Manhattan*. She is camouflaged in varied shades of gray to resemble waves. Later we are to see how those colors do melt into the waves and the ship is visible for a short distance only. We are established in stateroom 50H—five of the Fort Knox gang, Boyd,

The main body of the 48th Surgical Hospital was shipped from New York to Scotland aboard a converted luxury liner, the U.S.S. Wakefield. *The ship (below) was originally called the* Manhattan, *built in 1932 as a trans-Atlantic liner with a passenger capacity of 1,239. Re-fitted for wartime service, it carried thousands of soldiers to the European Theatre.*

White, O'Connor, Kaelin and I, and a little girl named Rogers from Texas. Later, Martin and Rogers trade places, and O'Connor and Hall. Someone reports a good meal is being served upstairs to lunch and are amazed when they serve us cornflakes.

Dr. Leonard Schwade would join the 48th in England three weeks later. His diary describes his separate departure from New York Harbor and the ensuing trip.

August 18, 1942:
"Marched to boat in Ft. Hamilton Bay – boarded the boat Queen of the Pacific – stateroom 518, sailed about 4 a.m."

August 19, 1942:
"Three transports, two cruisers, one battleship (New York), one oil tanker. Meals good on ship."

August 20, 1942:
"Spotted sub at 4 p.m. – sunk by plane and cruisers. Played poker – won $4.35."

August 21, 1942:
"Entered bay at Halifax, Nova Scotia at about noon. Picked up many ships from Boston and Halifax and sailed again at 5 a.m. Going to England or Ireland?"

Then we discover they're still serving breakfast and its only 10:30 a.m. Troops are loading throughout the day. They are awfully crowded. There will be two divisions of them. "Standees and Bunkees," there being only half enough bunks to go around. They occupy the bunks in twelve-hour shifts. On each side of us we see similar vessels loading. To our left is the renowned *West Point*. They have a group of nurses too, we see. We all stay on the sun deck as late as possible, to spy

The trans-Atlantic trip was accomplished in convoy, with destroyers, cruisers and battleships forming a ring around the unarmed troop ships. This shot of the convoy was taken from the main deck by Margaret Hornback. (Photo courtesy of Margaret Hornback)

out the land. Apparently no one knows the time of our sailing or our destination."

Down the hall, another group of nurses were settling in. The situation is described by Lt. Theresa Archard in the book, *G.I. Nightingale*:

"We were assigned staterooms. I was glad my name began with an A— I got to the stateroom first. What had been a three-bed room had been converted into a six-bed boudoir. Well, I'd get the stationary bed near the portholes—first come, first served. The door opened and Krusic and French popped in. I was glad to have them as roommates.

'I think it's just silly of them to rush us like this,' a girl with a southern

One week after the Wakefield delivered the 48th to Great Britain it was totally destroyed by fire on the return trip to the United States.

THEY HAD A STORY TO TELL: At his Pawtucket home, Robert Crabtree (left) tells of his rescue from the burning Navy transport Wakefield while a fellow-survivor, Sven Gothe of Cambridge, Mass., enjoys some of the coffee Mrs. Crabtree is brewing. The Wakefield, formerly the S. S. Manhattan, is shown below in an official Navy photo taken at sea during transport duty.

accent cried. 'I just bet we'll stay here for days and days.' She introduced herself—Evelyn Hodges from South Carolina—and was followed by two other girls, Dorothy Cox from Rock Island, Illinois, and Eva Sacks from Philadelphia. They had been together at Camp Croft and knew each other very well. Their beds were selected and we settled down to talk. Did anyone know what kind of outfit we were in? No one did. Who's our commanding officer and how soon do you think we'll get started?"

Hornback continues:

August 6, 1942:

"5:00 a.m. We are on our way. Whistles have been blowing for a long time it seems. I have been watching a crack in the dock, and suddenly it begins to slip backward. We dress madly and dash up to the sundeck to see our convoy take shape. There are ten troop ships beside our own, a light cruiser, a battleship, and a British vessel we cannot identify. It's several days before we're told that she's a merchant raider disguised as a cargo ship. It is a most beautiful morning. We never imagined the sky could be so blue. We've quite a group of destroyers making a circle around us, and flying continually back and forth the planes soar overhead, and two navy blimps follow. We wonder if they're going all the way. Evening brings our first blackout. Our neighbors ships all snuggle in closer for the nite. We respond to 2400 o'clock bed check and all is quiet."

August 6, 1942: New York:

"We liked New York but I was disappointed in it, too. I guess the lights being dimmed made lots of difference. There are so many lovely things I'd like to share with you all. We sometimes wonder how we are being paid to have a part in anything so beautiful. I'm writing down the most impressive things so I can tell you when I get back.

"We had a lovely church service on deck this morning – the first worthwhile message I've heard in sometime. Also found one Texas Baptist chaplain. To think one would have to come this distance to find one. After which we had a swell chicken dinner, same as you did, I betcha. I considered saving the bones for my dog, Mac Kendrick – wonder if they would pass the censor?

"Speaking of the censor, we cannot describe any dates, numbers, places, or things, so don't imagine that I'm any dumber than usual when I write. Your letters will be censored too so write on one side of the paper, so he may sniff out the parts that don't appeal to him.

"Try not to worry about me or even think about me much. We are all well and quite happy even. Were it not for you all and especially for your being worried

August 31, 1942:

"In North Sea – many mines, but ship knows way. Docked at Liverpool at 12:30 p.m. Met our CO) – Lt. Col. Ringer. We are to be stationed near Tidworth 60 minutes from Bristol. We are known as the 48th Surgical Hospital Unit."

Nurses on the Wakefield *deck on the way to England. (Photo courtesy of Agatha Griebel)*

CONTENTS OF A
MUSETTE BAG:

ESSENTIALS
Rations
Flashlight
Extra bulbs and batteries
Change of underwear &
socks
Matches
Candle
Washcloth
Towel
Soap
Tooth-brush
Tooth-paste
Mess-kit
Kotex
Sanitary belt
Toilet paper

DESIRABLE
Cigarettes
Cosmetics
Delicacies
Stationary & pencil
Playing cards
Book
Can-opener
Kleenex
Band-aids

*Nurse armed
with a musette
bag and mop.
(Photo courtesy
of G. Jesse
Flynn)*

about me, I wouldn't trade places with anybody. I am to have the kind of work I wanted. I think, as far as my safety, I am not in the least afraid, for the Lord God who has kept me thus far certainly seems nearer than before, and I know he'll be with me still, and the chaplain said this morning, 'God's hour of peace will come when the smoke of this battle has cleared away.'

"We've just learned that we will be able to mail some letters now, so I'll sign off til the next time. Orie sends her love and Martin, too."

August 7, 1942:
"4:30 a.m. General alarm sounds. We roll out, don clothes, life preservers, etc. and are on deck in 5 minutes. There, we are told, there is no danger; the navy does this each a.m. at this time. Properly impressed with the vigilance of the navy, we crawl back to bed again not for long though, for breakfast is at seven. We must necessarily economize on water, so we have water one hour in each four. None of these hours come before breakfast, so no wash face. We must make arrangements about that. We open the portholes and it's such a clear, sparkling morning. We hasten on deck to drink in its beauty. Our neighbors are all back in their old positions again. What a marvelous thing to bring these great ships thru the darkness in exact formation. So must God pilot our lives among the dangers of life's sea?

"At 10:00 a.m. we have our first assembly of nurses. We meet our Commanding Officer Col. Ringer, Majors Snyder and Murphy, and our Capt. Proffitt. We are told what the well-dressed woman is wearing (and apparently, we need it) where the well-behaved woman will consider off limits, etc. Maybe we'll get some order out of this by and by.

"The hospital has been organized about one year, having been stationed in Wyoming. Its personnel consist of: 22 medical officers, 1 chaplain, 60 nurses, and 250 enlisted personnel."

Lt. Archard adds her recollection of the meeting:

"Now, girls," said the colonel, "you probably want to know what kind of outfit you've joined. Its name is the 48th Surgical Hospital Unit, and we are going to function as a field hospital. We will be a mobile surgical installation, divided into three units: the First, the Second, and the Surgical Auxiliary. We will leap-frog one another on the field of battle and the Surgical Auxiliary will always be with the forward unit. Just how close to the fighting line we will be, will depend upon battle conditions. Do I make myself clear?"

August 8, 1942:
"A beautiful clear morning. About nine AM we see land on port side. How can it be? We rush topside to learn that this is Nova Scotia. Now we come in closer and can see the 'murmuring fires and the hemlocks.' It's a beautiful country; little church spires gleaming on every hilltop, and some of them are quite level and green. They look like golf courses, but they tell us there are fortifications there. We drop anchor in Halifax harbor about 10:00 a.m. This is a lovely natural harbor and today it's certainly full of ships when all our convoy gets in. Here the destroyers get refueled and we add two more transports to our number. All afternoon we expect

to take off but toward evening we give up hopes. It's been a nice days rest lying at anchor. We will not realize until later how much the days rest helped us to accustom ourselves to the roll of the ship. There's blackout on deck tonite but there are lights on in the lounge tonite for the last time til we reach land again. So the orchestra plays and a few couples dance. The men are singing on lower decks. *Carolina Moon* seems to be the favorite number."

August 9, 1942:

"This morning we have our first fog. We can't even see the ship next to us. At breakfast, the crewmembers tell us we'll have to wait til the fog lifts before leaving harbor. Finally it clears about nine, and we're on our way. Church begins at 10:00. Chaplain Pate of the Amphibian Engineers brings the message and it is a most auspicious one. He served in World War I as an enlisted man, and he knows what these men are up against. Sunday afternoon is quiet, and at nite, a hymn sing is held. The boys really put their heart into it."

August 10, 1942:

"Today were greeted by rough weather – rain and wind. It's rather disagreeable but the crew says it's most healthful. Planes can't fly in it and subs can't come in close either. We barge around thru the rain, get wet several times and our hair is so full of salt it stands straight out. Some of the girls are not very well but this Fort Knox bunch is really rugged."

August 11, 1942:

"Very little new taking place today. The weather has cleared considerably and early in the morning, various guns are fired to see if the rain has damaged them. They certainly sound ominous enough. We all got our second typhus shot in the PM."

August 12, 1942:

"The girls are kinda tired today. It's all we can do to get the house ready for inspection. Hall has a terrible sore throat but seems to be receiving adequate treatment. Boat drill is held in the p.m. Apparently we won't drown if we are attacked. Things are a bit tenser. We, the officers, especially are looking for trouble. Guess it will be most unexpected if we get by without a scratch."

THE MALE OFFICERS

Frank Burton, Leonard Schwade, Frederick Mackenbrock, George McShatko, Louis Forman, Harry Connelly, Frank Duffy, John Fast, J.W. Findley, Ellis Grabau, Henry Kavitt, George Mc Donald, Milan Predovich, Ed Rohlf, Edward Rosenbaum, W.B. Schafer, Kirby Shiffler, John Snyder, Roco Tello, Frank Tropea, Howard Weinberger, Wilson Weisel, Thomas Burgess, John Gordon, John Leinbach, Milton Marmer, Samuel Rifkin, Richard Stappenbeck and William Wheeler were

Margaret Hornback, in 1943...

...and in 1995. (Photos courtesy of Marnie Terhune)

doctors who served in the 48th Surgical Hospital. They had come out of residencies, private practice, volunteer reserve and some were draftees. Lt. John Flynn and Lt. John Ford were "90-day wonders," men who were college educated and had attended officer candidate schools in the States.

Since the primary task of the unit was medicine, I was fortunate to have a prominent physician and former soldier take us through much of this story— Dr. Edward E. Rosenbaum, 1st Lt. to Major 1941– 1946.

I first met with Dr. Rosenbaum in March 2001 at his beautiful home in Portland, Oregon. He made available to me extensive records of his days in the army along with many photos and books that related stories of the unit. I

Lt. John Flynn.(Photo courtesy of G. Jesse Flynn)

interviewed him for two days, met his wife Divida, one of his sons, his daughter-in-law and a grandson.

Dr. Rosenbaum later introduced me to his brother, who also served as an army medical officer in another unit in France during WW II. By chance, I was also fortunate enough to meet a neighbor, Verne Tossey, a famous artist who had served in the Italian campaign as an enlisted man, and had been in Viet Nam as an artist doing a documentary of that war.

Dr. Rosenbaum returned from WWII to become immensely successful in the field of medicine. In addition, he and his wife raised four talented children. He authored the book, *A Taste of My Own Medicine*, which became the basis for the 1991 movie, *The Doctor.* The theme of the story is that of a physician stopped short when he is diagnosed with a malignancy. Suddenly he finds himself in the role of the patient and the object of the old adage, "physician heal thyself." His illness, including the ordeal of the physician's waiting room, the aloof delivery of the cold, hard facts of his diagnosis, etc., provided lessons that humbled him and led to a major change in his bedside manner. The movie starred William Hurt and it is now mandatory viewing for most medical students. What follows is his description of the formation of the 48th Surgical Hospital as told to me, and taken from excerpts of a letter to one of his sons:

In July of 1941 Rosenbaum, a 1938 graduate of the University of Nebraska Medical School, was snug in his third year of medical residency at the Mayo Clinic. He was ordered

Dr. Edward Rosenbaum. (Photo courtesy of Edward Rosenbaum)

Dr. Lou Forman. (Photo courtesy of Edward Rosenbaum)

Dr. Frank Burton

Photo courtesy of Isabel Anthony

to interrupt his schooling and report as a first lieutenant in the United States Army Medical Corps.

At graduation, every member of his class was offered a commission in the Reserve Corps of the United States Army, which Rosenbaum accepted. In medical school, his entire military training consisted of four lectures on public health given by a retired Army Colonel. Since a military officer had conducted these lectures, the Government reasoned that the class had had enough military training for Reserve Officers. At this time the entire United States Army consisted of about 175,000 men. The country could see no reason to tax themselves for a larger military force and conscription was a dirty word. A largely untrained Reserve and National Guard were to take up the slack if an emergency arose. The war was far from the minds of Rosenbaum and his fellow students as they accepted their medical degrees on that sunny June afternoon.

President Roosevelt had promised in the campaign of 1940 and many times since, "I have said this before and I'll say it again and again and again: Your boys are not going to be sent to foreign wars." Many Americans believed him.

By September 1941, with war for America three months away, Congress, (by only one vote) extended the draft law. With the induction of the draftees, Reserve Medical Officers were ordered to active duty. At first, Rosenbaum was left alone since he was still in training but as medical officers became scarce, those in training were called. In August of 1941, he was ordered to Fort Snelling, Minnesota.

Rosenbaum had mixed feelings as he prepared to leave his residency. His pay for a twenty-four-hour-a-day, seven-day-week was a mere seventy-five dollars a month. For seven years he had studied, slaved and scrimped. The fact that his orders were only for one year, coupled with the prospect of almost two-hundred dollars a month Army pay, tempered the bitterness he felt at leaving one of the finest medical residencies in the world.

". . . You have to understand that the peacetime Army between wars was about a couple hundred thousand men. And how many doctors did they need for a couple hundred thousand men? So the medical corps was very small...these men are in good health, so there isn't much medical work. I was inducted in August of 1941 and the Army had just been raised to a million and they were continuing. But as medical officer, my first two weeks at Fort Snelling, I would have ward rounds from 9 to 10. I'd have sick call and be through at three o'clock in the afternoon. So you played tennis or golf, a little bit of drinking. And that was the life of a regular Army medical officer. Part of your medical training was a continuing ongoing practice where you saw patients. For all practical purposes that was fun. So you were a doctor in theory only."

After a short tour of duty at Fort Snelling, Rosenbaum was ordered to Fort Warren, Wyoming. When he arrived in Cheyenne, he was surprised to find that it was a bonafide city. Upon his arrival, Rosenbaum saw a bustling main street crowded with cowboys and soldiers in uniform. There were honky-tonk bars and decent hotels, motels, restaurants and clothing stores featuring western clothes and military

Dr. George McDonald. (Photo courtesy of Edward Rosenbaum)

Dr. Hyman Katzovitz. (Photo courtesy of Edward Rosenbaum)

Dr. Leonard Schwade. (Photo courtesy of Sandy Schmidt)

uniforms. The Post was on the outskirts of the city. And like Fort Snelling, there were the usual low rectangular red brick buildings along tree-lined streets. Just across the creek from the old Post a new cantonment was being built for the rapidly arriving inductees. These were white, wood, two-story rectangular barracks stretching for blocks along newly paved streets. There was no grass or shrubs, only wide-open areas around the barracks for drills, calisthenics and target practice.

Capt. Rosenbaum remembered in indelible images his first days in Cheyenne at Ft. Warren:

Above and below, Fort Warren exercises in the field, 1941. (Photos courtesy of George Willett)

"Now Cheyenne, Wyoming was already an established Army Post. It had probably been used in the Indian Wars. There were these old red brick buildings that housed the offices and the apartments for the officer personnel. They were just building the new division, which was to train quartermaster soldiers. And they built a new hospital for the quartermaster soldiers. Now when I first came there I was assigned to do medical work in the new wing of the quartermaster corps.

"In addition to our medical work we were given military assignments in order to train us. I was made a supply officer and one of us was made a motor division officer. Another doctor was made a mess officer. They were trying to break us from civilian life.

"About twenty of us physicians began learning how to read a map and set up a tent. We were assigned to work with a group of enlisted men. Together we would practice setting up and taking down the hospital. Then we would give the guys lectures on how to perform the duties of a medical technician and soldier nurse.

"The unit would do field exercises about two hours from Fort Warren at Pole Mountain. We had a two-week encampment there and spent our time setting

Max Lanning (third from left, back row) with other enlisted men at Fort Warren, 1942. (Photo courtesy of Jane Van Dyke)

up tents and taking them down. The object was to be able to set up and be operating in four hours and then break it all down and pull out as fast as possible.

"We were in a transition phase between the peacetime Army and the wartime Army. For relaxation we had an officer's mess and there was an officer's club where we'd go for drinks. Sometimes we'd have a dance. Most of us were single, but with time there were a good number of marriages with local girls.

"We had no idea of what was coming. The rumor was that we were going to go to the Philippines or to Alaska. And that's the way life was in 1941."

Rosenbaum's duties as battalion surgeon consisted of holding sick-call every morning. He was appalled by the morning line-up. Sick-call was supposed to last thirty minutes, and thirty to sixty men were reporting every day. It was impossible to examine this number of men in a short period of time. The physician who had preceded him had made this observation and had instituted an appointment schedule much like the one he had used in private practice. He did not last. He was reassigned to a post in Alaska. By now Dr. Rosenbaum had accommodated to military life and was determined to do his best as an army physician. During sick call each man walked past him in line, Rosenbaum's clerk would hand the patient some aspirin and mark his sick call slip "return to duty." Rosenbaum had an infallible rule. He never examined a man for any complaint unless he appeared on sick-call three times in a row or had a temperature over 102. This procedure proved to be effective and efficient.

Enlisted men, including Pvt. Max Lanning, far right, at Fort Warren. (Photo courtesy of Jane Van Dyke)

Some of the doctors attached to the 48th are grouped above. In front, John Leinbach, George McDonald, Leonard Schwade, Hyman Katzovitz. Back row, Russell McIntosh, Louis Kingston, Sam Rutledge, Louis Forman, Frederick Mackenbrock, Ellis Gorishek, Fred Geist, David Solomon, and Henry Borgmeyer. (Photo courtesy of Isabel Anthony)

As time passed, the army weeded out and reassigned the more qualified soldiers; the "less than perfect" GIs remained. Normally a battalion of 800 men would have been expected to produce a sick-call list of forty or fifty men a day but when this group held sick-call, as many as 400 men at a time would report. Rosenbaum stuck to his rule and soon was using a method of triage in which he would line them up, blow his whistle for attention, raise his arm high above his head and shout, "All men with sore feet report in this corner, all men with colds report in this corner, all men with backaches report in this corner, all men with the drips report in this corner and all men with fever report in the middle." This quickly separated them into five groups. His aides would then circulate among each group rapidly passing out little packets of aspirin and sending every man back to duty. He conducted sick-call with speed.

As the soldiers finished their training at Fort Warren, they were sent to other posts for advanced training. In those days, the Army did not waste money. Men were not given tickets or travel allowances and told to take off and reach their destinations on their own. To provide low-cost travel, a series of old railroad coaches was attached to a regular train. As a further money saver, the Army conducted its own mess by providing a boxcar which served as a gasoline field kitchen.

Since more and more men were being inducted into the Army, Dr. Rosenbaum would be sent downtown periodically to help perform physicals at the Army Induction Center. The procedure was simple. The new men were ordered to strip nude, then line up like sheep. In a large room, each medical officer would stand in front of a small table with an enlisted man as a clerk. Each officer was assigned a special part of the physical examination—a true medical specialist. One officer would look into the ears, another officer would check the eyes, while an officer would listen to the heart, another officer would check blood pressure and yet another officer would take the pulse. The process resembled a rapid moving assembly line. According to Dr. Rosenbaum, the attitude of the medical officers was, "If they can breathe, they're in." They would not have seen a defect if there had been one.

Some of the men tried tricks to raise their blood pressure or increase their pulse rate by taking drugs—but to no avail. No matter what the blood pressure machine recorded, the clerk always reported a normal blood pressure. There were certain physical defects that would keep a man out of the army, such as a hernia. Since a repair of a hernia involved an assault upon a person's body, there was no way that a man could be forced to repair his hernia in order to be inducted into military service. Unless a man called special attention to his hernia, the medical officer rarely acknowledged it and the man was inducted. Once in the Army, a man's body no longer belonged to him, and the commanding officer simply ordered the hernia repaired. Rosenbaum was sure that some of the young surgeons passed those boys with hernias just so they would have some surgery to do.

In his Bachelor's Officers' Quarters (BOQ), Lt. Rosenbaum received the news of the Japanese attack on Pearl Harbor calmly. Despite the news, he and his companions continued to play cards and drink their beer. In a week, they expected to leave for the Pacific and within the year, to be back home. They felt sorry for the civilians who would have to decide whether to volunteer or try to shirk military service. For them, the decision had been made and they did not regret it. They had no concept of the disaster that had befallen our country and what it meant. By noon of the first day, they were placed on a twenty-four-hour alert. All leaves were canceled. They received with pride the order not to take off their uniforms for the duration of the war.

Fort Warren enlisted men, 1942. (Photo courtesy of G. Jesse Flynn)

Their orders to develop a mobile surgical hospital were now clearly defined. A combat battalion had as part of its organization a few enlisted men who served as medical first-aid personnel to render first aid to the wounded. The first aid medics could inject morphine, stop bleeding and apply bandages. As part of their duties, the medics would attach an Emergency Medical Tag (EMT) to the wounded man's wrist. The EMT listed the man's name, his wounds, and what drugs and treatment he had received. A battalion surgeon worked at the front with these aid men. He supervised the collection of wounded into a sheltered area and could administer more definitive treatment, even giving intravenous plasma and performing some

Tented hospital units in the field; these were able to be erected or dismantled in four hours or less. (Photo courtesy of G. Jesse Flynn)

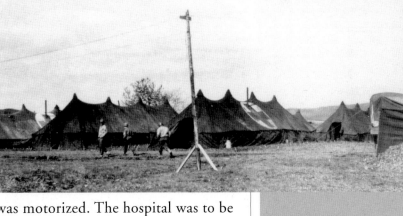

surgery. From this battalion aid station, the men were transported as soon as possible to a collecting station usually located further to the rear. The next destination in the evacuation chain was the clearing station. A mobile surgical hospital was to operate as close to the clearing station as battle conditions permitted. The hospital consisted of three elements: a mobile surgical unit which included a team of surgeons and two hospitalization units— units one and two. The entire organization was motorized. The hospital was to be housed in tents. It was to be entirely self-sufficient with its own water system, gasoline generators for lights, gas sterilizers, oil heating stoves, cots and hospital beds. The hospital was expected to be erected or dismantled and ready for action in four hours. The surgical unit would always operate at the most forward position.

Pvt. Harm Sanders in training near Pole Mountain, Wyoming. (Photo courtesy of Dora Sanders)

The hospital units would leapfrog each other; as one became full of patients, the other would move forward while the full hospital unit began the slow process of evacuation.

Rosenbaum was informed that he was to be a member of the forward surgical team. He argued that the tables of organization called for surgeons in the forward unit and he was an internist. The colonel studied the tables of organization and found a job for him—shock officer. This was the advance man of the surgical team. He took charge of the wounded as they arrived in shock and prepared them for surgery.

The staff developed a training program to teach the enlisted men their duties in the new surgical hospital. Some men were assigned to the station hospitals to learn operating room procedures and nursing; some were assigned to the motor pool to learn truck maintenance; others were appointed clerks; and still others were assigned to the labor pool to learn to erect tents, build latrines and manage sanitation. Whatever his assignment, an enlisted man was taught multiple jobs so that he could function in any capacity in an emergency.

Just as the men were becoming proficient, the Colonel received a request to recommend enlisted men for Officer Candidate School. If the Colonel recommended his best men, the efficiency of the unit would suffer. Even in wartime, military leaders at times did not consider the good of the whole. The Colonel recommended the second-stringers. He retained his best men.

Rosenbaum learned his second important lesson: if you want to advance in the Army, don't do your job well.

By July 1942, seven months after the attack on Pearl Harbor, rumors of imminent departure were rife within the 48th Surgical Hospital. One July morning when hospital personnel reported for duty, the colonel gave orders to pack and be ready to leave that night for an unnamed destination. That destination turned out to be Indiantown Gap, Pennsylvania.

Dr. Rosenbaum remembered sitting in an old dirty chair car for four days and nights as the train lumbered across the plains. The cars were crowded; there was no room to move around; the meals were brought to them. When they arrived in Indiantown Gap they were crowded into barracks jammed with cots.

On August 1, 1942, thirty-nine nurses in the charge of Lt. L.A. Salter arrived in Indiantown Gap. On the same day, seventy-seven enlisted men reported for duty with the 48th Surgical Hospital.

In the early morning hours of August 4, 1942, the members of the 48th Surgical Hospital were awakened and issued steel helmets and gas masks. These tools of combat brought the reality of their situation into focus for them. War had begun. The fun and training were over. They were in the fight. Crammed into Army trucks that were completely enclosed with canvas so that no lurking spy could count the troops, members of the 48th Surgical Hospital were driven to the docks of New York Harbor and at dawn, hustled aboard waiting ships.

Ed Rosenbaum recalled that journey:

"We were assembled on the S.S. *Manhattan*, which was a passenger ship belonging to the American line. Now in peacetime I don't know how many people it would carry. But now this is the first ground troops of the United States Army and it was important to get as many of them over as they could. So on our ship, I think there were 3,000. The way they managed to carry that many was for the enlisted men to use hammocks, three high they were strung. And there weren't enough hammocks for these enlisted men so they shared them. Twelve hours on and twelve hours off. Two men shared a hammock. By the way, they had toilets but they obviously didn't have enough so they used gutter piping on the deck. When we got on we were each given lifejackets and told not to take them off until we landed. We traveled in convoy and it took us 17 days to cross, zigging and zagging. The only other way that the troops went was on the *Queen Mary*. Now the *Queen Mary* was so fast that she could outrun any sub and she only took 5 days. But I remember our crossing was 17 days.

"The chow line never ended. You'd go through twice a day and they had big steam vats and you'd carry your mess kit. They would fill it up and then you'd clean your kit by dipping it in big 50 gallon cans of hot soapy water and then rinse water. We developed an epidemic of diarrhea. It wasn't bacterial. It was because the soap was being left in the mess kit and was not being cleaned out. But imagine when you don't have enough toilets and you're using gutter pipe for latrines and you have thousands of men that develop diarrhea. GIs were just lying in the passageways. But it only lasted a couple weeks."

Gas mask training, Fort Warren. (Photo courtesy of G. Jesse Flynn)

Walter Larson, Chief of Supply for the 48th Surgical.

ENLISTED MEN

With a few exceptions, the enlisted men of the 48th Surgical Hospital entered the Army in 1941 through April of 1942. They were mostly draftees, with a few volunteers. In one case, four men from the county that surrounded the tiny town of Hudson, South Dakota ended up in the 48th. Oliver Sorlye, Arnum Sorlie, Gilbert Smith and Charles Thorson entered the service on the same day. Gilbert became a surgical assistant and the others worked in the motor pool and maintenance.

The young men from Hudson, South Dakota— Charlie Thorson, Oliver Sorlye, Gilbert Smith. (Photo courtesy of Gilbert Smith)

Thorson, Sorlye and Smith were among the 18 well dressed men (below) from the Hudson area who reported for the draft in early 1942. (Photo courtesy of Bill Thorson)

Jodie Harmon was drafted off the farm in Robert Lee, Texas in April 1942. Jodie, a twenty-four-year-old and one of eleven children, was inducted in Abilene and sent to Fort Bliss for training. The new recruits were quartered in tents, given uniforms, fatigues, blankets, bedclothes, footlockers and WWI vintage rifles. They received haircuts and training on how to march and clean the old rifles. After about a month, Jodie was sent to El Paso where he was assigned to train at a medical replacement school. The training involved a half-day of classes and the other half working in the hospital. The classes involved anatomy, physiology, pharmacy and X-Ray. They learned how to set up instruments for surgery.

They were essentially taking a three-year nursing curriculum in eight weeks. Similar classes were attended by Gilbert Smith (South Dakota), George Willett (Kentucky), George Howe (Wisconsin) and more than fifty other enlisted soldiers.

Private Harmon completed the course and was entrained to New York City to join the 77th Evacuation Hospital to go overseas. He and thirty-eight other graduates arrived at the Brooklyn Naval Yard to meet the 77th Evacuation Hospital... but the unit wasn't there. They waited almost three weeks and the 77th still had not arrived. They were finally put on a train to Boston where they boarded the British liner HMST *Ormandy* for a convoy to Scotland. Shortly after arriving in the British Isles, they were sent south, and the orphaned group was taken in by the 48th Surgical Hospital. This did not sit well because all of them lost rating and had to start from the bottom with a new unit.

I visited Jodie Harmon at his home in Robert Lee, Texas in January 2001. I spent time with him and his lovely wife, Mary Jo, who was suffering through the final stages of an illness. She died July 31, 2002. Mr. Harmon had extensive notes and tapes of his time in the army. His was typical of the enlisted man's experience, and I offer here his combination of notes, contemporaneous tape-recordings and interviews of the enlisted man's perspective of life in the 48ᵗʰ from induction through the trip to Scotland.

JODIE HARMON – FROM INDUCTION TO ENGLAND

"I was drafted in the Army and inducted on April 14ᵗʰ 1942. I reported to Abilene, Texas with about thirty others. I was put in charge of the group and sent to the El Paso receiving station. We traveled overnight on a train. We got in to El Paso about eight o'clock in the morning and they sent trucks from Fort Bliss to come and pick us up. The first meal furnished by the Army was breakfast. We rested for a short time and then we were assigned to a tent. We were quartered in peramvle tents, which were square tents built on a plank base with plank walls about three feet high covered with a pointed top tent.

"Our day began with being issued uniforms, fatigues, blankets, bedclothes, footlocker and musket. We had to take the muskets, which had been used by World War I troops, out in the dry dirt and scrub them, polish them up and get them ready for use. Then we had to get a haircut and were shown how to make our beds and how to fix our footlockers for inspection. I spent two or three weeks at the reception center and then I was sent back to Abilene Camp Barkley and placed in medical basic training.

"The first thing I had to do after I got there was pull guard duty. We had just regular basic training and KP. This lasted through the month of May and I was called out and put on a train for an overnight trip back to El Paso where I was assigned to the medical replacement training school. We trained there to be medical and surgical technicians. Training was half a day in classes and the other half day working in William Vermont General Hospital. We studied anatomy and physiology and we also had a little schooling in Pharmacy, X-ray, how to prepare and set up surgical instruments for sterilization and set up surgical trays. In essence we were trained as nurses. I had two aunts who lived in El Paso and they said we were taking the same training that took them three years to become RNs. Of course, we didn't get as proficient as they did in that short a time, but we did get the basics.

"After my first month there I was told if we passed our grades at the end of that month we'd get a few days leave time to go home. Well, it came to the end of that month and everybody (or a good many of them) got their leave and I didn't; but I knew I had passed the grade. I went to talk to the sergeant in the office about it and told him

Pvt. Jodie Harmon (right) with Kenneth Willis (left) and Hilton Leudecke. (Photo courtesy of Jodie Harmon)

Walter Larson (left) and Loren Butts. (Photo courtesy of Walter Larson)

I'd been promised a leave if I passed the test. He checked it out and they gave me a weekend pass plus four days leave time. I planned to leave on Friday evening after the workday was over and have a weekend pass on top of a four-day leave. Then we had a visit from some "high brass" and they demanded we have a parade on Saturday. They refused to give us the pass until it was over on Saturday afternoon. That cut my leave short coming home. But by paying my way on the travel car and hitchhiking half the night I got home on Sunday morning. When my leave was about over I took a bus back to El Paso and it took all day and into the night to get there because the speed limit had been lowered to 45 mph during wartime.

"I spent the month of July finishing school. I graduated at the end of July and was assigned to the 77th Evacuation Hospital, which I was to join at the port of embarkation in Brooklyn, New York. There was a group of us—it seemed like there were thirty-nine of us that finished school and were assigned as technicians to a hospital unit. We were put on a Pullman car with a major in charge, attached to a civilian train. We went to El Paso and traveled to Chicago and arrived just before noon one day. We were supposed to have a two-hour layover and then change over to another track, which would be the New York Central. The major told us not to get so drunk that we couldn't find our way back in time to get on the train. So we had very little time to look around in Chicago.

"We arrived in Grand Central Station in New York the next morning about 7 AM and evidently no one had gotten the word that we were coming. No one knew where we were supposed to be. The major finally contacted somebody. Trucks were sent to pick us up. We had breakfast at Grand Central Station. The trucks took us down through New York City and across the Brooklyn Bridge to the Brooklyn Naval Base where the 77th was supposed to be. They weren't there, so we were taken to Fort Hamilton. We were dumped there and put up in barracks. We were then issued newer field equipment.

"After about three weeks we were taken back to the Brooklyn Navy Yard and put on a train in day coaches. We were given a sandwich, with an apple or an orange, and then we rode overnight in day coaches to an unknown destination.

"We got into Boston just before sun-up and got off the train, walked through a large warehouse and right up the gangplank onto a ship. We were aboard a British ship named HMST *Ormandy*. We hadn't had a full meal since lunch the day before so we were kind of hungry and sleepy because the train was cold and the day coach didn't allow much sleep. I was assigned to a stateroom. I thought, this doesn't look right. (It wasn't right because they thought from my name I was a woman). But I took it and didn't say anything. We were sent to the dining room to have breakfast and we had what the British call porridge. It was poor, alright. It was terrible. Anyway, I managed to get part of it down. I got in the bunk in the stateroom and took a good nap. They woke me up sometime during the day to take my ID picture. We had our pictures and cards returned to us the same day. It was about 5:20 that afternoon when the tugboats began to nudge us out from the docks and out in the bay. We sailed out of Boston harbor on the 20th of August at about 5:30 in the evening.

"When we started out we were all alone in the dark. No other ships were around that we could see. When I got to my bed in the stateroom, I had a roommate in the other bed. We woke up the next morning and it was foggy. You couldn't see anything and we were traveling at a pretty good speed for a ship. It was much later in the day before the fog lifted enough that we could see any distance. We could see now that we had a destroyer escort. By late or mid-afternoon it cleared off completely and it was just as bright and pretty as it could be. We were still traveling with one escort but later in the evening we began to see ships up ahead and we pulled into Halifax, Nova Scotia, where we joined a large convoy. Later on that night more troops loaded on our ship. That night, when they discovered I wasn't a woman, I lost my stateroom and was assigned to a hammock in the mess hall! I did enjoy my one night of upper class.

"When we sailed out from Halifax we didn't know where we were going. We just knew we were going. We knew the Atlantic was a dangerous place to be at that time. We pulled out and the patrol planes were flying

Many different kinds of ships were pressed into service as troop transports, but all of them were full, and many of the enlisted men spent much of their trans-Atlantic time on deck. (Photo courtesy of U.S. Army Signal Corps)

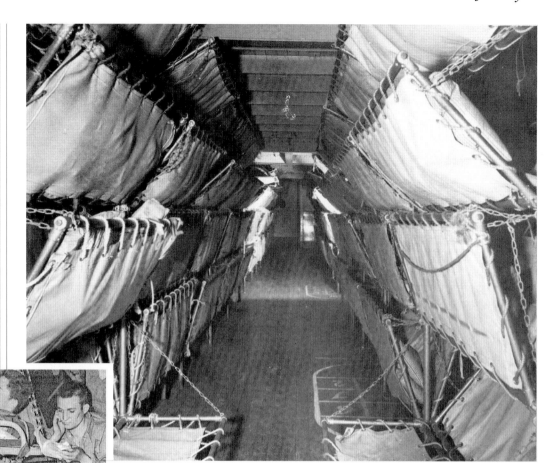

Right and below: The enlisted men crossed the Atlantic in crowded spaces below decks, sleeping two to a bunk in 12-hour shifts. (Photos courtesy of U.S. Army Signal Corps)

around us up ahead and back until we got out of their range. As I recall, on that first night I had swung a hammock over a dining table to go to sleep. That's quite a comedown from a private stateroom! I had just gotten onto the hammock when an explosion shook the ship. We were not allowed to go out on deck. All doors were locked down and guarded. The escort ships had begun to drop depth charges. That went on for awhile, and then it quieted down. We went on without a scratch.

"We sailed into Reykjavik, Iceland. I was put in charge of a work detail and ran into a friend of mine who had been on guard detail on the top deck when the explosions had occurred. He said a torpedo went behind us and struck a ship on our left side. He thought that the escorts had gotten the submarine that had hit the ship. At Reykjavik they unloaded all the American troops except the 30-odd men that were in my group. We were ordered to clean up the ship. We were soon joined by British troops that were being rotated back home and some American civilian construction workers that had been in Reykjavik working on bases.

"It was about the last day of August, I guess, when we left Reykjavik and it was snowing. The *Ormandy*, another troop ship and two British corvette sub-chasers formed a small convoy. The second night I woke up and the ship was a rockin' and reelin' and pitchin.' A large footlocker came sliding down the aisle and hit the wall on one side and then the ship would roll the other way and the footlocker would slide down the aisle to the other side. Everything loose was moving around. I put my shoes on and had to get up and tie that footlocker down before someone got hurt. The sea was really rough and when daylight came I went out on deck. In that rough weather I spent as much time as I could outside on deck because the fresh air helped prevent getting seasick. All the British soldiers were sick and vomited all over the place. The weather didn't get any better.

"That day, the next night and next day, it was still quite rough. You'd stand on deck and hang onto the rail and when it rolled to one side it looked like you were 100 feet from the water. When it rolled back to the other side it looked like you could just about touch the water."

Jodie comments on the British/American rivalry:

"There were three of us standing against the rail and one of the British soldiers came up and said, "Yank, you ain't got nothing to worry about now, that's the Royal Navy with you." Well, none of us commented much about it. After a bit he said again, "Yank, you sure don't have anything to worry about. That Royal Navy out there will protect you." One of my buddies was a pretty good-sized old boy, probably six feet tall, weighed over 200 pounds and was a former deputy sheriff out of Oklahoma. He said, "Is that the Royal Navy?" The British soldier says, "You betcha, that's the Royal Navy, you got nothing to worry about." And the guy says, "Well, two GIs, a rowboat and a sawed-off shotgun could sink those outfits." I

"I got on the boat, went to bed that night and when I got up the next morning all I could see was water. We were assigned below in the hold. Everyone got seasick. It's an awful feeling."
—*Oliver Sorlye*

"Stuck down in the hold, hammocks as our beds, we were so sick in there you could not move. We just lay there retching...the smell was awful"
—*Marcus Duxbury*

Convoys were a transportation tactic of the Allies, since there was the constant threat of attack by German U-boats. Here in the summer of 1942 the likelihood of attack was not as great as it would be seven months later, when merchant ships and transports were hunted by Axis submarines in record numbers. (Photo courtesy of U.S. Army Signal Corps)

thought we were going to have to pull him out from under some of those British boys because they're pretty proud of their Navy but we didn't hear any more after that."

"Finally after about two and a half days and nights of bad weather it calmed down and we were getting close to our destination, which turned out to be Glasgow, Scotland. We sailed right into the city. The river went right up in to town. As we docked, the kids lined the pier and we began pitching chewing gum and even hard candy that we had gotten at the PX out to them. I'm sure that's why they had lined up."

ENGLAND

THE AMERICAN BUILDUP IN THE BRITISH Isles was accompanied by various rumors about where the invasion force would strike. The most obvious was a cross-channel invasion of France, with a dual advance into Germany. Other considerations were a northern advance against Nazi-occupied Norway or the Winston Churchill idea of attacking southern Europe through the Balkans. This brought back memories of the Churchill-led disaster at Gallipoli in 1916 during World War I, when thousands of British and Australian soldiers died on the beaches of southern Turkey, leaving the surviving troops to withdraw months later.

Early in the war the British commanders felt that forces were not at a sufficient level for a direct assault on the French coast. The Balkans and Norway would stretch logistics, so a compromise was reached to attack French North Africa. From Morocco in the west, to Tunisia in the east, the French controlled thousands of miles of coastline from the Atlantic Ocean to the central Mediterranean Sea.

As the 48th Surgical Hospital—packed into trucks—drove along the streets of Glasgow, the people lined the curbs. Windows were flung open, flowers were thrown and children pointed their thumbs up—the British sign of stoicism and courage. Adults held their fingers up in the form of a V, the sign of victory. It was a rousing welcome and thrilling to all the soldiers.

A train carried them across the countryside and they arrived at Salisbury

Dr. Hyman Katzovitz (left) and Dr. Ed Rosenbaum in England. (Photo courtesy of Anna Clark)

The former luxury liner Wakefield *carried the 48th in a convoy from New York through Halifax, Nova Scotia to Glasgow, Scotland.*

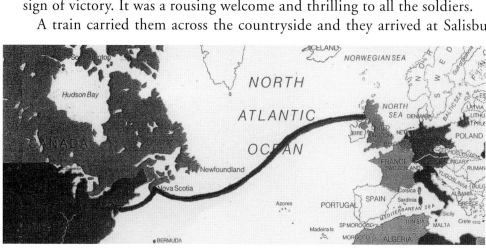

plain. There, where the battle of Hastings had been fought in 1066, the British had erected a tent camp for them. Officers and men all had tents and near each tent was a trench for shelter in case of an air raid.

There were adequate cots and blankets but food supplies were limited. American supplies had not yet arrived, so they were fed English Army rations—dark bread, orange marmalade, porridge and tea for breakfast; brussel sprouts, cabbage and a small piece of fish for lunch; for the evening meal more brussel sprouts, cabbage, tea, bread and occasionally a small piece of canned corn beef. The British knew what rationing was. Milk, oranges, butter, eggs, fresh fruits, vegetables and sweets were so strictly rationed that they were almost unknown to the civilian population.

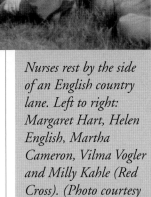

Nurses rest by the side of an English country lane. Left to right: Margaret Hart, Helen English, Martha Cameron, Vilma Vogler and Milly Kahle (Red Cross). (Photo courtesy of Anna Clark)

Private Harmon talked about his orphaned group after they off-loaded in Glasgow:

"We offloaded, took our barracks bags and our packs and went straight to the railroad station and got loaded on the train about dark. We were assigned to day coaches.

"By now it was early September and quite cold at night. We were on the train all night and part of the next day. That afternoon we arrived in England near a place called Tidworth. We unloaded and made camp where there were just American tents. They took us to a hospital unit but it wasn't the 77th; it was the 128th or, at that time, the 48th mobile surgical. The 77th had left Indiantown Gap, Pennsylvania while we were in Brooklyn at Fort Hamilton. They had been waiting for us there and when we didn't show up there was a group of recruits who had no medical training that were taken as our replacements. The 48th was waiting for the same number of basic trainees that was in our number to fill their contingency. We were just transferred from the 77th to the 48th and that put us back to the bottom of the barrel. Our technical training meant nothing anymore as far as our ratings were concerned. We were supposed to have been promoted to T-4's but we remained privates. I don't know why the 77th didn't demand to have us back because they were the ones that were needing the technicians."

The soldiers in England; marching, drilling, guarding and eating. (Photo courtesy of Isabel Anthony)

Harmon gives an example of how the enlisted man was sometimes treated as a second class soldier by some officers:

"We had to begin going through the individual interviews, as you had to do anytime you changed locations or units. When the captain was interviewing us, one of my buddies in front of me was asked what he did in civilian life. He informed the captain that he worked for Boeing Aircraft 2 Company in Seattle, Washington. The captain said, "A non-essential job, huh?" I thought he could have gotten by without making that remark. It was implied that he was holding down an essential job but apparently it wasn't essential enough that they let him be drafted. I got through my interview with him. I don't know why but he and I just didn't hit it off very well. Unfortunately, this captain was a commander of one of the units.

The 48th had two units plus the mobile surgical unit, which was designed as a small unit with an operating room, set up in back of a two-and-half ton truck.

Both the first and second unit had a head surgeon and an operating room and equipment.

"Our group had become permanently assigned to the 48th Surgical. Our days at Tidworth consisted of marching, drilling and guarding. Then we were moved to another camp that had quonset huts instead of tents. Still it was routine; we just had better living quarters and a little more comfort. We now had wooden beds with mattresses filled with straw and coal-burning stoves for heat. A short time later we moved. A rumor began that we would be attached to a unit on a hit-and-run raid on the continent.

Cooks attached to the 48th prepare a chicken dinner in the field. (Photo courtesy of Isabel Anthony)

"It wasn't long before a group of twenty of us were called out. I hadn't had a full paycheck since I'd been in the Army, so I was called in and paid. I took out ten thousand dollars worth of life insurance and we marched off to the railroad station. We spent a night on the train and ended up in Glasgow, Scotland. The next morning we got off the train, took our barracks bags and our equipment and marched up there to the edge of town on the highway, lined up, sat down and waited in the cold damp air. We waited, waited and waited. Finally, a couple of trucks picked us up and headed up into the mountains outside of Glasgow. We hadn't had anything to eat since we ate sandwiches the night before. We finally arrived at a camp high up in the mountains among tall trees and we were quartered in quonset huts. It was after dark when they showed us the way to the kitchen to try and get something to eat. They had some herring and orange marmalade. I never thought I would like orange marmalade and I never had eaten herring but I really enjoyed it; it was something to eat."

THE PERSONNEL OF THE 48TH WERE TO BEGIN a new type of life. Comforts that they had taken for granted were now nearly non-existent. Dr. Rosenbaum had been reared on a typical American diet of orange juice, milk, eggs, meat, butter and cheese at breakfast. He was not to taste another glass of milk for two years. Oranges came at Christmas time and were only for the children. An Englishman was allowed one egg a week, very few sweets and rare amounts of butter. While the members of the 48th Surgical Hospital remained in England awaiting orders, they were largely to share this diet.

Things they had taken for granted no longer existed. There was no laundry

Dr. Leonard Schwade

service; there were no showers; no running water, no sink. From now on they would have to do their own laundry. Their helmets became washbasins. They would fill their helmets with water from canvas bags and use this for their personal hygiene and laundry, then dump the dirty water and wear the hats on their heads. A simple thing like getting a haircut was a problem. One of the enlisted men had been a barber and he was pressed into service at this task for the duration.

Lt. Archard laments the new living conditions for the nurses:

"Nissen huts of corrugated iron! There were twelve iron cots to a hut—no place but the floor to hang our clothing. A small stove, which did nothing but smoke while in use, was in the center of the hut. And topping off the scene were the so-called washroom facilities—another Nissen hut with no beds at this time, just a wooden trough about ten feet long, a foot wide and waist high, with six spigots, spaced three on each side. One was very careful how one spat when cleaning one's teeth, otherwise the friend on the other side was apt to be a friend no longer. And the toilets were really something—eight ordinary buckets, each crowned with a toidy seat. We were simply appalled—and yet before we moved from there we had reached the stage where one sat enthroned and discussed the affairs of the nations with seven companions."

Another factor that added to the discomfort experienced by the Americans in England was the Dieppe Raid that took place two days after their arrival in England. The Dieppe Raid involved an amphibious landing of about ten thousand Allied soldiers, mostly Canadians, on the French Coast. It was a reconnaissance attack and it proved the strength of the German defenses. Only half of the Allied troops returned. This added to Allied tensions, as they believed they would be engaging in similar raids shortly. The Dieppe Raid had proved a miserable failure.

Members of the 48th Surgical Hospital settled into a routine and their main preoccupation became food. Officers and men constantly talked about hamburgers, steaks, milk shakes and French-fried potatoes. Their predominant malady became homesickness. It seemed to Rosenbaum that no other army suffered as much from homesickness as did the U.S. Army. From the day they arrived, they began speculating about how soon they would be rotated home. They maintained an air of optimism and assured each other that the war would be over in a short time.

To help combat homesickness, Hornback wrote home frequently and read copies of her hometown newspaper sent by her family. In her letters she writes:

September 27, 1942: England:

"I keep forgetting to tell you that the *Shelby News* (Shelby County, Kentucky) arrived and is enjoyed by all concerned. Orie, Martin and I read it, the other girls and finally some of the boys who are from Kentucky but have never been near Shelby County.

"Orie is well again. Guess she must have had flu or something. She was most unhappy, cause she missed having lots of fun with us. Yes, we try doing other

Felix H. Rascop became the unit barber. He is giving Paul Riesenberg a "field haircut." (Photo courtesy of Isabel Anthony)

things besides play sometimes but playing is our major occupation."

Shortly after they arrived, new officers and nurses joined them, bringing the number of personnel assigned to the hospital to full strength. The nurses had been working in station or general hospitals in the States and had volunteered for overseas services. Most of the enlisted men were from the east coast and had only 13 weeks of basic training. The medical officers, by Army standards, were generally older men, thirty to forty years of age. The majority had been directly commissioned as Captains from private practice and, without any preliminary training, sent overseas.

The last wave of new personnel arrived in the middle of the night during an air raid. For those experiencing an air raid for the first time, the situation was terrifying.

Dr. Rosenbaum recalls the scene: "They bumped into and fell over each other in their attempts to occupy trenches that had been dug as a protection against enemy planes. For the experienced soldiers who had been through more than a couple of air raids, the behavior of the newcomers was a source of hilarity and joking."

After touring the bomb damage in London and observing the blackouts, nurse Archard reflects on a new awareness:

"We began to have a realization of what war really meant. Up to this time it had been an adventure, not without danger, but with new lands to explore, perhaps romance, and all at the government's expense. Most of us had felt that way—we didn't know any better. England had a decidedly sobering effect.

"The blackout was really frightening. At first we scarcely dared put a foot out of the barracks at night, but gradually we became accustomed to it."

Much of the 48th's time in England was spent assembling supplies. Officers would go with men and trucks to the ports for tents, drugs, foods and surgical instruments. The trips were made under blackout conditions and it was not easy to find one's way through strange terrain in all-but-total darkness. An added danger was presented by the English custom of driving on the left side of the road and as a consequence, accidents were not infrequent.

Rosenbaum recalled being sent with another officer to Bristol for a truckload of bandages. "The only place serving an evening meal was the British Red Cross Club and we had to drive all evening just to find the place. When we got there, we were rewarded with a meat dish. The other medical officer was delighted; he could not eat enough. When we finished, we thanked the waitress, tipped her generously and asked what it was we had eaten. When she told us "sheep's heart", my

Dr. Leonard Schwade. (Photo courtesy of Sandy Schmidt)

A stainless steel sterilizer field unit. (Photo courtesy of G. Jesse Flynn)

companion gave up his entire dinner."

Other days were spent in idleness. The weather was pleasant. They played cards, chess, dice and read.

American PX supplies began to arrive. The Army furnished the troops with tobacco. Other armies gave rum and wine but the only things American enlisted men got free was tobacco and chocolate bars. Most of them smoked heavily.

One day the Colonel advised Dr. Rosenbaum that he was being sent on a secret mission, destination unknown. The Colonel was responding to a request from headquarters for six officers, six nurses and twenty enlisted men.

GIs with time on their hands always found a card game. (Photo courtesy of G. Jesse Flynn)

Rosenbaum recalled those days:

"We traveled overland to Bristol, England and settled in the field somewhere near where the Battle of Hastings had been fought. We were near Salisbury Cathedral in tents in an English encampment. We didn't know why we were there, or what we were going to do.

"One day I got a call from the Colonel and he said, 'I'm going to send you on a secret mission.' He didn't tell me any more than that. He did explain, 'I've been asked for six nurses, six officers and twenty enlisted men. I picked them and I sent them but I felt guilty because I didn't send a single trained man with them.' By trained man he meant someone who had received some military training as my group had before shipping out. 'So, I've selected you. At five in the morning you'll be at this and this street corner in Bristol. A truck will come along and you'll give them this code word and they'll let you get on the truck.' That's all I was told."

What neither the Colonel nor Dr. Rosenbaum knew at the time was that the 48th had been selected to provide medical personnel for the Roosevelt Group as the invasion of North Africa got underway. Troops were on the move.

Dr. Frank Burton and "Olle" share stories at a 400 year-old English pub. (Photo courtesy of Isabel Anthony)

Jodie Harmon, one of the enlisted men selected for the Roosevelt Group, described the training leading up to departure:

"We trained there for amphibious landing, climbing the rope net ladders and going over obstacles. We were not there very long. One day it was raining hard. It was about an hour before lunchtime and they called us down in a big rush to get all of our equipment and line up. We lined up and headed down the road double-time. It was two or three miles and we marched through the slow steady rain until we got to a shoreline that I thought was just a big lake.

"There was a large ship sitting about half to three-quarters of a mile out from shore, a three-stacker. One of the little Higgins boats was moving troops and supplies from shore out to it. We stood out there and waited in the cold rain. We waited and waited. They just kept coming in and filling up with troops and going out to the ship and coming back and getting more. Finally, about seven in the

Dr. Schwade's diary,
October 20, 1942:

"Go on absolute alert
at midnight. Probably
leave tomorrow.
Going to Glasgow,
Scotland for
embarkation to our
destination–Africa?
Expect to be on trip
for 6 weeks–wow."

*As the poster (above right)
indicates, The* Monarch
of Bermuda *(above) was
a luxury passenger ship
built in the 1930s for
vacation travel between
America and Bermuda.
The accommodations on
the ship, such as the main
lounge (right) were lavish,
and were not altered for
wartime service.*

evening it was our time to load in the hole. We boarded the Higgins boat with all our equipment but the tide had gone out, leaving us on the shore. We sat in the rain until four the next morning, waiting for the incoming tide.

Rosenbaum remembers the training and loading:

"We arrived at Inverary, Scotland and were assigned to the English barracks. It was raining, wet and cold. Every day we'd be sent to practice boarding one of the ships in the harbor. We'd climb on and off the ship with rope ladders. That's the way we spent our days.

"When we finally got underway, the wind and waves were high. We pulled alongside the big ship, and we had to time the crest of the waves in order to grab the rope ladder. After this tough ordeal, we were finally aboard the *Monarch of Bermuda* and ready to go somewhere. My thought was: could war be worse than this?"

"Finally one day, without any prior warning, the ship pulled out to sea. We had no orders, no knowledge of plans to deploy. We'd taken our bedrolls with us but we'd been doing that right along every day. And we hadn't the remotest idea in the world where we were going on that boat. Actually, we were going for the African invasion. I had this small group of six officers with me. I was not in charge; Burton outranked me. I was a Captain then and Burton was a Major. We also had these enlisted men and nurses. We were on the ship with the 26th Infantry, the 1st Division and Theodore Roosevelt's son, General Roosevelt. It was almost like being on a peacetime cruise. We were allowed a shot of liquor at dinner. We ordered from menus."

CHAPTER THREE
FROM ENGLAND TO AFRICA

THE FARMERS, NURSES, DOCTORS AND STUDENTS who had answered the call less than a year earlier to fight Japanese and German aggression were now about to be killed and wounded by the thousands with French bullets. There would be more casualties at Oran, Algeria than at Utah Beach in the invasion of Normandy eighteen months later. It was a page of history purposefully buried by the press, military and politicians. Americans were there to free the people of France and they were killing us. Why was this happening?

The French hatred of the British had been intensifying for 18 months. France had not been anxious to declare war against Germany after the invasion of Poland despite their alliance with Britain. Many saw the German move as one to re-establish the borders of Germany to their pre-WWI alignment. The British eventually goaded France into declaring war. French and German troops faced off along the Maginot line in late 1939 but there were no significant battles, rather a simple posturing. This period of September 1939 to April 1940 became known as the "sitzkrieg." England sent troops (the British Expeditionary Force, BEF) in support of the French but conveniently (according to many Frenchmen) stationed them along the French border with Belgium where there were no German soldiers within 120 kilometers. When the Germans attacked in earnest, on May 10, 1940, they moved through the Ardennes Forest, Holland and across Belgium in the direction of the British lines. After a brief advance into Belgium, the British forces abandoned their French allies, running for Dunkirk and evacuation (beginning on May 27 and completed June 1st) rather than joining the fight. French requests for planes and general armaments from their "ally" were turned down based on Britains' expressed need to retain their resources for the defense of their homeland. France sustained 92,000 dead, 250,000

> "On this ship to Africa we were with the 26th infantry. There was a young Lieutenant; we called him the "Mad Russian." He had a signal. He'd have his men kneel; point their rifles in the air and fire. This was to be their anti-aircraft protection. So I said to him 'that seems silly to me, I doubt they could stop an aircraft with machine gun fire that way.' He says 'we have to give them some hope or something they can do to defend themselves.' That Lieutenant was the first guy killed in Africa."
> —Dr. Ed Rosenbaum

The invasion of North Africa was launched from ports in Scotland, England, and Norfolk, Virginia. The objective was the capture of all French-held ports from Morocco to Tunisia.

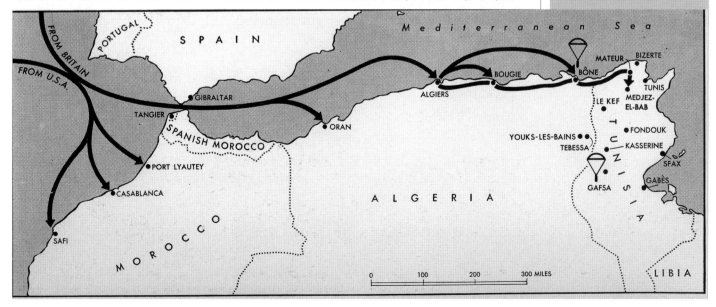

wounded and 1.5 million captured in a little over one month of war. On June 22, 1940, the French declared themselves neutral and signed an armistice with the Germans. The armistice gave the Germans control of that portion of France that would allow them to protect against an invasion from England while allowing the French government to control a portion of the country as a "sovereign power" as well as retain their military based in French colonies such as Morocco, Algeria, Tunisia and Indochina.

It was under this neutrality that a large British Naval Task Force approached the French colony port of Oran, Algeria on July 3, 1940 (at this time there were no German military units on the African continent). The battle cruiser *HMS Hood*, the aircraft carrier *Ark Royal* and two battleships, *Valiant* and *Resolution*, blocked the port and demanded the French surrender. The French fleet at Oran included two battleships, two battle-carriers, five destroyers, a seaplane carrier and many smaller ships. All were at anchor but were attempting to fire up their engines to get under way.

The French reply was sent indicating that they were in the process of disarming their ships and demobilizing their troops. Tragically, the message arrived too late. The British opened fire, almost immediately sinking the battleship *Bretagne* and killing over one thousand sailors in her crew. The battle-cruiser *Dunkerque* was next, along with the destroyers, *Provence* and *Magador*. All suffered loss of life, the final tally being 1300 French crewmen in a matter of ten minutes. The British commander would later explain that in the absence of a reply from the French, he gave the order to fire as the light of day was waning and he was under orders to complete his mission by dark. Following the battle, the British simply withdrew.

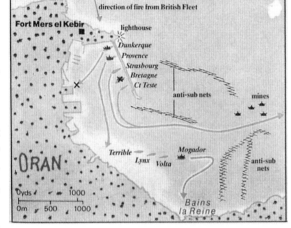

In September, 1940, just two months after the attempts by the British at Oran, the British fleet and a landing force of 5,000 attempted to seize another French African colony at Dakar. The colony resisted, damaging four British warships and driving off the landing force.

Twenty-six months later when a seven hundred ship convoy of British and American soldiers and sailors approached French North Africa, the mood on the shore was to fight.

THE TRIP

The members of the 48th were separated on two different ships for the voyage to North Africa. The *Orbita* and the *Monarch of Bermuda* were polar

---

A photograph of Fort Mers el Kebir (above) was taken by Lt. Ora White in December 1942. Eighteen months earlier it had been a scene of destruction. The British Navy took the French fleet in Oran by surprise and sunk several ships, killing over 1,000 French sailors. (Photo courtesy of Anna Clark)

Dr. Schwade's diary, October 22, 1942:

"Boarded HMS Orbita at 8:30pm. Don't know when we'll sail."

October 23, 1942:
"Still in dock on board Orbita. Was O.D. for the enlisted men in hold(deck L6)—12 noon to 6:00pm—what a hole."

October 26,1942:

"We are on our way—Cheerio."

opposites. The former was a mothballed World War I rustbucket and the latter a modern luxury liner. The *Orbita* required a great deal of cleanup by the 48th just to make it semi-livable, while the *Monarch* was clean and staffed with Indian servants.

Captain George McShatko described the *Orbita*: "The ship was a dirty, rusted, slow, rough and unpleasant hulk that was dragged from the scrap heap for our transportation to Arzew."

PFC Jodie Harmon remembered the trip from England to North Africa from an enlisted man's point of view. After sitting all night in the rain in an open Higgins boat, he finally boarded the *Monarch of Bermuda*, the second ship that would transport personnel of the 48th in the Invasion of North Africa.

"After I got my berthing card with the stateroom number on it, I unloaded my bag and reported to the kitchen for breakfast. The food was much better than what was served on the ship we had previously been on. The cooks were excellent— I think they were Indian.

"The ship was the *Monarch of Bermuda*, the British luxury liner that, in peacetime, had run from New York to Bermuda and London. It was called a honeymoon cruise ship. It had three stacks, a sundeck. Nice. Seven times around the sundeck was equal to a mile.

We finally set sail to 'destination unknown'. There are always rumors when you've got that many people together. I learned earlier not to pay much attention to rumors. We were moving along quite slowly. I was standing there on deck watching the scenery when I noticed a beer can floating alongside the ship. Someone had looped a string or a cord down over the beer can. When they pulled the thing up, they'd caught a little shark on the end of that rope. It was probably about three or four pounds!

We kept moving along and finally we came out through Glasgow, the same route we'd sailed when I came into Scotland. We got out into open waters and we joined a large convoy. That's when we knew it wasn't going to be a 'hit and run deal.' It looked to us like we were going somewhere to stay. It was extremely smooth. The ship was so large we didn't feel any movement in rough water or in ordinary seas.

"We were assigned to the 126th Infantry Regiment from the 1st Army Division. There were about twenty of us altogether, counting doctors, surgeons and I think there were several nurses on the ship. There might have been more but there were about twenty enlisted personnel and three or four doctors. The doctor in charge was a Captain by the name of Burton—a man that I learned to respect and admire as time went on. He was in command and he was a real steady type of person. A good man, an honest and good worker, he wasn't trying to make a name for himself. One of our men had appendicitis and he did surgery on him on the ship. And the man was able to go ashore with us when we landed in Africa a few days later.

"Our trip was uneventful as far as any military action was concerned. The infantry personnel put up machine guns, two on either side of the ship along the deck rails and had one machine gun on top of the third stack, which wasn't in use.

October 27, 1942:
"Got seasick after breakfast—was really sick. What a feeling—went to bed and stayed there."

October 28, 1942:
"Tried to make it on deck this a.m.—but just could not stay up. Got sick and went to bed again. Could not eat a thing."

October 29, 1942:
"Up on deck this a.m. Ate small piece of roll and tea, but still feel queasy. Tried to eat supper but got sick—went to bed and stayed there."

October 30, 1942:
"Ate very little—got kind of woozy again. Felt lousy and went to bed."

Dr. Frank Burton of Hot Springs, Arkansas, was the team leader of the medical unit aboard the Monarch of Bermuda. (Photo courtesy of Isabel Anthony)

The ship had a six-inch stern gun. The infantry had two water-cooled 50mm machine guns, one on each side of the ship. The ship also had a battery of pom-pom 20mm or 40mm anti-aircraft guns in front of the bridge."

Below the deck of the ancient *Orbita,* the enlisted men endured various indignities. Pvt. George Willett explained the toilet situation: "The toilet consisted of narrow troughs running the length of the ship that had fast running cold water that pumped in one end and went into the sea on the other. A soldier could be sitting reading the *Stars & Stripes* when a prankster some 75 to 100 feet away would light a toilet paper ship and send it down stream to heat up the unsuspecting reader."

Another incident that occurred on the trip to Africa aboard the *Orbita* is recounted by Sgt. Loren Butts:

"The officers had to take turns being the Officer of the Day. That usually meant that they had to stay in the enlisted men's quarters, eat with them and otherwise associate for a day with them. A requirement of the Officer of the Day was to wear a sidearm...a .45 caliber semi-automatic pistol. This particualr night Dr. Leonard Schwade, who had never shot or even handled a pistol, was the Officer of the Day. As he met with us he examined the pistol and placed a clip in the grip and it discharged. GIs hit the floor as the bullet careened from wall to ceiling to floor. Fortunately, no one was hurt and Dr. Schwade was a great doctor and not needed on the front lines."

Harmon relates the events of the days aboard the *Monarch*:

"We had many boat drills to stay prepared for disaster. My job was to evacuate any wounded. I was assigned to carry them up the stairs from the lower decks and to get them to the sundeck and the life rafts. Fortunately, we didn't have that problem. After more than a week on the ship we approached the Strait of Gibraltar late in the evening. It was night when we entered the Straits. Tangiers and Spanish Morocco were to our right; we were surprised that their lights were on. It was quite a sight to see a city lit up after so many nights being blacked out. New York City was on a "dim out" but it wasn't blacked out. We were standing on the deck and it was relaxing to see light like that. While we were going through the Straits, somebody shot a flare in the air up over the convoy of ships. It lit us up like daylight but nothing ever happened from it, so apparently they were friendly, whoever it was. By next morning we were in the Mediterranean. The water was so calm it looked like glass reflecting sunlight. We remained sailing all day. The Mediterranean wasn't very safe during those days. Later that evening I was lying in my bunk listening to the Army-Navy football game piped over the PA system. About 9:00 to 9:30 the captain of the ship came on the PA system and said a signal had been spotted from our Uboat or submarine to guide us in to our landing area. Just before midnight we dropped anchor about three miles offshore and started unloading troops into barges. The first group went ashore about midnight on the eighth of November. I was assigned to the ship's hospital sick bay. My duty was to help with any wounded coming back from the beaches.

"They went ashore and took the village right on the beach. They took it by complete surprise without any casualties. The captain announced over the PA that they would now pull in anchor and move in to within about one mile of the beach and anchor again. We had to pause in loading the landing craft until the ship got reset. That was done without a problem. The troops began to go ashore again. About 3:00 AM I was relieved of my duties, so I thought that it would be a good idea if I got some sleep before they called our group ashore. I also had no idea when I might get the chance to sleep again once we started landing. I went back down to my stateroom, which was just about water level. It had portholes instead of windows and they were sealed tightly. The water line came up almost to the porthole. I had a comfortable mattress and bunk. All the air vents were closed in case of fire and it was hot but I had no trouble going to sleep.

"I woke up at about 7:00 AM with the PA system. Someone was describing a naval battle just off shore, a little further out to sea than we were. But he could see it and he was describing the maneuvers just like a boxing match over the radio, blow by blow. I listened to it, kind of fascinated for a little bit and thought, I better get up to where I can see it. I may not have a chance to see anything like that again. So I hopped out of the bunk and ran upstairs and out on deck but I was too late. The British destroyer and a French destroyer were the two ships engaged in the battle."

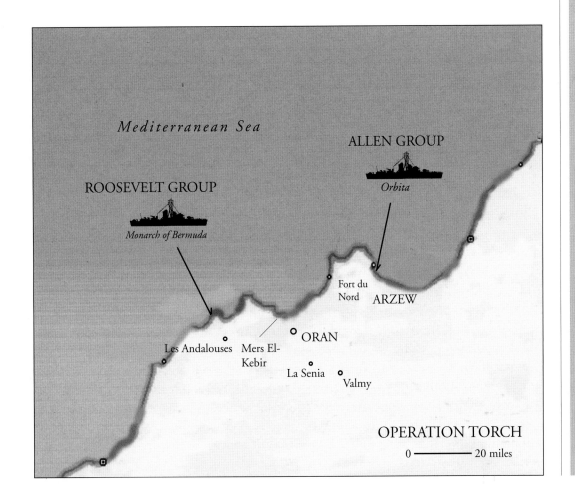

Mediterranean Sea

ALLEN GROUP

Orbita

ROOSEVELT GROUP

Monarch of Bermuda

Fort du Nord

ARZEW

Les Andalouses Mers El-Kebir

○ ORAN

La Senia ○ Valmy

OPERATION TORCH

0 —————— 20 miles

Dr. Schwade's diary, November 6, 1942:

"Began to see lights at 6 p.m. from lighthouses along Spanish coast and saw more and more as we approached Gibraltar (port side)...Expect to go through Straits of Gibraltar by 10:30 or 11 p.m. Now we are only 250 miles from our objective, Oran. 11 p.m passed Rock of Gibraltar. Stands out in black outline against the lights of Gibraltar in the background. Quite a thrill to see the Rock. Too bad we can't see it during the daytime "

Aboard the Monarch of Bermuda *Dr. Burton, Dr. Rosenbaum, and their medical unit of about twenty were with the Roosevelt Group (left) west of Oran, landing at the village of Les Andalouses. The balance of the unit was in the Allen Group aboard the* Orbita *(right), landing at Arzew, east of Oran.*

THE LANDINGS

ABOUT ONE A.M., NOVEMBER 8, 1942, the *Monarch of Bermuda* and more than one hundred other transports and warships had eased into position off the coast of Algeria, a few miles east of the port city of Oran, population 200,000.

The landings east and west of Oran were conducted in the early hours of Sunday, November 8, 1942. (Photo courtesy U.S. Army Signal Corps)

The second unit of the 48th was aboard the *HMS Orbita* just west of the city at the fishing village of Arzew.

The allied plan was to attack in three waves; the first to occur was a "coup de main" on the port of Oran by the 3rd Battalion of the 6th Armored Infantry Regiment.

Three hundred ninety-two American soldiers from the Battalion were to be carried into the harbor aboard two British ships and attempt to capture the harbor intact. The ships were former Great Lakes cutters that had been given to England in the "Lend-Lease" program. They were each two hundred fifty feet in length and named *HMS Walney* and *HMS Hartland*. Twenty-six American naval officers and men, seven Marines and over one hundred British sailors joined the battle group.

The ships had been loaded for combat in Gibraltar on the seventh and headed across the Mediterranean to crash through the boom at the harbor entrance at three AM on the 8th. The harbor was the most heavily defended in the Mediterranean. It had numerous shore batteries and forts, along with many French warships.

As the *Walney* cut the cable and entered the harbor, machine gun fire raked her. The heavy shore batteries and those of destroyers and submarines soon joined the battle. The *Walney* and *Hartland* were sent to the harbor floor. Three hundred forty-six of the 392 American soldiers were dead or wounded. In addition, five American and 113 British sailors were dead, along with eighty-six wounded.

Teresa Archard spoke to a French woman in Oran four days after the battle and was given this description of the carnage:

"She told us about the ships, American and British, coming in and firing upon the town and how they in turn were fired upon. Their house was high on the hill overlooking the harbor, and they could see everything from their balcony. They told of the ships exploding in the harbor, how men were catapulted into the air only to fall into the flaming water. She said the screams of those tortured men would stay with her for the rest of her life. All the horrors of that frightful morning and the days that followed were mirrored in her expressive face. We sat and listened, hardly breathing."

At daylight the 30,000 American soldiers in the Central Task Force, along with the 48ᵗʰ Surgical Hospital units one and two prepared to disembark to the African shore. They were totally unaware of the major disaster that had occurred a few miles away in the pre-dawn darkness.

Nurse Margaret Hornback later wrote home about the invasion experience: "We were alerted about 3:00 AM of that morning—that is, to battle stations, which we were previously assigned. Off on shore we could hear our first artillery fire and saw our first tracer bullets. It was a terrible feeling not to be able to know what was happening. As dawn came slowly we observed little flags along at intervals, which to our inexperienced eyes could be nothing but submarines. They were actually set to indicate a channel cleared of mines. I'm still wondering how the Royal Navy arranged that without being seen. At least it was day, and nobody shelled us from shore, and no flames came to molest us, for our able Rangers had done their job well. So we dropped anchor, and waited patiently for disembarking, which had to be done in small boats, which we brought along. The whole sea was full of them, looked like little ducks swimming along. We didn't go ashore 'til about three in the afternoon. The barges of course wouldn't go all the way to shore, so the boys carried us, and we didn't get very wet which was a very good thing for we carried nothing with us but iron rations, tooth brush, canteen and make-up which we sneaked in. There were a few summer cottages boarded up for the winter, and forgetting all instructions about booby traps etc. we went into them for the nite. No fires of course were allowed, so we nibbled a chocolate bar for supper, and a little after dark we lay down close together on the floor to keep each other warm."

It should be noted that Hornback consistently sanitized the actual events of the day, most likely to avoid upsetting the folks at home.

Jodie Harmon, on the other hand, described the more difficult landing of his unit 20 miles west of Oran:

"The British Navy was escorting us, and the *Monarch of Bermuda* was a

<u>Dr. Schwade's diary, November 8, 1942:</u>

"2 p.m. told to get men ready for disembarking. 3:15 p.m. disembarking in commando boat–20 enlisted men, 5 nurses and Rutledge, Markham and myself. Off on beach wading through the sea waist deep at 3:30 all wet from waist down. Has been lots of sniping going on–a few American casualties. Told that the native soldiers surrendered and then opened fire on our boys as they landed—the rats."

American soldiers waved flags and had "Old Glory" armbands in the hope that the French troops would not fire on them. This did not prove to be effective. (photo courtesy U.S. Army Signal Corps)

Transport ships unloaded men and materiel onto smaller landing craft for the push ashore. (Photo courtesy U.S. Army Signal Corps)

Dr. Schwade's diary, November 8, 1942:

"Still dark outside. Cannon and machine gun fire very visible in distance off portside. Looks like it's all from our side onto the shore. Can hear the rumblings of the big guns and see the sky lit up–like 4th of July celebration. 6:15 a.m. dawn breaking– see our convoy and large cruisers and corvettes scurrying around. Our first unloading took place at 9:30 a.m. President Roosevelt spoke to the French people last night at 1 a.m. in French telling we're their pals, etc. and we were invading."

British ship. Some of the escorts were big battleships with 16-inch guns, but the battle I missed had been between a French and a British destroyer. The French ship was sunk before I reached the deck. I missed even seeing the ship go down let alone any of the guns going off. I stayed up on deck and had everything ready to go ashore once they called us. The sun had just about come up and we had high clouds. It was not a bright morning. I could see mountains behind the beach a few miles from our location. Two of my buddies and I went out to the fantail of the ship just below the mounted six inch gun. We were standing leaning on the rail watching the boats shuttling back and forth to the beach and the activity on the shore. We happened to be looking back toward the mountains and saw three bright flashes. I made the remark, 'We'll hear the reports of that in a minute,' and one of them agreed with me, but we thought it was our shells bursting on shore. To our surprise three shells came over us just one right after the other. The first one went further out and then another just closer in and another closer than that... oh probably just about a couple hundred yards apart or in line of each other. Well, the next three shots fell short of our ship. The next three went over again and were getting closer. Our little group quickly decided that we were in trouble. The next shell came through the lifeboat that was hanging above the sundeck. It went through the wall of the ship about the edge of the deck. By that time we had been called to go ashore and had assembled in C deck square ready go down the rope ladders into the landing boat. The next shell came through the hull leading out of C deck about 100 feet from us. It hit a British Navy officer about the shoulders and it went on through the floor and down in the ship where it exploded. The poor fellow didn't know what hit him. It shredded one of his shoes that came off his foot and the other was shredded on his foot. The next shell that came through exploded below the deck we were on. A decision was made to move away from shore and the alarm was sounded for us to go to our station. As we pulled up the anchor, the battleship *Rodney* threw up a smoke screen to protect us. This battleship had 16 inch guns and it began firing back at the shore batteries. Covered by the smoke screen, we headed quickly back to sea. Once we had gotten out of range, the British destroyer that had sunk the French ship earlier, pulled alongside. They were having a burial ceremony for several of their crew who were killed in the earlier battle. We witnessed the burial from our deck rail.

"We soon turned around and came back in to our original location. This time we went down the rope ladder into the Higgins boat landing craft.

"Shortly the ramp dropped and we stepped off the boat into shallow water and ran onto a sandy beach. There was a small building on a seawall a hundred yards from the water. We ran for the cover of the seawall and building. One of the guys in my outfit just went right up the steps and into the building. I think it was a small store. He came back with a bottle of wine, enjoying himself and laughing loudly. We paused there long enough to regroup and went on through the town, up through some tangerine orchards, circled back and turned left and then back toward the beach.

"The *Rodney* was firing over our heads at the bunkers in the hills as the French artillery was firing shells at our ships. That went on till about 11:00 the next day. We took over a beach house to use as an aid station. The first injured we got were from the French ship. They had picked up the survivors and we got five or six of them.

"That evening I was placed on guard duty but didn't have a gun. I wasn't supposed to have a gun, being a Medic, but I was on guard duty to warn others in case anything began to happen. I wasn't concerned because our infantry had a machine gun set up on top of a little sand hill nearby. That night passed without incident.

"We took care of some injured there. They brought in nine dead GIs from the field and we buried them there in the shallow sand. In that tropical climate we had to bury them until a place could be found to set up a permanent cemetery. The fight was over in about three days. The grave registration sent a crew down to get the soldiers. A chaplain was leader of the crew. I helped them load the bodies. One of their crew, a sergeant, just couldn't take it and the Chaplain told him to 'get hisself on out of there if he couldn't stand it, get on out of the way, out of sight.' He didn't need him if he couldn't stand it. So, he left and we went ahead and took care of the job. I felt sorry for those boys mother's and father's. I knew it wouldn't be long till they'd be hearing about their death.

"After that battle was over we didn't have much to do. Some time during the day we'd go down to the beach and swim. There's a pretty sandy beach and the water was nice, the weather was nice and it was just a way to kind of kill time, to just enjoy ourselves. Finally we were called back to our unit. The main unit had set up over in Arzew. They sent trucks to pick us up. We had to go through a tunnel through the mountains to get to Oran and then on to Arzew.

"Still had snipers around Arzew and they'd set up a hospital unit there on the edge of town. Their password or challenge was 'High ho Silver' and the answer was 'Away.' We got in there late in the afternoon and it began to get dark before we got to the place where we were supposed to be. So I just waited and I got next to a building and unrolled my blanket. It began to get dark and I pulled my blanket over my head so that I could smoke a cigarette and have the light. We still had snipers near but the rangers were on the other side of town. Anyway, about dark I

"They were buried in a mattress cover and had one dog tag on them; the other went back to the government. That's the way it was...something terrible."
—Oliver Sorlye

After the hostilities ended in Oran, the bodies were exhumed and placed in the permanent American cemetery. (Photo courtesy of Vaughn Pulice)

Dressed in the latest fashion, the nurses of the 1st Unit pose for a picture on the shore at Arzew. (photo courtesy of G. Jesse Flynn)

Soldiers descend to waiting boats on rope ladders. (Photo courtesy of U.S. Army Corps of Engineers)

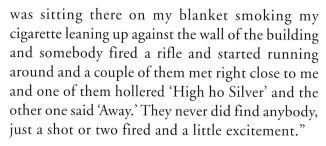

was sitting there on my blanket smoking my cigarette leaning up against the wall of the building and somebody fired a rifle and started running around and a couple of them met right close to me and one of them hollered 'High ho Silver' and the other one said 'Away.' They never did find anybody, just a shot or two fired and a little excitement."

Dr. Rosenbaum describes the trip and landings:

"Once again I wound up on a former cruise ship, this time the *Monarch of Bermuda*, along with 1,000 combat-ready infantrymen and six unarmed nurses, including Lt. Vilma Vogler. We dropped anchor on the evening of November 7 about a mile east of Oran, Algeria. I was up all night watching the infantrymen with full packs and loaded rifles climb over the ship rails, down rope ladders, and then jump into bouncing steel barges, which carried them to shore. But the beach was too narrow and the barge couldn't land, so for the last few yards the soldiers waded ashore with their rifles over their heads. By daybreak most of the soldiers had left the ship, and it was time for the medical team to follow.

"We had begun to hear sporadic rifle fire on the shore, but it seemed remote to us as we prepared to disembark. The nurses had to carry quite a load – they wore steel helmets, gas masks and 26-pound packs loaded with three day's worth of rations and canteens of water. In addition, some of them hauled knapsacks filled with extra bandages and morphine. I remember a brief feeling of surprise at seeing that women could be so physically strong.

"Then suddenly I heard the swish and whistle of an artillery shell and saw the splash as it landed near our ship. Seconds later we suffered a direct hit. A crewman was killed instantly, and smoke began to billow from the gaping hole the shell had made in the deck. The *Monarch of Bermuda* would survive the bombing, but our immediate goal was to get ashore. I'll never forget our frantic scrambling down the rope ladders. I could hear the commotion on deck, and I instantly broke out in a cold sweat. I spotted Lt. Vogler descending a ladder at my side. Our eyes met for a moment in mutual shock, and then we quickly continued downward into a waiting barge. At that moment she and the other nurses had ceased to be 'the women.' We were all comrades on equally dangerous footing, trying to survive the insanity of combat."

Margaret Hornback wrote to her family about the days following the invasion:

"About two AM on 9 November 1942, they took the town nearby, so they called us to go down to the city hospital on duty. It was undoubtedly the dirtiest hospital I'd seen although I've seen some more like it since. Perfectly huge rats had their abode there. Of course, we, the invaders, had destroyed the city water and light supply. So they lined the stretchers up side by side on the floor and we scrambled through them with flashlights, while the rats discreetly kept their distance near the walls. We had only the most meager supplies, which we could carry ashore in our hands. Guess it was logical to give combat supplies priority in unloading off the ships, but that nite we felt ours were most important. I don't suppose any morning was ever so welcomed. We did major operations with equipment that heretofore we'd have thought insufficient to run an emergency room at Shelbyville even. Throughout all this and since, too, our boys have been the best sports. They never whimper or complain. They hold on to your hand tightly during painful procedures if you've time to stand there. If not, they just take it alone."

MEDICAL OPERATIONS

The First Hospitalization Unit and the Mobile Surgical Unit took over the old military barracks, and after cleaning as thoroughly as possible, began operating four surgical tables. The Second Hospitalization Unit took over the old Infirmary two blocks away. Both units continued to operate in these places for four days. They accomplished the mission by using some captured out-dated instruments, operating with bare hands, without drapes, using alcohol-burning sterilizers and Lysol cold sterilization and using ethyl chloride and chloroform for general anesthesia. These conditions prevailed for the first thirty-six hours because the only instruments available were those of the clearing station. The infantry moved on a few miles and the port refused to unload even one of the trucks of the unit, all combat loaded. They were forced to work almost empty-handed. Despite these conditions, over 300 patients were operated upon in the three day period, with only three deaths during or following surgery. In the group there were 12 abdominal laporatomies, only one dying (and he seven weeks later), some major amputations done by flashlight for want of other light,

Arzew "city hospital" on November 9, 1942.

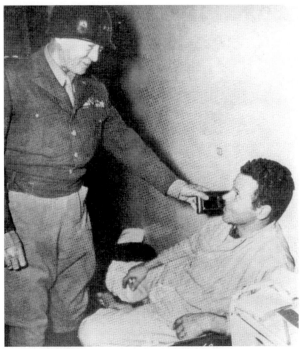

General George Patton made regular visits to the unit. He did not create fond memories for most of the medical personnel.

Dr. Schwade's diary, November 10, 1942:

"Cleaned up my building and arranged the beds, blankets, etc. amidst lots of sniping from the natives in the hills and a madhouse of confusion making arrangements about admitting patients to hospital. Still eating stew from cans–whew, I'm sick of it. Lots of bad injuries coming in– gunshot and shrapnel, fractures, etc. Air Corps, Drivers, everyone. It's a terrible mess and all in between time there is sniping going on and our boys are returning the fire– some fun."

and many wounds surgically treated. During the period there was constant sniper fire between the barracks buildings as well as sniper fire into the courtyard of the Infirmary. By the morning of the third day, conditions had improved somewhat for the hospital personnel and its patients.

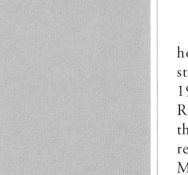

Hugh Reinier leans against his "home away from home."

Margaret Hornback described that morning when she wrote a letter to her parents:

"I shall never forget their (the patients') gratitude when on the morning of the 3rd day the chaplain melted chocolate bars and served hot chocolate on the wards. That's a good way to make hot chocolate by the way—melt a bar to about three cups of water."

Jodie Harmon told about the days that followed the invasion:

"Pretty soon it all settled down and we had the hospital units set up—part of them in tents and part of them in buildings. I had a pup tent set up out in an open city block. It began to rain and it continued for a whole week. The pup tents looked like they were a bunch of sheep in water up to their bellies. The nights were cold. I had lost my equipment or it hadn't come off the boat with me. I just had my pack with one blanket and pup tent. My legs stuck out from half the blanket and I covered myself with the other half; I almost froze to death every night. I used my cigarette lighter at night to read. It didn't furnish much light, but I could pass some time writing letters home. We stayed at Arzew through the month of December and part of January, just routine work, routine hospital operation. We treated mainly sickness and a few accidents. We were not too far from the beach, so we could take a swim to break the monotony."

After the cessation of hostilities, the unit served as a station hospital until 14 January 1943. During this period, Col. Ringer was relieved of command of the 48th Surgical Hospital and was replaced by Lt. Col. Chester A. Mellies on 24 November 1942.

When the focus of the war moved east toward Tunisia, the members of the 48th Surgical Hospital remained in Arzew. As their patients were either evacuated, or were getting well, the hospital personnel allowed time for some sight-seeing.

Mary Meyers and Margie Hart pose with a local elder.

Dr. Ed Rosenbaum remembered a special trip:

"The destination was Sidi-Bel-Abbes, headquarters of the French Foreign Legion. Movies, books, and magazine articles had glamorized this famous, volunteer French fighting force composed of men of many nations. The Legion had been evacuated to Africa after the collapse of the French Army—and was spoiling for a fight."

When they landed in Africa, the Legion had marched to meet them. They had nothing against them; they just wanted a fight for a fight's sake. Allied planes from an aircraft carrier found them on the road and, fortunately, immobilized them by destroying their trucks.

Now that they were close, a visit to this glamorous headquarters was virtually mandatory. The Colonel could not furnish Army transportation for the fifty-mile trip into the interior, so they rented a native bus. Since gasoline was in short supply, buses were fitted with converters to burn alcohol.

Twenty officers and ten nurses started on the trip. The first stop was a native village of humble mud huts. The single street was narrow, crooked and crowded with naked children, goats, and donkeys. A sizeable crowd, attracted by the nurses, soon surrounded them. One of the officers snapped a picture and this added to the excitement, for the natives objected to pictures, regarding them as an "evil eye." The gestures of the crowd toward the girls gave them cause for apprehension.

Enlisted men doing business with a local. (Photo courtesy of Isabel Anthony)

Most U.S. Army nurses were pretty and young, all of them volunteers in the strictest sense of the word. Their motivations for joining were various; some came out of pure patriotism, some because of a boyfriend in service, some for adventure, some to escape home, and some for reasons unknown.

This group of women was as brave as any men Rosenbaum knew. In the field they shared the fortunes and hardships of the soldier. Their work uniform was khaki Army coveralls, men's heavy shoes, and steel helmets. In spite of this they were feminine with hairdos, rouge, powder, lipstick, and perfume.

During the invasion they had gone ashore through the surf under enemy

fire. They had the same fears and anxieties as the men, but they never complained, shirked or shed a tear publicly. If the going became tough, it would have been easy for them to go home. No medical officer would have denied them a disability discharge if they had shown fear or anxiety.

Yet few of them took this road. They chose to share that life, and they were the jewels in the crown of the medical corps.

Dr. Burton trades for a tobacco pouch. (photo courtesy of Isabel Anthony)

Sometimes the enlisted men were jealous of the nurses' popularity. Handsome young officers pursued them. There was the excitement of a flight to Cairo with the young pilots, headquarters parties with Generals and Colonels, or dinners of steak and lobster aboard Navy ships.

Relationships between the men of the hospital and the nurses were like that of brother and sister. In spite of being with sex-starved men, they were never in danger of insult or assault. In spite of the jealousy, everyone was proud of them.

To the wounded men the nurses were an unbelievable miracle. When a soldier was wounded, he lay in pain and terror on the field. He was exposed to enemy fire and the elements. He was apprehensive that he would not be found or would be killed by enemy fire. When he was found, and transportation began to the rear, he was still terrified. Like a drowning swimmer who sees the shore, but fears his strength will fail before he can make it, the wounded soldier is weak with blood loss, fatigue, and pain. The noises of battle are around him, and he fears further wounds.

When he reaches the field hospital, he is still in artillery range and lies in dirt and blood. The sight of a woman brings a sense of relief. Surely, he thinks, the Army would not subject women to danger. He can relax into peaceful slumber and forget the war. Trained enlisted men functioned efficiently in the wards and operating rooms, but only the female could bring the comforting touch.

Rosemary McNeive and Margaret Stanfill. (Photo courtesy of G. Jesse Flynn)

On the excursion to visit the headquarters of the French Foreign Legion, it was the feminine quality of the girls that attracted the Arabs. Their coveralls bulged, their faces were rouged, their lips were red, and their hair peeked out from under their helmets. The crowd had decided that the girls were fighting soldiers, Amazons. In a culture that regarded the female as chattel, this could not be great. Their instructions were that loss of face with the natives was dangerous.

They tried to make the Arabs understand that the girls were nurses, but they misinterpreted and took it to mean that they were their mistresses—camp followers. This was a mutually acceptable conclusion for the men, because it meant an increase in male stature, a saving of face.

The girls would not leave it so. One of them pulled a bandage from her pockets, and the crowd understood. They pushed a scabby child forward, and when the nurse bandaged it, the crowd parted respectfully to let them pass.

Sidi-Bel-Abbes proved to be a modern city of sixty thousand. There were palm-lined boulevards, modern shops, sidewalk cafes, and cinemas. The Legion lived in immaculate, concrete barracks, and the men were the pictures of the correct soldier.

The Legionnaires fussed over the nurses, invited them to rendezvous, strolls or dinner. When it came time to leave, they assembled at the agreed-upon spot; everyone was prompt except one nurse. When she was still missing after an hour, Dr. Rosenbaum became apprehensive. Had they left her in the Arab village? Had someone assaulted her? Where could she be in this strange place?

Her roommate finally told. Against regulations, the missing girl had been seeing one of the sergeants. A nurse ranked as a Second Lieutenant; regulations forbade association with enlisted men. The sergeant had come to town with another group, and now they were together. When the girl appeared, no one said a word; no one reported the incident to the Colonel.

As the Christmas season approached, the weather became drizzly and cold, increasing the sense of gloom and homesickness. The abundant arrival of letters, packages and newspapers from home, for the lucky ones, lessened the depression. The packages from home were welcome Christmas gifts. They contained cans of food, candies, books, warm socks, pipes and, in rare cases, such luxuries as small cameras or radios. A few packages demonstrated poor judgment on the part of the senders. One boy received cigarettes, aspirin, razor blades, stationery, and the final insult, C rations—all items furnished by the Army.

Margaret Hornback wrote home about the packages she had received:

"Quite a few Christmas packages arrived. I had a jar of candy from cousin Ruby, and the girls at Knox sent a box for each of us—Kleenex, soap, etc. I was awfully glad to see that Woodbury soap. It's wonderful to get boxes but you'd better not send any more, for we know lots of them get lost. The hose are lovely. The British girls wear anklets, the French no socks at all and the Arabs go barefooted, and so we've resigned ourselves to our fate. But Christmas will postpone that awhile."

The nurses would not let Christmas pass without some observance. While the women proved they could be as tough as any man caught up in war, they also added a homey touch that reminded all of life without war. Christmas 1942 promised to be as dreary as any other day in that bloody winter, but at the last minute Lt. Vogler and her associates sewed up Christmas stockings for all of the patients, and filled them with a few candy bars, a comb and packs of cigarettes provided by the Red Cross.

They sent out scouting parties for an appropriate tree and found one, a scrawny specimen fourteen miles away. "The scraggly, gunshot-scarred trunk of wood looked like a beaten-up telephone pole and we labeled it a Christmas tree," Edward Rosenbaum remembered. "The women cut up strips of tin from the C-ration cans and used them for decorations. Art Carney, the dental officer, was

Ruth Haskell at Arzew, Christmas 1942. (Photo courtesy of G. Jesse Flynn)

Below: Christmas in Arzew, 1942. Capt. Art Carney played Santa Claus. (Photo courtesy of G. Jesse Flynn)

(Photos courtesy of Isabel Anthony)

Santa Claus. Then we gathered around to distribute the stockings and to sing carols. The wounded soldiers were thrilled at this ramshackle touch of home."

The lobby of the old infirmary was fittingly decorated and Father Power celebrated with Midnight Mass. Chaplain Grove and Father Power conducted services on Christmas morning for Protestants and Catholics respectively.

For Christmas Day entertainment, the men staged a musical review using their own talents. A skit in which one of the soldiers imitated a burlesque strip teaser brought down the house, but the favorite skit was on censorship. The Officer read aloud enlisted men's letters, and as he did so, deleted forbidden phrases. When he reached the end of the letter there were so many that he had to destroy the entire letter. The punch line came when the censor read the signature on the letter—it was his own letter to his wife.

The Christmas dinner was still luncheon meat and stew (turkeys arrived three days later.) "The weather was gloomy, but the girls had brought some cheer," Ed Rosenbaum recalled. "And if later that night some of the nurses shed a few tears at the sheer poignancy of it all, well, I can tell you at least one doctor went to bed that night shedding a few tears of his own." Thus passed Christmas, 1942, in North Africa.

MOVING EAST TO TUNISIA

During the entire period the winter rains were with them. Anywhere off the hard surfaced roads or walks everything was a sea of mud. Most of the enlisted men were moved into wards that were not in use. Admiral Darlan, commander of French forces in North Africa, was assassinated during this time and the unit was confined to the area. A company of Rangers was assigned to protect the unit in both locations.

On 15 January 1943, the entire unit left Arzew eastbound for Constantine, Algeria. Some equipment was sent by sea, 55 Officers and enlisted men by motor convoy, and the remainder of the personnel by rail.

They were moving forward to support their troops. They were the first American hospital moving into combat again. Trucks, tents, supplies and personnel were loaded onto wooden railcars, and they rambled forward. The four-hundred mile trip took over two days. Off the train, they loaded their trucks and began to roll to the front. The battle was fluid and the front lines fluctuated rapidly.

The convoy moved along the road on a fixed time schedule, so that there could be a free flow of military traffic. They were not within range of enemy artillery but were in range of their aircraft. Truck tops were off. At the corners of each truckbed stood a man scanning the skies. If he spotted an enemy plane, a signal was given, the trucks stopped and they scattered along the roadside.

It was a clear, sunny day and Major Rosenbaum recalls: "We were to move from the first bivouac in Africa. We got into the truck and we had guys in the trucks with rifles scanning the sky for aircraft. It was a beautiful day and I thought to myself, if I ever reach a point in life where I can ride on the road and not look up at the sky for an airplane, I'll be very happy. You know, it was just so disturbing to think that something would come out of the sky and shoot at you. You really didn't have any defense.

Nurses having lunch at Tebessa, Algeria. (Photo courtesy of Jesse Flynn)

"Every few hours the convoy stopped for a rest and the men answered the call of nature. At the first stop the nurses sat quietly in their trucks, and no one gave them a thought. At the second stop, the chief nurse, a fiery little Irish girl, ran up to the Colonel's lead car.

"She was furious: 'Sir, what about the girls?'

"The Colonel looked at her with a start; then he looked around. The land was flat, uninhabited and semi-desert. There wasn't a shelter, tree, hill or bush in sight. He looked at the nurse and shrugged his shoulders helplessly.

"She was not to be brushed aside; 'Some of my girls are ready to bust.'

"The Colonel looked hopefully at the Executive Officer. The Exec was at a loss. Army training manuals did not cover this situation. The manuals were filled with details but no one thought about a mixed convoy, carrying men and nurses, traveling through desert country. This was a problem to be referred to the first sergeant.

Nurses of the 48th in their desert taxi. (Photo courtesy of Isabel Anthony)

"He suggested erecting a tent but this was impossible; the time involved would delay the convoy and block the road for the columns behind. Someone thought of leaving the girls, driving on out of sight and then coming back for them. This wasn't practical. There were wandering tribesmen and to leave sixty American women alone on the desert even for a few minutes was unthinkable.

"After aimless discussion the little Irish gal had a twinkle in her eye. She demanded an extra ten minutes. She marched the girls a hundred yards off the road. Four girls formed a square and held up blankets between them. There could be no false modesty in the field. The proprieties had been met."

Jodie Harmon describes the trip:

"In January, it came time to move forward again. They took us over to Oran and we got on a train. It was a passenger train pulling just regular day coaches. I don't know whether they had such a thing as Pullman top coaches in that country or not. The train was old and the cars didn't have all the window glasses in them. The seats were wooden-slatted seats, facing each other. They had a fishnet basket above them for luggage or carry-on equipment. Instead of having the aisle in the middle of the car like they do here, the aisle ran down one side and then came around the end to the middle to go from one car to the other. It had a bathroom— or not really a bathroom, just a commode and sink. I suppose it was 20 to 25 people to the car. We had to place three cases of C rations in the end of the aisle where it made the turn at the end to go into the next car. Of course, there wasn't room to lie down and sleep in those seats because they had at least four men to the seats, or two to each seat. So, I checked out those C ration cases for a bed the first night. Those nights were cold out there; I slept on top of those cases fully clothed and wearing my overcoat. It was cold almost all night. The next day we got off out in the desert somewhere; we broke down and sat out there for hours. During the day it went to extreme temperatures the other way. It got hot and we sat there in that heat and waited and waited. Finally, we got going again. The next night, the second night, since we had eaten one of those cases of C rations, it left me only two to sleep on. So I left a gap between them and I managed to get by through that night. The next morning we were getting into the mountains and it was getting colder still. There would be frost over everything in the early morning."

Both the convoy and rail shipments arrived in Constantine on 17 January and the unit bivouacked in the Foreign Legion Park. The hills of Constantine made an indelible mark on Margaret Hornback:

"There was never anything to compare with the sunrises and the nights here. I can see why people who live here don't feel satisfied elsewhere, but think I'll have enough to last me."

1st Lt. Roberta Tayhoe in the book *Combat Nurse* describes Constantine January 17, 1943:

"Next day a walk into one of the most unusual cities I have ever seen. Constantine has a very deep narrow canyon right through the middle. Several bridges connect the two parts, and there is an ancient fort on the very top which, of course, I had to see. Quite a walk up there, but what a panorama—picturesque valleys, mountains, and hills north and west; in fact, a view in every direction; the African colors with changing lights!"

⁓

The following day, 18 January 1943, the sea shipment was transported to the unit and the 48th moved out intact to the vicinity of Tebessa, and would set up camp in the wooded hills eleven miles north of the city.

On 24 January the First Hospitalization Unit was ordered to set up a hospital near Thala, Tunisia. On 27 January the Second Hospital Unit with the Mobile Surgical Unit were ordered to Feriana, Tunisia to set up a hospital in the old French outpost barracks. These barracks were of the one-story type and were in an advanced state of disrepair. Large holes in the roofs, windows out, and no doors were the rule, not the exception. These were repaired with cardboard,

Nurses relaxing at the Constantine National Forest. (Photo courtesy of G. Jesse Flynn)

Helen Moloney at Feriana, Tunisia. (Photo courtesy of G. Jesse Flynn)

Nurses at Feriana prior to the German attack. Back: Gladys Martin, Teresa Archard, (unidentified), Doris Brittingham, Mildred Harris, Vivian Sheridan, Marie Kelly. Front: Mildred Kaelin, (unidentified), Margaret Hart, (unidentified), (unidentified). (Photo courtesy of G. Jesse Flynn)

canvas, and any materials available. GI pot-bellied stoves were placed in each ward. Tents were erected for the mess and supply tents.

On 1 February the First unit closed down at Thala and rejoined the Second and mobile units. After three days the unit was ordered again to Thala to set up and reopen. 10 February 1943, organization day, found all units operating.

THE GERMANS ATTACK AT KASSERINE PASS

On 15 February 1943, German forces under the command of Field Marshall Erwin Rommel launched a counter-offensive against the American sector. The Second Unit and the Mobile Unit with Headquarters were ordered to evacuate and clear the area immediately. Orders were received at 2030 hours and by 2400 they were closed, packed and moved. The Second Unit moved back and set up at Bou Chebka, and before patients could be received, it was forced to move again, this time back to Youks les Bains, Algeria. The First Unit was forced out of their area at Thala.

Jodie Harmon remembered those times:

"One day the whole Army began to move back past us coming from the front. The Germans were attacking and we were in full retreat. Late that evening the commander couldn't understand why we hadn't received orders. Why was everyone retreating and not us? So he and a first sergeant got in the command car and left to go to corps headquarters and find out. They sent word back for us to stack all of our equipment and get it ready to burn in case we had to surrender. We

Dr. Schwade's diary, February 1, 1943:

"We moved out at 11:00 a.m. to Feriana, where 2nd Unit is working. Nice barracks – don't think we'll stay here long. Many planes overhead at all times – 2 big airfields nearby. Saw many camel caravans on way here."

"I had just finished building a nice six-seat latrine for the unit, and the very next day we were ordered to leave. The Germans captured it the next day, and boy that made me mad."
—Oliver Sorlye

got everything torn down except one ward tent and maybe another small tent that had a few patients that we had no way to move. All vehicles were in use moving other units to the rear. We finished before nightfall. The wind was blowing hard and it was a cold February night. We just lay down and went to sleep expecting to be in enemy hands when we woke up or maybe wake up in time to torch our equipment. A little bit after midnight, a two and half ton truck came rolling in and a large sergeant came along and jerked the blanket off of us and said to get our equipment together and get on the truck.

"Going down those narrow dirt roads in the dark, I don't know if we were moving fast; we got into civilians that were running, too. We then began to meet the British tanks coming to take our place. They were being hauled on lowboys. The speedometers on those vehicles were luminous so you could read them at night. One of the guys riding in front said part of the time it was running at 70 mph.

"We got lost and almost drove into enemy lines. Finally, we found our way out and got to a location where we were to set up and start operating. We worked the rest of the night, the next day and the next night getting everything set up. When we finally got finished, they gave us orders to get some much-needed rest. I went and got my blankets and lay down and slept the rest of that day, ate chow that evening, went back to bed and slept that night. Next day we were ordered to tear down to move again. We never received a patient there."

Capt. Rosenbaum remembered their retreat at Kasserine Pass:

"Our training proved to be very important when we were trapped in the Kasserine Pass. We didn't abandon any troops and we got the trucks out and got all the equipment out because our men were trained like circus roustabouts. They knew how to move that stuff out.

"We, as soldiers—and this is standard military operation, I'm sure—knew nothing about what was to happen and what wasn't happening. We were just given orders. Move here, strike the hospital, let's move out as fast as we can. Get in line with the convoy. We weren't told where we were going or what we were going to do because in case we were captured we couldn't give any information."

Two days later the First Unit moved to La Meskiana, Algeria. After handling patients from the large Evacuation Hospitals so they might retreat further, the Second Unit closed the hospital and went to Montesquieu, Algeria and set up a hospital.

Margaret Hornback's letter two months after Kasserine read:

"Most of our travels have been forward except that incident of Kasserine

KASSERINE PASS 14-22 February 1943

On February 14, 1943, German Field Marshal Rommel made a bold attack on the American positions in southern Tunisia. The 1st Unit of the 48th was located in Thala; the 2nd Unit was in Feriana. The positions at Feriana were overrun on February 16, and the unit experienced a hair-raising nightime escape across 30 miles of mountains to Bou Chebka, Algeria. By the 17th the Germans had advanced to within five miles of Thala, and the 1st Unit evacuated to Le Kef, Tunisia.

"I remember one night in Feriana helping unload 83 wounded soldiers. The Germans had broken through."
–Oliver Sorlye

"I remember we went to Pole Mountain, Wyoming for two weeks training in setting up and tearing down tents as fast as possible. This proved to be very important when we were trapped at Kasserine Pass. We didn't abandon any troops and we got all trucks and equipment out. Our men were trained like circus roustabouts. They knew how to move that stuff out!"
–Dr. Ed Rosenbaum

Pass which, contrary to the reports of Time magazine and others, was not a disgraceful defeat. And if those guys think they could do better, they might come over and try it. It was part of the plan for the British to have the lion's share in this campaign to avenge Dunkirk. But it's no picnic to try to stand still and hold a sector without advancing until the British arrive for the kill. They're excellent fighters, it's true, but they should be, as they've been at it so long. I'm glad our boys don't hate as they do.

"We've covered most of the fighting until the last set-up here. We were worked as two separate units one covering north sector, the other south. We keep the more serious patients, sending the others on back.

"Boy, if we ever get back to the good old USA… still we have lots of fun. Our boys [the medical corpsmen] are such cute eggs and they're really a challenge to teach OR technique. I've expected them to hang themselves in suture material at times.

"Spring is at last coming to this charming country, I hope. It actually looks like there might be a little green around sometime. The almond orchards are certainly the ladies' things—white as snow. You remember in the last chapter of Ecclesiastes where it compares white hair to the almond tree? One can appreciate how they got that simile, for they are such marked contrast to all the dirt round about."

Dr. Schwade's diary describes the anxiety and confusion in the unit located in Thala as the Germans drew closer.

February 17:

"Started getting patients from Bou Chebka, not far from here. Boys hurt pretty badly. One died after 20 minutes. Heard Jerrie's are in Kasserine and a little

beyond. Things really are popping. Worked in shock ward and kept fairly busy.

February 19, 1943:

"We are the only medical unit between the German's ahead and Tebessa – everyone else has pulled out. Tanks, halftracks, trucks, guns, cannon – everything is just jamming the road back towards Tebessa. Can't get any satisfaction from C.O. (Lt. Col.) by phone. Decided to pack up and get ready to pull out; what a mess. At about 9 p.m. Col. M. pulled in and what a mix up. "A" section pulled out for bivouac on road to [Souh-Abras], past Le Kef. I slept in shock ward and up at 6:30 a.m. to the bivouac in ambulance – set up by noon. Visited a farmer across the road and got a dozen eggs and [Muscatel] wine. All set to stay for a while when at 5:30 field message arrived to move immediately, as soon as transportation arrives. What a M.F.U. we are. Men are all fired up and disgusted. Supposed to go past Tebessa and to Constantine – why? What? Who knows?"

The order to retreat from Thala finally came on the 20th as recorded by Dr. Schwade:

"Up at 7:30 a.m. Nice day, slept well, had breakfast. No trucks came for us during the nite or as yet. Shaved and sitting around in tent talking to Katz – reading "House Beautiful" magazine. I just don't give a damn whether we move or not. Day was nice until 3:00 p.m. when we got orders to move again – Sect. "B" this time. Trucks arrived at 4:00 p.m. We ate supper and pulled out at 5:30 – what a life.

"Muddy – slippery – we went into ditch once and almost turned over. Everybody bitching. Passed 100's tanks and U.S./British on way. Arrived at destination 10 miles from 2nd unit (Youks les Bains) at 2:00 a.m. but we got orders to move 15 miles farther towards Constantine (La Meskiana). Finally found location up in hills under trees (camouflage) to set up and got to bed at 3:45 a.m. Mad and tired – this is three moves in three days – what an outfit."

Post-operative ward, Tunisia.

February 22, 1943:

"We are supposed to go to a place called Montesquieu. Moving in a.m. (had meeting with Maj. Mackenbrock at 6:00 p.m.) Germans are at Kasserine and also at Thala fighting Allies. Lost 14 tanks there (Germans did). Allies are supposed to have destroyed at least 70 German tanks by this a.m. according to the tank officer Mack talked to this a.m. Sure hope we do something pretty quick or these Germans will be going places and prolong this damn war in Africa. Well, we will see what tomorrow's news will bring."

February 23, 1943:

"Supposed to move today. I counted 50 Flying Fortresses going over us towards the east and 12 P-38's. Somebody's going to get bombed and *plenty*. Just heard we won't move today – probably tomorrow sometime."

February 25, 1943:

"News very good for us. Germans driven out of Kasserine Pass. Played poker in kitchen and won 175 francs."

On March 8, 1943 the second unit with the mobile unit and headquarters detachment moved forward as the American forces took the offensive again. Margaret Hornback wrote:

"We've been quite busy. I can't remember if I've written you since we've been here or not. In case I didn't, we have a marvelous surgery in an old schoolhouse, tile floors for most everything is a form of tile in Africa, plastered walls and ceiling over our head. The room I'd say would be about the size of Mattye Sees front yard. In it we run three tables and keep up all supplies, not to mention instrument water, sterilizers and autoclave and a charming tall French stove, with ornamental a plenty, but in which you cannot keep a fire to save your soul."

While at Youks les Bains, soldiers had an opportunity to avail themselves of the luxury of a bath. However, the bathhouse turned out to be a mixed blessing. Jodie Harmon remembered this:

"In Youks les Bains they had a public bathhouse, a mineral water bathhouse and natural hot water. It wasn't easy getting a bath in those days out in the field. I did get a chance to get one in that place. That mineral water didn't smell too good but I guess it did get us clean."

An operating tent, Tunisia.

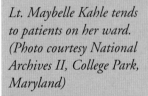

Lt. Maybelle Kahle tends to patients on her ward. (Photo courtesy National Archives II, College Park, Maryland)

At this time another change was made in the organization. Lt. Col. Chester A. Mellies was relieved of command and Col. Norman H. Wiley became the fourth commanding officer on 15 March 1943.

On 19 March, First Unit was ordered to set up in the old French Barracks at Feriana. The Mobile Unit and Headquarters accompanied them on this mission.

It was a mission that Dr. Rosenbaum would never forget:

". . . The shock officer was in charge of triage but it just went automatically. We took whoever was sickest into the surgical tent or shock tent first. There'd be nurses or enlisted men taking care of the patients. The enlisted men were getting pretty well

trained as they went along. The nurse was very important psychologically.

"We had a medical tag called the EMT, the emergency medical tag. We would put it around the patient's neck and write down on it what we had done, such as give him morphine, so that if he moved back, the guy who had him next would know what had been done. The first treatment was at a battalion aid station that was commanded by a doctor, with enlisted men assisting. Basically they were outfitted with morphine and bandages. Then they had what they called "collecting" stations and "clearing" stations and we would be right up there with them. In other

words, the battalion aid station would pick them up and bring them back to us. But we were always within a couple of miles. They had ambulances that would carry litters. And they'd bring them in on jeeps and trucks and ambulances."

One of Rosenbaum's duties that still stands out in his mind is blood transfusions, a simple procedure taken for granted today. It was much more complicated in the early days of the war. Dr. Rosenbaum explains:

This surgical team includes Evelyn Vaughn Fisher (second from left) and Larry Inderrieden (far right).

"Before WW II a blood transfusion was a major procedure. The way a blood transfusion was done—you matched the blood of the donor and the recipient to be sure that it was the compatible blood type. Then the donor would lie in one bed and the recipient in the other and you transfused from one human being to the other because the blood had to be sterile. It was very important that it matched and it had to be sterile and warm. So transfusions were 'live.' From 1938 until the war people were working on ways to preserve blood in case of war and also for civilian use. They came up with blood plasma. What they did was sterilize it and freeze it. You ended up with a powder in one bottle and a liquid in the other. You'd combine them and that would give you plasma. That is what you'd use for a transfusion. Now, that was better than nothing but it still wasn't the equal of whole blood because it lacked the red cells.

"The mobile unit was supposed to go ahead and be supported by one hospital unit. I was assigned to the mobile unit as a shock officer. At times of combat I was chief shock officer. When there was no combat I was assistant chief of medicine. As the combat officer, I got the wounded first and I had this plasma to give them. It was better than nothing but it didn't work perfectly. It was not as good as whole blood. So we came up (and I really take credit for this because it was my insistence) with this: we set up another tent and we'd get guys who had non-combatant jobs who would donate blood so we had whole

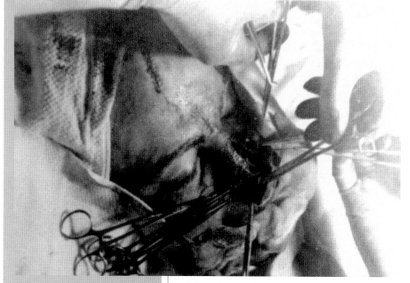

blood to treat some of the wounded. We'd give them a shot of whiskey for this. But we only did that in the African campaign. It would never have worked for mass casualties."

Devastating injuries, such as the facial reconstruction shown here, were routine in the heavy fighting in Tunisia.

Jodie Harmon reflected on their time at Feriana:

"They assigned me one of those old barracks buildings to set up a wardroom for patients. It was intended for post-operative shock patients, what we call I.C.U now. It was staffed by a doctor who happened to be the commanding officer of our unit and a nurse and me and another private. I was on daylight shift at the time. This room held about 18 maybe 20 patients. We had it full. A spot close to a stove for heat held our workbench and desk which took up about what an ordinary hospital bed would take up. It was about that much room, maybe a little more. Almost every bed stayed full. No sooner we had one out we would bring in another one. We'd keep them long enough to be moved back further behind lines or to another hospital ward in the area.

Dr. Frank Tropea, Jr., assisted by Lt. Mary Hatcher and Sgt. Gilbert Smith, successfully removed this live bazooka shell from a lucky GI's chest.

"One day, about noontime, I was sitting down on the floor eating my C rations. These little huts had a door at each end of them. The door opened and in comes General George Patton and his bodyguards. I glanced up when they came in and I knew immediately who it was. He had on his riding britches, his ivory-handled six shooters and riding boots; clean as a pin. He didn't have any mud, dust or dirt on him that I could see. His riding boots were shining like new money. He walked in…I moved my feet out of the aisle, so he wouldn't stumble over them. I went on about my business, eating my lunch. Well, he didn't tear in; he just walked through and looked at the patients on either side of the aisle as he went through. Then, later on, another three or four days, he came in again. This time I was working on a patient on one side of the aisle and he came through that same door. Between me and that door he stopped at the bed of one of my patients, fresh out of surgery—tubes in him, needles sticking in him and so forth, bandaged up. He was looking at the names on the charts hanging on the beds. We had old-style hospital beds, nothing fancy, just a little better than a litter. Anyway, he read this soldier's name and said, 'Young man…' I myself was around twenty-five years old. This kid was probably around 19, maybe 20. Anyway, he called his name and the boy was just barely able to answer him. He said, 'And you're the one who surrendered and when you came up and waved your flag they shot you?' And he affirmed that he was. The General then used some choice words and said, 'That's what they ought to have done. A soldier doesn't ever give up. You ought to have been shot.' Well, right about that time I would have hit him over the head with a club if I had had one. But I couldn't see that it would've done any good. Fact is, it did more harm than good to talk to the boy that way. The war was over for this kid, anyway. I wondered just what the General would have done had he been in the same position. Anyway, he got through chewing

Dr. Frank Burton attends a particularly gruesome leg wound.

Photo courtesy of Isabel Anthony

him out and he went on out the door. Didn't see him around there anymore.

"We operated there at full load for I don't know how long. The admission recorded a little over 700 casualties coming through in one 24-hour period. And those were rather busy times. Of course, it's always a balance, coming to a high point and then fading down. So it had cooled down as far as casualties were concerned and the fronts moved further away. I kept operating there and just dropped back to a routine. We had a couple of guys come down with the mumps, two of our own men. So they put up a [primal] tent out there, put some bunks in it, put them in isolation and gave me the job of taking care of them. The Army, in case of mumps, would keep a man in bed for 21 days. You don't need to get out of bed for anything. So, I had to wait on them hand and foot. They had another soldier come in from the field; they thought he had the mumps. His throat was so swollen that they were afraid it was gonna close up on him requiring a tracheotomy. They placed him in my tent, so that gave me three patients. They brought in a tracheotomy tray and left it on the desk for me in case he did become unable to breath. I don't know if I could have done an incision or not but I guess I could have if it had become necessary. But as it happened they found that he had a boil in his throat and he didn't have mumps at all. So they went to treat him properly and got him cleared up."

On 27 March 1943 the Second Unit was ordered to Gafsa to set up near this highly important battlefront. The Mobile Surgical Unit and Headquarters joined the Second immediately. During this period Ivan "Cy" Peterman, the well-known war correspondent, was brought to the hospital as a patient.

Peterman had broken his arm as he had jumped from his jeep into a ditch in an effort to avoid enemy planes that were strafing the road. Several days after his arm was set and he was feeling better, Peterman decided to write an article for a deadline that was fast approaching.

His broken arm prevented him from typing the article as he usually did and Sgt. Loren Butts offered to type the article for him. The two sat in the 1st Sergeant's tent and were working on the article when the air raid siren sounded and enemy planes flew over the hospital, strafing and bombing as they went. With bombs and tracer bullets streaking through the darkness of the night, the two men sat in total darkness. Peterman dictated the article while Butts used his skills as a touch typist to put the article down on paper.

The article, which appeared in *Liberty* magazine in 1943, was titled, "Medics Also Fought." Peterman's words were vivid and dramatic and painted a clear picture of the life of medics on or near the frontlines of battle:

"The third night under that hospital tent in Tunisia was the worst. Nobody slept because of the traffic, inside and out. The Army's 48th Surgical Hospital stood just twelve miles behind El Guettar, and as reinforcements and supplies cascaded toward the front, ambulances poured 416 wounded men through Admissions between dusk and dawn. Eighty-six required emergency operations; the rest, after examination, were sent back to Tebessa.

"At intervals a new arrival would brush the canvas flap of our tent, his litter-bearers searching for an empty cot. At the opposite exit, doctors huddled before bundling a short-term patient into the 'meat wagon.' It was a hundred-mile trek to

Cy Peterman. (Photo courtesy of Liberty Magazine)

Gladys Self. (Photo courtesy of Walter L. Jones, Jr.)

nurses of this outfit are the most veteran of any in Africa.

"There are nearly 60 of them, and they're living just like the soldiers at the front. They have run out of nearly everything feminine. They wear heavy issue shoes, and even men's G.I. underwear. Most of the time they wear Army coveralls instead of dresses.

"I asked them what to put in the column that they'd like sent from home, and here is what they want—cleansing creams and tissues, fountain pens, shampoos and underwear. That's all they ask. They don't want slips, for they don't wear them.

"These girls can really take it. They eat out of mess kits when they're on the move. They do their own washing. They stand regular duty hours all the time, and in emergencies they work without thought of the hours.

"During battles they are swamped. Then between battles they have little to do, for a front-line hospital must always be kept pretty free of patients to make room for a sudden influx. A surgical hospital seldom keeps a patient more than three days.

"They lead a miserably blank social life. There is absolutely no town life in Central Tunisia, even if they could get to a town...war is no fun for them." (Photo courtesy of Anna Clark)

"During these lax periods the nurses fill in their time by rolling bandages, sewing sheets and generally getting everything ready for the next storm.

"They lead a miserably blank social life. There is absolutely no town life in Central Tunisia, even if they could get to a town. Occasionally an officer will take them for a jeep ride, but usually they're not even permitted to walk up and down the road. They just work, and sleep, and sit, and write letters. War is no fun for them.

"They make $186 a month and pay $21 of it for mess. There's nothing to buy over here, so nearly all of them send money home.

"Like the soldiers, they have learned what a valuable implement the steel helmet is. They use it as a foot bath, as a wastebasket, as a dirty-clothes hamper, to carry water in, as a cooking utensil, as a chair, as a candleholder, as a rain-hat, and—er, ah—yes, even as an emergency toilet on cold nights!

"Being nurses and accustomed to physical misery, they have not been shocked or upset by the badly wounded men they care for. The thing that has impressed them most is the way the wounded men act. They say they've worked with wounded men lying knee-deep outside the operating rooms, and never does one whimper or complain. They say it's remarkable."

SHORTLY AFTER ERNIE PYLE'S ARTICLE appeared in print, the 48th Surgical Hospital was pulled back from the front lines, reorganized and reborn as the 128th

48TH TO THE 128TH

Evacuation Hospital. In her letters home, Margaret Hornback commented on the reorganization of their hospital:

> "We've covered most of the fighting until the last setup here. We were worked as two separate units one covering north sector, the other south. We keep the more serious patients sending the others on back. Since other hospitals arrived in the front, we were reorganized into one unit and became the 128th Evac. We disliked that idea, but we're growing accustomed to it now, and our work is much the same as before."

Hornback was not the only person at 128th Evacuation Hospital who longed for the days when they worked as the 48th Surgical Hospital. Jodie Harmon remembered the experience in detail:

Annie Cooney and Gladys Self near Hill 609, Tunisia.

"15 April 1943, both units shut down and all assembled at Feriana. The following day the entire organization moved on the long trip to the north of Tunisia. The unit was again supposed to set up in old French barracks, but they were dusty and dirty so Col. Wiley found a very nice location alongside a cork grove and there the old 48th Surgical Hospital set up for the last time on the 19th April."

Capt. Rosenbaum had vivid memories of the final days of the old 48th Surgical Hospital. General George Patton's wounded troops were among the hospital's patients:

<u>Dr. Schwade's diary, March 23, 1943:</u>

"Lt. Gen. George Patton visited today. He sure is a bruiser. Said that the 'German tanks were stopped and we would set them on their ass by tonight.' We still have plenty of casualties coming in."

"... What happened when an officer would come on the ward, the patients, if they were able, would jump out of bed and stand at attention. The wounded wouldn't do this, naturally, but somebody who was in for an emotional problem would. So Patton and his entourage came on this ward and these soldiers jumped out of bed and Patton goes up to this one guy and he wants to commend him, and he says, 'Son, what happened to you?' and the kid says he had combat fatigue and Patton slapped him. That happened in my tent. Now, the men used to say, "Blood and Guts Patton. He's got the guts and we've got the blood."

Rosenbaum also had memories of one of his fellow physicians:

"Ed Rohlf was from Waterloo, Iowa. He was a small-town surgeon but proficient in the operating room. He didn't have administrative duties, he worked strictly as a surgeon.

"Ed devised a great way to relax. He would fill an IV bottle with wine, attach a hose, then lay back on his cot and sip the wine by sucking on the tubing! What a character!

Gen. Patton visits wounded troops at the 48th. (Photo courtesy of the Patton Museum of Cavalry and Armor)

"He said something to me that I've never forgotten. After the African campaign we got some newspapers from home and one newspaper had the headline, 'GREAT VICTORY. ONLY 100 MEN KILLED.' And Rohlf said, 'Do you realize that for those 100 men and their families the mortality rate is 100%?'"

Rosenbaum spoke of another doctor apparently weary of war:

"There was another physician who shall go unnamed, a general practitioner who was a little older than the rest of us. One day—it's over 100 in the shade in Africa—he dresses himself up in a mac and scarf and earmuffs and walks up and down the company streets yelling, 'It's cold, it's cold, it's cold!' So they tackle him and take him in and figure that he's had a nervous breakdown. They send him home! After that everybody said, 'Crazy as _____.' You do understand what I'm saying?"

In this location and pursuant to CG #34, on 1 May 1943 the organization became the 128th Evacuation Hospital (Semi-Mobile). The strength of the command of the old 48th was at this time 48 officers, 56 nurses and 275 enlisted men. The new T O/E (Army structure) did not allow this number. A certain number had to be transferred and, in some instances, normal attrition was to take care of the excess personnel. The new 128th Evacuation Hospital moved on 4 May 1943 to the little station by famous hill 609 called Sidi Nisir. This new location presented previously unavailable opportunities to the personnel of the 128th Evacuation Hospital.

Margaret Hornback's letter of 8 May 1943, described some of these leisure-time activities:

"Yesterday there was a soft, warm rain that really felt like home. We went swimming the day before. It's really blue Mediterranean now. It was also exceedingly cold. I had just taken my second typhoid shot, which didn't help matters, but it was swell anyhow. You'd have loved it, the water was clear as a bell and it's so easy to swim in it. You can get out and ride in on the tide.

"We went up to one of the former battlefields last week, our first time to see one before it was cleared away. American troops were plotting the graves there. Ours on one side of the road, the Germans on the other. You remember that little poem, Under the Willow the Blue, Under the Laurel the Grey? Same kind of boys on both sides. What a pity!"

On 8 May 1943, the fighting stopped in Tunisia. Jodie Harmon noted the event in his diary:

"The unit remained in Sidi Nisir through the cease-fire order of 18 May 1943, and on 13 June 1943 moved to the area on Lac Bizerte east of Ferryville. Here the unit opened as a medical hospital, with malaria and dysentery the chief

The cemeteries at Hill 609. The American cemetery (top photo); the German cemetery (bottom photo).

Margaret Hornback writes, "Under the Willow the Blue, Under the Laurel the Gray? Same kind of boys on both sides..."

foes." Capt. Rosenbaum remembered that not only did their patients have malaria but members of the 128th were ill as well.

"Well, I think, considering our age and the time, we were pretty well trained and pretty confident. Now, one of the things was we were in Africa and American doctors were really not trained in tropical medicine. Because, after all, we never saw tropical diseases in Nebraska or in North Dakota. The only medical schools that taught tropical medicine were down south like Louisiana and we didn't have anybody from Louisiana. But what happened was, in the middle of the African campaign they sent me to an English school of tropical medicine in North Africa. The English had set up a school in a resort town on the coast called Hammet Muskateen and I was sent there for a week to learn tropical medicine. When I came, at the end of the fighting in Africa, soldiers started to come in with chills and fever. Mackenbrock, who was the Chief, had been trained in the Panama Canal. He knew malaria and he immediately diagnosed malaria. I think we had 400 cases of malaria admitted at one time. We treated them with quinine, which was the accepted treatment for malaria at that time. We didn't lose a single soldier. We thought we were gonna get some commendation; instead we were severely censored because we had used quinine, which was in very short supply because it's derived from the bark of a Cinchona tree.

They had just developed synthetic Atabrine and we had an ample supply. We were supposed to use the Atabrine instead of quinine. With the malaria under control, we suddenly began to see jaundiced patients who had hepatitis. Now the interesting thing is, doctors really knew very, very little about hepatitis; it's a viral disease. But in those days it was an exceedingly rare disease and we didn't understand it. We really didn't have any treatment except rest and a good diet. I had a ward full of hepatitis."

Capt. Frank Burton (far right) and three other officers pose by a sign that indicates 32 kilometers to Tunis. (Photo courtesy of Isabel Anthony)

The wrecked city of Bizerte was the last home for the MASH unit in Tunisia. The weather was hot and the flies thick before the late July embarkation to Sicily. (Photo courtesy of U.S. Army Corps of Engineers)

CHAPTER FOUR
THE SICILIAN CAMPAIGN

THE MILITARY AND POLITICAL decisions that were being made by the American Army in the spring of 1943 were simple. The objective was to keep pressure on the Germans without a direct confrontation in France. This meant that the Allied forces in Africa would invade the "underbelly" of Europe. The Axis-controlled areas that were in striking distance of Africa included Sardinia, Sicily, and the Balkans. The island of Sicily was chosen for its proximity to Tunisia and the purpose of knocking Italy out of the war.

The code name given to the invasion at the Casablanca conference in January 1943 was "HUSKY." The Allied force (British/American) would include 3,000 ships and 150,000 soldiers. Overall command was entrusted to American General Dwight Eisenhower, while British troops were commanded by Bernard Montgomery. The Americans were to be led by Gen. George S. Patton.

Patton's troops (The U.S. 7th Army) were to land in and around the port towns of Gela and Lacata. They consisted of one armored, one airborne and four infantry divisions. His objectives were to strike across the island to the north and west, then to push eastward to the town of Messina where he would join the British, who were to land in the southern port of Syracuse, then move north to Messina.

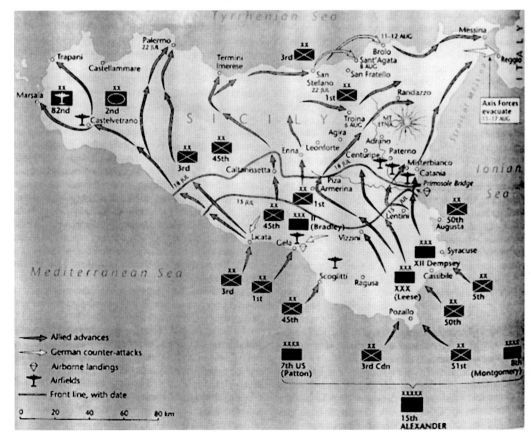

Dr. Schwade's diary, July 5, 1943:

"During the night at 4 a.m. terrific air barrage at Ferryville. Continuous shower of red and white lights. One bomber zoomed over us trying to evade the search-lights and barrage and two shells landed in our area. One landed three feet from message center tent and went about 20 feet in the ground. The other landed 200 feet from our latrine and exploded–sure a close call."

Castellammare (right) proved to be the most beautiful of the towns to which the 128th was assigned in Sicily.

Castellammare Beach, 1943. (Photo courtesy of Loren Butts)

Lacata, Sicily was the destination of the unit in late July, 1943. The 128th moved across the island following the 3rd Infantry to the area around Palermo. (Photo courtesy of U.S. Army Signal Corps)

The U.S. 7th Army sailed from the ports of Tunis and Bizerte on the ninth of July, landing on the tenth at Lacata and Gela in Sicily. The 128th Evacuation Hospital received the assignment to support the 7th Army that was commanded by General George Patton.

On 19 July 1943, the unit moved to a staging area near Bizerte to prepare for shipment again. On 22 July 1943, the first group of personnel of the 128th Evacuation Hospital landed at Lacata, Sicily.

Margaret Hornback remembered that rough sea voyage from Tunisia and her arrival on Sicily's shores:

"That was the rockingest boat that ever sailed the sea. Me thinks we were the sickest crowd that ever sailed the seas, too. There's nothing to equal it. Even our tail wagger dog was sick... We had a tiny little boat, only three officers and the crew besides the nurses and the thing really rode the waves. We just lay down on deck in the dirt and stayed there til we arrived. One thing tho, you feel so good when its over . . . My, but we were happy to set foot on dry land again.

"We landed on one side of the island and our post was on the opposite side, so we had another truck ride across country. Sicily is mostly mountainous, as you've probably already read. The country is terribly poor, but it's cleaner than Africa, and there are no Arabs, praise Allah!

"The people were quite glad to see us and quite a number of them gave us the Fascist salute. We'll have to correct that. Many of them speak English and not a few have lived in the States. One man (in whose vineyard we set up the hospital) told us he made lots of money in the States, and then came back here to retire. But Mussolini interfered with that taking everything he had.

"You've never seen the equal of the roads over here. Being mountainous, they have the sharpest of curves, and I don't think they had American traffic in mind when they built them. Then the Germans methodically burned all bridges behind them and that's a serious matter here for the streams are deep. So they made detours over old Roman roads. The same were built in stairs terraced about 4-6 inches high. So you can imagine driving down a steep curving staircase in a truck with a trailer. Betcha jerry would laugh up his sleeve at that. It was even funny to us."

Camp set-up in Castellammare del Golfo, Sicily, September 1943. (Photo courtesy of Vaughn Pulice)

Capt. Ed Rosenbaum will never forget his arrival on the beach in Sicily:

"We went into Sicily late—I say late, we weren't a part of the invasion, maybe D-10 or something like that. And we went in small groups. I was on an LST and the skipper of the LST probably had less experience than I'd had. We landed on the beach and we didn't have mess tents or anything like that, everybody had to take care of their own food. They had just issued K-rations for the first time, which were better than C-rations, which came in a tin can. One of the things we did, we would take a tin can and fill it half full with soil, then pour gasoline on it and light the gasoline and we'd have a flame with the soil acting as a wick and that's the way we'd heat our coffee and have hot water and do our cooking. Well, after we'd landed I made myself a tin-can burner and somebody lit a match close by and the thing exploded in my hands. I badly burned most of my hands and they were wrapped up in gauze bandages like boxing gloves. I couldn't work and they sort of just let me hang around."

Rosenbaum recalled his limited duty assignment on Sicily:

"The outfit started to move forward. Since I couldn't work (I couldn't use my hands), I was left with the wounded that couldn't be moved, in an olive grove. A man came along; he spoke perfect English, and was from Chicago. He'd been born in Sicily and had migrated to Chicago and had returned to Sicily to settle the family estate and was caught by the war. His wife was an American girl. So he invited the few soldiers in the olive grove to come to his house for dinner. So we had a good dinner, but the interesting thing was, according to the custom of the country, the women were not allowed to sit down and eat until all the men had eaten. I talked with this girl from Chicago and she said it was a man's country, the women did all the work, and all the men did was hunt and fish."

Capt. Ed Rosenbaum after his accident on the beach in Sicily. (Photo courtesy of Dr. Edward Rosenbaum)

Margaret Hornback wrote home about her life in Sicily:

"I miss vegetables cooked like home. Limas with good cream, or corn on the cob.

"We buy tomatoes, grapes, and melons almost as many as we can eat. Last night we had dinner in an Italian home. They had spaghetti cooked with chicken, much as we would dumplings, but with shredded cheese over it. It was delicious.

They then had the chicken, potatoes boiled and fried, tomato salad, fruit, watermelon, then cake and coffee. Each course is served separately on the most beautiful china."

Margaret Stanfill near the OR tent at Castellammare, Sicily, September 1943.(Photo courtesy of Vaughn Pulice)

A Friday night in 1943 – Margaret Hornback's letter home:

"Tonight I'm on night duty, and one of my wards are sick nurses. Everybody has been taking quinine and is practically deaf. The rest of the army is in attendance and such yelling you never heard. I'm expecting the officer of the day any minute now to tell me to tell them to be quiet."

While Jodie Harmon was a tonsillectomy patient at an army hospital in Palermo, he had an opportunity to observe a unique facet of Sicilian life. He remembered his experience in detail:

"This hospital was right downtown in Palermo. They put me in a room with three other fellas. One of them had a leg amputation. They were trying to clear up the infection in my throat so they could operate.

"I could look out the window of the hospital and watch people in the streets. They lived in the upper part of their homes and kept their animals in the lower part of the houses. Across the street there was a man who'd bring his horse out on the street and hose him down every morning, hook him to a cart and head out of town. A little later on, a man would come along with a couple of cows and milk goats. People would line up at the corner of the intersection with pots, pans, cups or whatever container to get the milk in. It was first-come, first-served, and he would just sit there, milk it direct from the cow or the goat, whichever they wanted, and fill their containers. That was the method of delivering milk. It was quite interesting what you could see on those streets during the day.

"In about a week the decision was made to remove my tonsils. I was given tranquilizers and painkillers early on the morning of my surgery. When the doctor came to take me to the operating room, I couldn't stand up alone. I had to lean up against him to walk. I got down there and they put me in what looked like a dental chair and the doctor proceeded with his little wire squeezer to remove my tonsils. My tonsils had had so many ulcers and scar tissue that they looked like an old corncob. I was managing to stay in the chair but it was hard to do. I was put back to bed and I bled a lot the rest of the day and night. It took me a good while to recover. I was in the hospital for about a week before I was discharged. I guess they wouldn't have discharged me then if our troops hadn't invaded Italy on 9 September 1943. They were going to need my bed for casualties coming from Italy.

Alcamo, Sicily, October 1943. (Photo courtesy of Isabel Anthony)

"The discharge men sent me out to the staging area, out there where the hundreds and hundreds of soldiers were coming through. They

Dr. Schwade's diary, August 18, 1943:

"Well, looks like we'll be moving again soon –evacuate patients. Whoops–changed again–what a screw up–sure wish they'd make up their minds. Hot and sticky day. Swimming couple times. Heard that all the Lt's would be promoted very soon – we will see. Today marks one year overseas duty for me. Like a dream. Well, all of Sicily is ours."

had an office right there at the entrance. I went into the office and asked them if they knew where my unit was. They didn't know. They said you can't leave here until you get somebody to sign for you. I didn't know what I was going to do then. I knew I was gonna have to wait so I just told him to pick me a spot where I could put my stuff down and stay with it. I walked out, maybe a hundred feet from the office. I could see everything coming and going out the gate and I sat under a scrubby tree. I put my pack down and leaned over on my elbow, propping my head on my hand. I was just sort of trying to get comfortable, trying to figure out what I was going to do next.

"If I stayed there I would have probably been shipped out to Italy as a replacement. I guess I probably hadn't been there twenty minutes when an ambulance came driving in through the gate. I recognized it as one from an outfit close to us. I jumped up and headed to the officer and asked him if he was driving that ambulance. I explained my situation and he agreed to "sign me out." I asked him, 'Are you still where you were a couple of weeks ago?' And he said yes he was. I told him what outfit I was with and I asked him if they were still there. He said yes they were still there. I said, "Well, come inside and sign me out. I'm going to go back with you.

"I got back to the 128th late that night. I wasn't yet ready to go back to duty because I couldn't eat solid foods, so they put me in our hospital for about three days. When I went back on duty we weren't doing a whole lot except routine – malaria cases, jaundice and accidents."

THE STORM

On the early morning (0700 British Double Summer time) of 2 October 1943, a very strong storm struck the 128th. Approximately 195 patients were then on the wards of the hospital. Within a five minute period every tent in the organization had been completely torn down by the force of the storm. Tent poles were broken, canvas ripped, the X-Ray equipment and laboratory equipment lay broken and ruined.

Margaret Hornback described that storm in a letter sent home:

October 10, 1943: Sicily:

"We've been well entertained lately in keeping soul and body together. The rainy season started about ten days ago, and with it a good twisting wind that just at dawn, one morning, simply flattened our hospital out, leaving about two tents standing. You've never seen a mess to quite equal it. Everything soaking and muddy. With our supplies all wet, we could only pray fervently while we tried to bail torrents of water out of the autoclaves and get them working."

August 24, 1943:
"Met Col. and he led us to area near Castellammare del Golfo – 20 miles from Trapani. Wow – what a place. Don't see how anyone could ever find this spot. Slept under the stars tonight. Bombing and flashing light over Palermo."

October 2, 1943:
"At 6:30 a.m. terrific rain storm and wind came up–blew all ward tents and most of officers tents down. X-ray, Dental, etc. all damaged. Katz and I had a hell of a time holding tent up–got soaked...funny and serious. Moved tents to another area."

In the aftermath of the storm, hospital personnel examined the destruction. (Photo courtesy of Isabel Anthony)

Directory of Camp Setup of the 128th Evacuation Hospital

1. Office of CO and XO
2. HQ
3. Registrat & Dispensary
4. Receiving Ward #1
5. Latrine/Amb. patients
6. Receiving Ward #2
7. X-Ray Department
8. Lab & Dental Clinic
9. Pharmacy/Blood Bank
10. Double Ward
11. Double Ward Pre-Op Shock
12. Op. Rooms & Central Supply
13. Double Ward Pre-Op Non Shock
14. Prof. Svcs. HQ & Library
15. Generators
16. Office of Head Nurse
17. Exhaustion-War Neurosis
18. Isolation Wards
19. Double Ward
20. Double Ward
21. Double Ward
22. Double Ward Post-Op
    Head & Abdominal
23. Double Ward Post-Op
    Orthopedic & Chest
24. Double Ward
25. Double Ward
26. Double Ward
27. Shower Tent
28. Guard Tent
29. Detachment HQ
30. Enl. Men Recreation Tent
31. Enl. Men Mess tent
32. Food Storage
33. Enl. Men Kitchen
34. Patient's Kitchen
35. Diet Kitchen
36. Officer Patient's Latrine
37. G.U. Latrine
38. Dysentery Latrine
39. Patient's Latrine
40. Utilities
41. Medical Supply
42. Linen Supply
43. Dirty Linen
44. QM & other storage
45. Morgue
46. Chapel
47. Dispatcher
48. CO HQ
49. Officers' Quarters
50. Officers' Latrine
51. Officers & Nurses
    Dishwashing Tent
52. Officers & Nurses Kitchen
53. Officers & Nurses Mess
54. Officers & Nurses Recreation Tent
55. Nurses' Latrine
56. Quarters of Chief Nurse
57. Nurses' Quarters
58. Special Service & ARC Tent

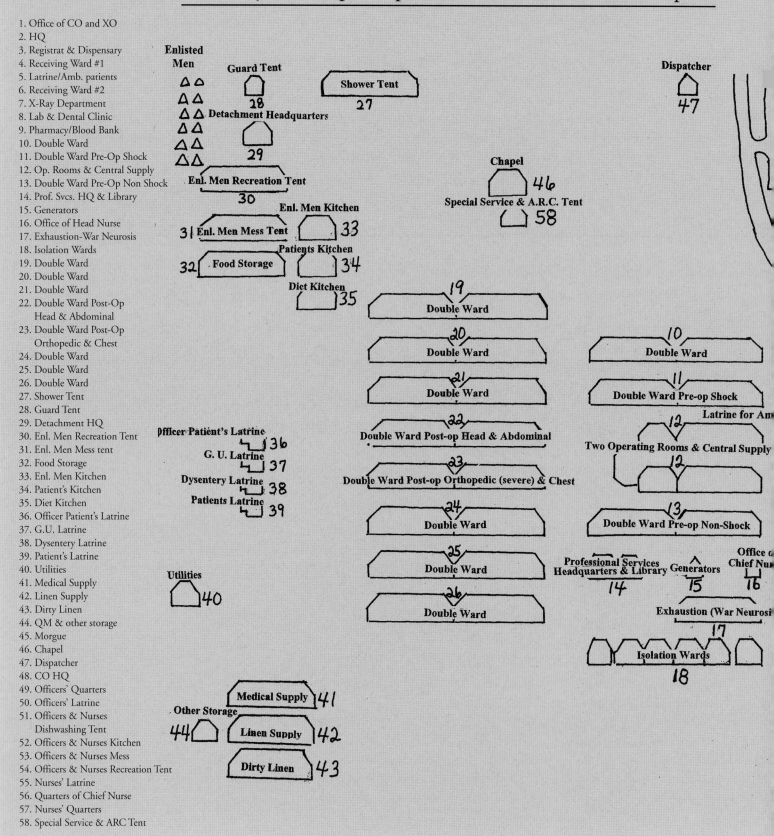

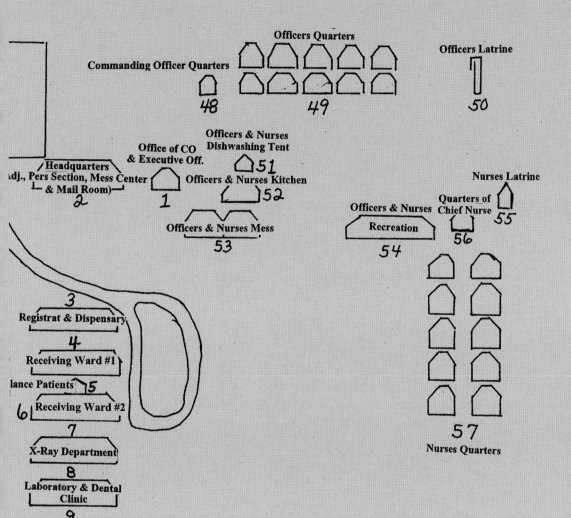

Officers Quarters

Commanding Officer Quarters

48

49

Officers Latrine

50

Headquarters
(Adj., Pers Section, Mess Center
& Mail Room)

2

**Office of CO
& Executive Off.**

1

**Officers & Nurses
Dishwashing Tent**

51

Officers & Nurses Kitchen

52

Officers & Nurses Mess

53

Registrat & Dispensary

3

Receiving Ward #1

4

Ambulance Patients

5

Receiving Ward #2

6

7

X-Ray Department

8

**Laboratory & Dental
Clinic**

9

**Pharmacy & Living
Blood Bank**

**Officers & Nurses
Recreation**

54

**Quarters of
Chief Nurse**

56

Nurses Latrine

55

57

Nurses Quarters

Morgue

45

The huge tent city depicted in the drawing was the home of the MASH unit for much of the war. It was efficiently laid out for fast processing of wounded soldiers. It has great similarities to hospitals of today. For example, the first stop (#3 Registrat), where the patient is booked is adjacent to #4 (Receiving Ward No. 1) and Pre-Operative Shock Ward (#11) for the most severely wounded soldiers. The Pre-Op Non-Shock (#13) has two operating rooms in between.

One of the "Main Streets" of the 128th, with double ward tents arranged in rows as neat as could be managed.

The enlisted men lived in these small pup tents; small but adequate, especially when placed under a shade tree.

In front: Doris Friedlund, (unknown), Helen Moloney; in back: Gladys Martin, Martha Cameron.

This view shows pup tents, wards, and surgical tents in the background.

Left: The Central Supply Tent, with Lawrence Inderrieden, Doris Friedlund, Holt, and Leo Weber.

Above, the tent complex in Heggin, Belgium, November 1944.

The personnel ward assignments below were reconstructted from unit records:

#1: Lt. Col. George McShatko, Col. Meritt Ringer, Maj. Frederick Mackenbrock, Maj. John Snyder, Lt. Col. Chester Mellies, Col. Norman Wiley, Col. Charles Gingles, Lt. Col. Wm Proffitt, M/Sgt. Loren Butts (Comm in HQ)

 # 2: Marcus Duxbury (mail), 2nd Lt. Vincent Klein (Adj.)

 # 3: Lt. John Ford, Jr., WOJG Thomas Dooken

Ward 4: Elizabeth Coates, Margaret Hornback, Genevieve Kruzic, Capt. Samuel Rutledge, Jr.

Ward 6: Capt. Max Mansfield

 # 7: Capt. William Wheeler

 # 8: Capt. Harold Rosencrans (dental), Capt. Louis Forman (lab)

Ward 10: Margaret Madigan, Margaret Miller, T/5 James Dick, T/4 Robert Hartman, Pvt. Peterson

Ward 11: Gladys Martin, Etoyl Grier, Catherine Cunningham, Cpl. Jack Dennis, Pvt. Fulks, T/4 Christ Kopan, T/5 James Whitman

Ward 12: Capt. Hyman Katzovitz, Capt. Leonard Schwade, Capt. John Leimbach, Jr., Capt. Arthur Leeroy, Capt. Samuel Rifkin, Maj. Frank Burton, Capt. Edward Rohlf, Capt. Michael DeVito, Capt. John Gordon, Capt. Harry Connelly, Capt. Frank Tropea, Jr., Capt. John Fast, Capt. Howard Weinberger, Capt. Thomas Burgess, Capt. James Findley, Capt. William Gorishek, Capt. Henry Kavitt

 # 12A (Supply): Walter Larson

 # 12B: Capt. Henry Borgmeyer, Maj. Richard Clark, Maj. Edward Rosenbaum, Capt. David Solomom, Capt. Richard Stappenbeck, Capt. Frederick Geist, Capt. Frank Duffy, Dr. Milton Marmer, Capt. George McDonald, Dr. Milan Predovitch,

Capt. Richard King, Capt. Wilson Weisel, Capt. Rocko Tello, Capt. Harry Kirby Shiffler, Capt. Russell McIntosh, Capt. Harold Klockseim, Capt. Ellis Grabau, Vaughn Fisher, T/3 Gilbert Smith

Ward 13: Carrie Smith, Cpl. Dexter Conner, T/5 John Mathistad, Cpl. Earl McCullough, Cpl. Raymond Nefstead

 # 16: Mary Ann Sullivan, Teresa Archard (unit 2)

Ward 17: Vivian Sheridan, Mildred Harris, Maj. Harry Rainey

Ward 18: Vivian Sheridan, Mildred Harris, T/5 Joseph Douglas, Cpl. Melvin Woodruff

Ward 19: Helen Moloney

Ward 20: Annie Gecke

Ward 21: Marie Kelly, T/5 Mario Calcaterra, T/4 Clarence Laurenson, Cpl. George Renninger, Pfc. John Swezey

Ward 22: Ora White, Doris H. Friedlund, Ruth Parks, Eva Sacks, Pvt. George Willett, Pfc. Jodie Harmon, Pfc. Al Davis, T/5 John Hoctor, T/5 McLaughlin, T/5 Donald Wertz

Ward 23: Doris Brittingham, Emily Nickerson, Mary Francis, Vilma Vogler, Mary Hamaker, Ella Ferree, Mary Hatcher, Pvt. Aragon, Pfc. Donald Chinn, Cpl. Delmer Smith

Ward 24: Helen English, Phyllis MacDonald, Beryl Karban, T/4 Frank Kukowski, Cpl. Julian Sagan

Ward 25: Nell Williams, T/4 Burton Hurley, Cpl. Oliver Tarr

 # 29: 2nd Lt. Rupert Meier, Jr.

 # 35: Helen Hobson

 # 41: Capt. Charles Ebbert

 # 46: Samuel "Chappie" Grove, Frank Arsenault, Father Paniera, John Power

 # 53: 1st Lt. Ray Moore

The storm ripped away the tents that provided shelter in the patient wards.

Jodie Harmon described the destruction of that storm:

"We had a rain squall, high winds come through. It didn't last long but when it passed over we didn't have a hospital tent standing. No one was seriously hurt. We had an amputee in a pyramidal tent and there were two or three guys handy that managed to hold the tent pole up, to keep it from falling on him. I think every other tent pole in the outfit was broken. My pup tent was still standing. I had it tied to a tree from both ends and somehow it didn't affect it."

The devastation of the storm convinced the 128th CO to move into a nearby town and operate the hospital in buildings.

Margaret Hornback describes relocation after the storm:

"After the storm, we moved to town, and what a town! We took over a military hospital, which houses some of the patients. We have a hotel for nurses' quarters. You should see it. In this country, windows all open on a central courtyard —a kind of skylight effect. The rooms are small, dark, and smell like the goats that live in the aforementioned courtyard, but their rooms are heaven when it rains. Some of the rooms have electrical current, but mine doesn't . . . but candlelight is swell when the wind doesn't blow. I have a wardrobe for my clothes (which I don't need much since the storm), a vanity, two chairs and a cot. I feel like a queen. We have water, too, 7-11 AM daily. We're not moving about much during that time. The population is not accustomed to more water than that; in fact, I'm sure they don't take full advantage of those four hours. These are the filthiest places—this town (Alcamo) has a population of around 50-60 thousand and no more area than Shelbyville (Kentucky, population 5,000).

"The streets are narrow, and the sheep and goats sit on the sidewalk so the people must walk in the streets. We're the first Americans in this town and they really mob you."

ON AUGUST 17, 1943, the Americans and British met in Messina. The whole island was now in the hands of the Allies. The total Allied wounded and killed was 16,000, with 7,000 of those casualties coming from Patton's army. The campaign had taken only 38 days due to the fighting retreat and the Germans' successful evacuation across the Straits of Messina to mainland Italy.

Capt. Rosenbaum recalled one incident that occurred while the 128th Evacuation Hospital was stationed in Palermo:

"The American troops were marching through Palermo and the Sicilians were standing on the sidewalk, watching. This old Sicilian ran up and grabbed one of the American soldiers and hugged him and said, 'My son, my son.' It was this man's grandson. He'd never seen him but the daughter had written that their son was in the Army and he stood and watched and he recognized similarities. I think that story was written up in *Stars and Stripes*.

Although Sicily proved to be one of the shortest campaigns, lasting only thirty-eight days, the 128th remained in Sicily for weeks after the fighting had ceased. On 8 November 1943 members of the 128th Evacuation Hospital packed and boarded a ship heading for England, where they would train inexperienced hospital personnel for the promised invasion of the European continent.

November 8, 1943 was the one-year anniversary of the unit's entry into combat in Operation Torch. They departed the combat zone as the most experienced field hospital in the American Army. They had received and treated 21,305 patients in the twelve preceding months. 2,586 soldiers received surgery and the unit had moved and set up thirty times. At this point in the war it was the prototype MASH unit and was well deserving of a rest.

Capt. Rosenbaum remembered their trip to England:

"After the Sicilian campaign, we were put on board a ship to go back to England. On this ship we were served a hot meal for the first time in months. We hadn't had anything like it in Africa. It was steak and potatoes, a real meal and I couldn't eat it. I was so nauseated, I thought I was having a nervous breakdown. So I left the table and went into my bunk to sort of sleep it off. Major Mackenbrock, who was chief of medicine (I was assistant chief of medicine), came up and looked at me and he says, 'You're a Chinaman.' I had turned yellow. I had one of the early cases of hepatitis. I was jaundiced. So I laid in my bunk the whole trip. I got all the oranges I wanted. That's one of the things I had missed the most—fresh oranges."

Capt. Rosenbaum and other exhausted and ill members of the 128th Evac. would have time and leisure to recuperate in England before their next assignment.

November 5, 1943:
"Muddy out–rained almost every day for the past week. Lee Roy fined $25–ain't war great fun?"

November 7, 1943:
"Rained all night again– boy, this is sure a rainy place. Our Italian prisoners left today to be reclassified. They all feel pretty bad leaving– some cried. Beni, one who worked for us and did our laundry, said we American officers were 'good and kind.'"

November 11, 1943, Palermo harbor aboard the USAT *Santa Paula*:
"We're out in harbor. We pulled out at 10 p.m. Where to?"

Capt. Leonard Schwade

Dr. Schwade's diary, November 24, 1943:

"Boat pitched and rolled all night. Thought it would fall apart. In Irish Channel now. We'll land tonight probably and debark tomorrow morning. Going to dock in Newport (near Bristol)."

November 25, 1943:
"To Newport at 5:30 p.m. and docked. Debarked at 10:30 and on train. Started for Charfield at 11:45 p.m. Arrived 4 p.m. in trucks to a castle (Tortworth Court) at 4:30 p.m.–really swell. 120 rooms. Five in a room. Fin, Meier, Flynn, Katz and me. To bed at 6 a.m. Really nice. Up at 10, shaved, and took walk on grounds with Katz–just beautiful."

CHAPTER FIVE
ENGLAND: NOVEMBER 1943-JUNE 1944

THE TRANSFER OF THE 128TH by the Army to England in November 1943 was ordered for three reasons. First, there was preparation needed for the planned invasion of France set for the spring of 1944. Millions of Allied soldiers were assembling in the British Isles for the final thrust into Nazi Germany. Second, there was the need to share the knowledge gained in a year of combat with new medical units arriving in Europe. This phase also included additional medical and logistical schooling for members of the unit. Third, there was a need for rest and recreation for this weary group.

The arrival of the 128th Evacuation Hospital in England marked the beginning of a new teaching and learning period for the 128th Evac. Since this unit was the most experienced hospital in the European Theater of Operations, it was selected to train personnel of hospitals destined to land in Normandy on D-Day.

Home base for the 128th Evac. while in England was Tortworth Castle near Bristol, England, but not all personnel arrived at the same time. Capt. Rosenbaum and other ill soldiers arrived at Tortworth after hospitalization and treatment for various diseases including hepatitis and malaria.

Dr. Rosenbaum spoke of fond memories of the castle:

"Tortworth was a huge castle. It was very striking. I got a picture of Tortworth, which was one of the best pictures I ever took! We had plenty of room and showers for the first time and good food.

Tortworth Castle, a 120-room estate near Bristol, England. (Photo courtesy of Dr. Edward Rosenbaum)

"Now the one story I'll never forget is, we hadn't had any fresh food or anything and they served steaks. It was the first time we'd had steaks in months. At that time, Catholics did not eat meat on Friday. And this was wartime, nobody was going to violate the rules, so the Catholic boys got their steaks and they wrapped them in napkins and put them under their pillows. At midnight they blew a whistle and they all got up and ate their steaks."

Early December brought assignments of personnel to civilian hospitals in London where they were to learn the British way of handling war casualties and ill patients. In a letter dated 12 December 1943, Lt. Margaret Hornback mentioned that experience:

"We came today to London where we are to observe in civilian hospitals for awhile. The one we will join was the same one Florence Nightingale had for her first training school. We're all agog to get started. We'll live in town, so we can see some plays and things. They're wonderful to us here.

"We live at the Red Cross rooms. The club was originally organized by Mrs. Anthony J. Drexel Biddle. It was small when we first visited it. Now it occupies several buildings, some of which were mansions reconditioned by the US after the Blitz. We live five or six to a room but it only costs three shillings, which is about sixty cents a night. Our bathroom is about the size of the kitchen, has a built-in tub and basin of marble and full-length beveled mirrors on three sides. Guess it must have escaped the bombing. But the water is hot always and the tub is longer than I am. Just about the nicest thing this side of the Atlantic."

One of the fondest memories of the 128th Evac. while stationed in England

Left: Members of the 128th dressed in costumes for the ball held at Tortworth Castle, January 1944.(Photo courtesy of Vaughn Pulice)

was the ball held at the castle. Some of the fun came from personnel dressing in 19th Century costumes to attend the party.

The following are excerpts from Margaret Hornback's letters home during their respite in England:

<u>January 1, 1944, England:</u>

"Happy New Year! Think that wish will come true too don't you and this terrible thing will this year be over."

<u>January 4, 1944, England, Homeless Germans:</u>

"We have so much for which to be thankful. I even feel sorry for the poor homeless Germans. Todays paper shows them serving soup in the bombed areas – quite as much to be pitied as any peoples we've seen."

The group photograph from the costume ball. (Photo courtesy of Vaughn Pulice)

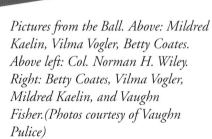

January 18, 1944, England:

"The biggest thrill of all is Mike's gang in Ireland. I haven't heard from him since Thanksgiving, but I never even guessed what was happening. Andy (Capt. W.J. Anderson) and associates should support them, so, here's hoping. Andy has bad jaundice and been pretty sick. He was still in the hospital Christmas, so I wonder. Some of them are coming here for their convalescence. The nicest thing is—I haven't used a day of my leave yet."

January 24, 1944: England, Uncle John Kelly going to see Gladys Martin:

"It's quite cold this AM. I'm wondering how you're doing with frosty or icy roads.

"We really keep on the go here, classes, exercises, drills, tests and everything in order in our rooms.

"I still haven't' seen John Rob't. He was coming to see Martin this weekend. I missed that and our party too. That surely grieves me."

February 14, 1944, England:

"Orie is just planning to stir off a batch of scrambled eggs. Guess you'd like that, wouldn't you? I eat them. I even ate British lamb stew for supper. Worse than that is steak and kidney pie.

"I think Orie will be an old married lady maybe when you see her again. One never knows tho, does one? She seems quite happy. This is once she's sure with what she wants. Hope she'll be happy. I don't like the guy much, but then she didn't like Dick either."

February 24, 1944, England:

"Orie recently lost her luggage on one of our night

Pictures from the Ball. Above: Mildred Kaelin, Vilma Vogler, Betty Coates. Above left: Col. Norman H. Wiley. Right: Betty Coates, Vilma Vogler, Mildred Kaelin, and Vaughn Fisher.(Photos courtesy of Vaughn Pulice)

safaris. It was found by some officers in an armored division who did not know there were girls within miles. Since it was open they examined silk pajamas, smelled her perfume and enjoyed themselves greatly."

March 11, 1944, England, Tortworth:

The radio is giving "God Save the King", so it's a most bad time, but I'll scribble in haste. Yes, the radio works wonderfully—I've never had the States on short wave here, but I used to get it last summer. Isn't that funny? We get rebroadcasts from home. The British programs are excellent. We surely enjoy it but I wish it wasn't so big. It's about half as big as the one at home. I wonder how I'll move it next time? It traveled here in one of the ovens.

"We're having a party tonite—think everyone had a pretty good time. Had an awfully good supper. Big steaks, but I wish they'd send them to the fighting troops instead. Heard from Mike today. He'd had my Christmas package with the cokes, the first they'd seen in a year. I'll have to collect them another box but I don't have much to send. Could you find some cheese packed to mail, or some nuts in cans, cookies, tuna fish, boned chicken or such for me and I'll send it to them. I've been sending one sock at a time in an envelope. Mike had received one so far."

March 15, 1944, England, New Uniforms & Worry for Andy:

"Today has been a busy one. A very high up inspection of our dollhouse. We appeared in our new combat uniform—like the armored corps. It's deliciously warm, but so bundlesome. The legs are so wide, we wobble like ducks.

"No word as yet from Andy. I continue to hope that he may be on some strategy where he can't write or maybe a prisoner. Guess my letters will begin to return soon. He's such a grand guy. One just can't afford to think about it."

Above and below: Officers and enlisted men enjoy the pleasant gardens and grounds of Tortworth. (Photos courtesy of Dr. Edward Rosenbaum)

March 21, 1944, England, Seeing Plays:

"Tonite we saw "Chocolate Soldier." It was so pretty and colorful. I've so enjoyed getting to see so many plays. They're always reduced rates for the armed forces, as one can afford to go every night if there are that many."

April 1, 1944, England:

"I've thought so much about penicillin for you, but I don't think it would work, as they claim E-Coli is one of the few things for which it isn't specific.

"We've nurses used it much. We're only allowed to use it for special things such as gas gangrene and once for a boy stung by a jellyfish on the neck. It swelled even with his chin and they did an emergency tracheotomy. Then they gave penicillin and it came down like a balloon."

April 17, 1944, England:

"We accidentally got tickets last night for the London Philharmonic. It was

"Tortworth was a huge castle. It was very striking. We had plenty of room and showers for the first time and good food." –Dr. Ed Rosenbaum

"We're sitting out on the hill which over-looks Tortworth Lake. Lilacs and chestnuts are in full bloom–pink and white." –Margaret Hornback

Maj. Frank Burton at Tortworth, 1944. (Photo courtesy of Isabel Anthony)

Left: Tortworth Castle. (Photo courtesy of Vaughn Pulice)

Right: Formation in front of the castle. (Photo courtesy of Vaughn Pulice)

SCENES FROM TORTWORTH CASTLE, NOVEMBER 1943-JUNE 1944

Gladys Martin (left) and Ora White in the Tortworth gardens. (Photo courtesy of G. Jesse Flynn)

Photo courtesy of Vaughn Pulice

Photo courtesy of Ed Rosenbaum

Photo courtesy of Vaughn Pulice

The officers mess hall at Tortworth set an awfully grand standard for veterans of the 128th. (Photo courtesy of Agatha Griebel)

Nurses relaxing on the lawn at Tortworth.

beautiful and you'd have loved it. They played parts of Nutcracker Suite, Schubert's Unfinished – two hours in all, but it seemed only thirty minutes.

"Big plans are under way for our promotion party. We even hope to have ice cream."

April 19, 1944, England, Description of England:

"I wish you could see the flowers here. Even snap dragons are in bloom already and I've never seen such gorgeous colors. Guess we've much to be thankful for. We could never have found a lovelier place in which to while away time.

April 21, 1944, England, Conditions at Tortworth:

"It's now the hour to scrub for inspection. It's not my turn this week, so it's my duty to stay out of the way til Hobby and Kelly finish. I can hear the refreshing sounds of swishing water on all sides.

"This has been a lovely rest for us. There are some objectionable sides to scrubbing floors but we've appreciated the opportunity of getting cleaned up.

"Our promotion party was held night before last. Think it went pretty well. I learned a bit more about dancing. Its great fun believe, though I wouldn't have learned if I hadn't had to."

April 21, 1944, England, Concern by nurses of being split up due to increase in rank:

"Today was a red-letter mail day. Two letters from you and the scrumptious cookies. My roommates had such a lean and hungry look that we were compelled to eat all but a few that I took to the hospital to some of our boys who were sick.

We surely enjoyed them. If you should ever want Andy to have some, guess you'll have to send them to him.

"Now to take care of some of the points of interest in your letter. Orie and I aren't married, neither is Martin, in fact neither are any of us. It is not considered good policy in this theater. Then there's always the question of a man and though they're relatively plentiful in these parts, I've no designs on any at present. Think I'm about as far from Italy as from you, and I wouldn't be marrying anyhow, no matter how short the distance.

"Guess that rumor got confused with our promotion, which we all described but nobody got (had anticipated a unit citation). Orie, Martin, my best pal, Genevieve Kruzic, our roommates Hobson and Kelly, Beryl Karban and Smitty, who is ill here, got promoted. It was a blanket affair and we weren't too happy to get them. We felt that all the girls who've been over the entire time deserved a promotion. That, of course, meant that some would have to leave the unit for so much rank wouldn't do in one group. So we were supposedly picked for merit but I don't know. Rank doesn't mean too much to us anyhow."

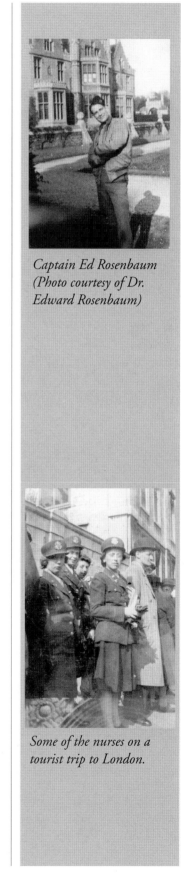

Captain Ed Rosenbaum (Photo courtesy of Dr. Edward Rosenbaum)

April 30, 1944, Heard from Andy:

"Today was an awful good mail day. Heard from each of the boys and they're all fine. Andy has been sick a lot during the winter but guess he got the best of it."

May 2, 1944, England, Andy:

"Had a nice fat letter from Andy yesterday. I had to give him just one gentle scolding to improve his letter writing. He named it "gentle sarcasm." Do you think I'd be guilty of such? For a long time I'd written often whether I heard or not as he said it was good for his morale. However, it works better just to answer his, I think. Guess you can't feel too sorry for a guy even if he lives in a foxhole."

May 3, 1944, England, Description:

"This has been one of the nicest days. First of all, army got at few watches for nurses and I got to buy one.

"Then we visited a little village down in the country. There they'll have strawberries next month almost as big as a teacup—in any case, only two are required for a serving. I hope to pay them a return visit during the season. We found some more junk to add to the coming home box. Think it will soon require a whole ship. They had some lovely caves and we went through them."

May 14, 1944, England, Tortworth Lake – Shakespeare:

"We're sitting out on the hill which, as I described, slopes off down to the lake. Lilacs are in full bloom now and our hedges contain only the best. Chestnuts are in bloom now, too. They're much like hickory nut blooms and some are pink and some are white.

"Yesterday we went by truck to Stratford-upon Avon. They have there a Shakespeare Festival lasting from April til September and give a different play each night. This one was Hamlet and you'll find it hard to believe that it was better than

Some of the nurses on a tourist trip to London.

D-Day!

The Nurse Corps departs Tortworth June 6, 1944. Left to right are Capt. Kathlyn Helm, Margaret Stanfill, Capt. Mike DeVito, Helen Molony, Edna Browning, Martha Cameron, Gladys Martin, Margie Hart, and Doris Brittingham. (Photo courtesy of Army Life)

any movie I ever saw but it was true. I think if I were making my home in England I'd want to live in Stratford. We went in the ferry little boats on the Avon like the pictures you've seen and it was such fun. Wish you could see the gardens in the Shakespeare memorial. Every color you can imagine, pansies almost as big as teacups and gorgeous oriental poppies."

May 21, 1944, England, Love Life:

"It looks like rain today and we're still looking for some. Kinda cold, too. The orchards were loaded with blooms, but guess Jack Frost got all of it. They usually use smoke pots like they do in California to prevent that, but of course one can't very well light a fire in war. Just another of its nuisances, I suppose.

"You'd approve of Andy, I think. He's such a screwball. Don't think you'll ever be called upon for your stamp of approval though. Mike's sweet but awfully serious for an Irishman. Besides, in civilian life he belongs to the FBI and I couldn't stand that. I've determined to go home, and chase those turkeys."

<u>May 28, 1944, England, Application for Voting Ballot:</u>

"We got our cards to apply for voting ballots this week. I wouldn't be greatly interested except that Congress must be afraid to have the soldier vote. The president, it seems, must be the only soul in Washington who knows there's a war going on. Probably he'd be glad if he weren't reelected. I wish to state that I didn't say prohibition wasn't right. All I said was I didn't have the faith of a mustard seed. Guess nothing can be accomplished unless it's tried, though."

<u>May 29, 1944, England:</u>

"Orie's charges didn't sleep long enough, as you see. They're the best patients having the most radical sort of surgery and getting well. There's barely room to get between cots on our wards. Still you can do all sorts of changing, getting Wangensteens, etc., to one's next door neighbor without disturbing the adjoining ones. You can even give some of them penicillin without waking them. They really ruin one for civilian nursing."

The nurses board the ship taking them to a new and more dangerous combat zone in France, where Allied soldiers had already begun the invasion of Europe. (Photo courtesy of Army Life)

Despite the pleasant surroundings of Tortworth Castle and the interesting diversion of historic sites to be visited, personnel of the 128th never lost sight of their mission. Time and again they instructed hospital units which had not yet served in a combat zone about the easiest and quickest way to set up and take down hospital tents, the best placement of supplies and OR tables for the operating room tent and the best way to pack equipment for quick access at a new hospital site. During their time in England, they taught hundreds of hospital personnel, hosted discussion groups for visiting medical personnel and passed on the priceless techniques and skills they had learned under fire.

As spring 1944 drew to an end, the mission became clearer as thousands of troops bivouacked in England awaiting the invasion of France. Several soldiers slated to take part in that invasion were not happy with their upcoming assignments. Capt. Rosenbaum commented on some of the methods used by a small minority to ensure that they would stay in England rather than leave with the invasion force:

"Now, one of the things that began to happen in England before the invasion—some of these guys would shoot themselves in the foot. Eisenhower blew up about that. He told the psychiatrist who was with us that he wanted some [criminal] convictions for that. This one guy had tried to blow his foot off. A psychiatrist gave him a low dose of sodium pentothal, which is a sedative, that put him half to sleep and then started to question him under the sedative in order to get a confession. And the guy said, 'You're doping me up in hopes that I'll confess and I'll tell you right now, I won't do it.' That was rare but not unusual."

In the early morning of 6 June 1944, American and Allied troops invaded Normandy, and the 128th was packed and ready to leave Tortworth. They were soon on the road to the port of embarkation.

CHAPTER SIX
THE INVASION OF NORMANDY

The 128th sailed out of Falmouth, England to Utah Beach 8 June, 1944. They were among thousands of troops and millions of tons of materiel shipped across the English Channel on ships of every description (far right).

THE ALLIED CROSS-CHANNEL INVASION of France was going to be the largest amphibious landing in history. The early morning of June 6, 1944 found 287,000 American and British fighting men aboard thousands of ships preparing to invade. Twenty thousand airborne troops were either already in France or on their way. Ten thousand aircraft flew over the ships that had formed an armada fifty miles wide.

The 128th Surgical Hospital had been preparing to embark in early June and began movement toward the coast on June 6. It was during this transit that they were informed that the invasion had begun.

After a train ride to Falmouth, personnel of the 128th Evacuation Hospital boarded the troop ship *William Pendleton* to begin their sea voyage to France. In the early morning of 8 June the *William Pendleton* sailed for the coast of Normandy. The trip was not uneventful.

Lt. Margaret Hornback described the journey in her 10 June 1944 letter home:

"The 128th Evacuation Hospital sailed aboard the ship *William Pendleton*,

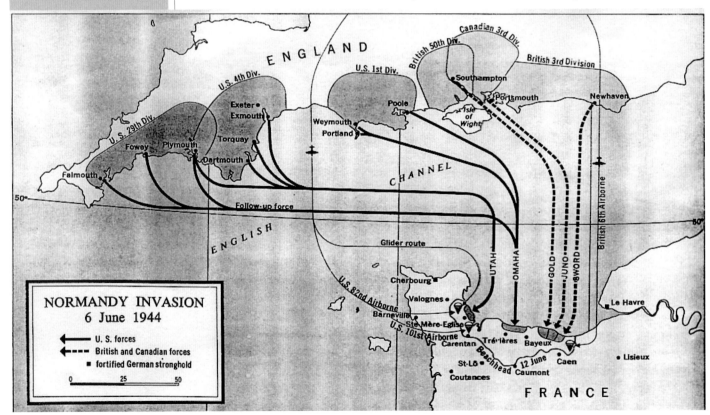

NORMANDY INVASION
6 June 1944

⟵ U.S. forces
⟵--- British and Canadian forces
■ fortified German stronghold

0   25   50

On June 8, 1944 the 128th was aboard the Liberty ship *William N. Pendleton* in Falmouth harbor, England, preparing to make the cross-channel trip. The 128th Evacuation Hospital sailed aboard the ship, and on 8 June 1944, at 0315, the ship was alerted because one of the ships in the convoy was sunk by enemy action or possibly a mine hit. Again at 0400, she was alerted because of an attack by a German aircraft that launched a glider bomb, causing a near miss and damage to the ship. The force of the explosion bulged in several side plates on the port side sufficiently to buckle one of the bulkheads and cause an oil leak into a water tank. The Liberty ship finally unloaded her cargo on the Normandy beaches and put the 4th Division of the 128th Medical Field Unit on shore. The ship remained off Normandy until 25 June. She then began shuttling troops and equipment between Southampton, England and France. In December 1944, she headed north to Norway and Belgium. She continued service until after the war. She was then placed in the Reserve Fleet on the Hudson River, New York. She remained there until 1968 when she was removed and scrapped. *William N. Pendleton* earned one battle star."

Dr. Schwade's diary,
June 8, 9 & 10, 1944:

Normandy:
"Trip – along coast of Southampton – met convoy of 25 LCI's and across channel to France. 4 a.m. attacked by Jerries. Got four ships of convoy in rear. One glider bomb missed us by 100 yards – some fun. Ate good and slept in cabin while others were in hold and eating K-rations. Met nice chap – Jerry Hale, 2nd Engineer on ship who took good care of us. Landed at Utah, red beach at 4:30 – waded in again and walked to area. 42nd Field Hospital set up and busier than hell. We're first Evacuation Hospital to land – even 42nd Field Hospital nurses beat their outfit in – some fun.
Slept in field – in pup tent with fire artillery and planes going day and night. Saw one Jerry shot down – good site. Lots of gliders smashed in fields. Many colored parachutes and supplies around in trees."

and on 8 June 1944, at 0315, the ship was alerted because one of the ships in the convoy was sunk by enemy action or possibly a mine hit. Again at 0400, she was alerted because of an attack by a German aircraft that launched a glider bomb, causing a near miss and damage to the ship. The force of the explosion bulged in several side plates on the port side sufficiently to buckle one of the bulkheads and cause an oil leak into a water tank."

Gilbert Smith described the explosion and what happened next:

"When that bomb went off, we stood on the first deck below; we jumped up that high right now! My feet were numb, I could hardly stand, I was sure I had a concussion. And that officer stood up there with a revolver in his hand and said, 'The first one that comes up here I'll drop ya.' And nobody ran up those steps..."

Lt. Ora White, one of the nurses, recalled her reactions to the events of those first hours when arriving in sight of Normandy:

"The African and Sicilian invasion seemed very small compared to the invasion of France. We landed in France four days after D-Day. As our ship came near the shore, a bomb landed just behind it. For the first time, I was really frightened. We thought we were going down. Then I began to wonder what I had to sustain me. Would my family, my background, friends or environment be enough? It was as if I were stripped bare of everything except the promises of God. They seemed to act as a bridge over a deep chasm. If we would keep looking to Him, he would take us safely across."

On 10 June at 1530 hours, hospital personnel waded ashore on Utah beach and began their work of unloading the ships, setting up the hospital and caring for the wounded.

Gilbert Smith recalled the problems they encountered during the process of unloading the ship:

"The Germans were still lobbing 88s on the beach and the captain of the ship would not beach his craft. The beachmaster would radio him out there, 'Beach your craft, beach your craft.' He just simply refused, period. So finally the only way they could offload us was they brought DUKWs (amphibious trucks) out. We unloaded the boat into the DUKWs and that's the way we landed in Normandy."

Lt. Ora White described the scene that greeted her group.

"We landed safely and moved in to assist a small field hospital that had been working night and day. It seemed there were fields of wounded soldiers on stretchers waiting for us. I had never seen our unit work so efficiently. By midnight, they were all cared for. We crawled into our pup tents to await the morning. There was so much bombing, it was difficult to sleep."

Gilbert Smith joined the 128th Evac's enlisted men at their new hospital site on Normandy. He recalled that trip.

"I remember the sand dunes . . . when we finally got out of the water and finally got up on the beach, we went over the sand dunes and onto a road and went right to the area where the hospital was set up. I remember we unloaded the supplies and that night I

Nurses landing at Normandy, France on Utah Beach, June 10, 1944. The nurses include (left to right) Lt. Amy Nickles, Lt. Doris Brittingham, Lt. Vilma Vogler, and Lt. Rusty Miller. (Photo courtesy of Agatha Griebel)

think we got strafed . . . I woke up the next morning with holes in the tent. Somebody had gone by and clamped my helmet on me. All I could smell was creosote . . . a fifty caliber shell had gone through a five gallon pail containing creosote in the front of the tent and it leaked out and stunk up the whole place."

The 128th Evacuation Hospital's first site was in Boutteville, about 5 miles from the coast. On 11 June 1944, Carentan was taken by American and allied forces, and the 128th Evac. received 223 patients. The hospitals' patient load remained high, but began to slacken off on 18 June when only 63 patients were admitted. All hospital personnel appreciated a little more breathing room and on 20 June, Lt. Margaret Hornback wrote a letter home:

June 20, 1944, France: Normandy:

"Things are shaping up nicely now. Guess operations in general are going according to plan and ours are, too. I'm night snoop-ovisor and believe me it is snooping. We only have total darkness from about twelve to four, but last night it was really pitch black. You couldn't even see the silhouette of the tents against the sky, and I fell over every rope, hole etc. within a mile. Everything happened; most remarkably we had a baby! That was the first time we've had that happen. A little French woman both of whose legs we'd amputated about two hours before. Neither of them lived. Guess we'll have to stick to army practice after all. Twas quite pathetic though she was probably a sniper by trade. One isn't supposed to bear a grudge, though, just because people shoot at you.

"The people, especially the women, are not too happy to see us anyhow. The Germans having been here four years, have married the natives and all was peaceful til we arrived to upset the works again and the German prisoners, army of

The village of Boutteville, five miles from the Normandy coast, was the 128th's first hospital site.

occupation, now working for us, give us pointers on how to get on with the French, keep down inflation etc. – a funny world, huh?"

Cpl. Jodie Harmon recalled some of his most hassled days at Boutteville:
Normandy

"It was about midnight or a little after when the Germans staged an air raid and the noise startled many of the patients. They jumped up off their cots like they were fixin' to stampede. We had an Indian patient by the name of 'Bigback.' He was a big man and I guess that is how he got his name. He jumped up all excited and I happened to be close. I walked over and tried to calm him down as I usually did in those situations. I had to shove him down on his bed and put a pillow over his head to muffle the sound. The patients would usually calm down after you started talking to them. I started walking back and forth down the aisle talking nonchalantly and it seemed to settle all of them down. A lot of them didn't know what was going on because of brain damage and some of them were paralyzed. It was a scene that, if you were there, you could never forget.

Boutteville, France appears the same today as it did in 1944—a beautiful small village in the middle of a huge, ugly war. (Photo courtesy of G. Jesse Flynn)

"Head wounds were very common. The surgeons would work for hours getting metal slivers out of the brain. They would then put a plaster cast on the head of the soldier. It was learned early on that if they didn't cast the head, the patient would scratch the bandages off and get their fingers in the wound. We would sometimes cast their arms so they would be unable to reach their heads. Many nights my heart would ache listening to some young man eighteen, nineteen years old say, 'Mama…Mama. Help me. Mama…help me.' And somebody not far from him would say the same thing. They always called for Mama. 'Mama, it hurts. Mama, help me. Somebody help me.' It would kind of tear you up. But, you just had to brush it aside and do the best you could."

Even in faraway places like Boutteville, hospital personnel sometimes came face-to-face with a soldier from home. Pvt. Jodie Harmon recalled such an incident:

"About three o'clock in the morning the doctor and I were on duty. I was working with the patients and he was seated at the desk. They brought in a wounded soldier on a litter. I had an empty cot where the soldier was placed. I spoke to him and he was rather apprehensive. I came to find out it was his first day in the line. He had been hit and given a dose of morphine. While I settled him in he recognized my voice and asked me where I was from. He was from Sanko, (a town near Robert Lee, Texas). I hadn't recognized him because it was subdued light and he had two days' growth of beard. We weren't close friends but we were from the same county in Texas. We talked of things back home. I'd been overseas nearly two years and he'd been there a few weeks. The doctor heard us talking and asked, "Do you know this fellow?" I informed him that the man was from my hometown. He examined

Dr. Schwade's diary, June 26, 1944:

"Big guns going all night – couldn't sleep. Sure wish things would slow down. Cherbourg should be ours completely today or tomorrow. Got German Naval doctor this evening to care for POW's. Some enlisted man, I think a Jew, interpreting for us for a Nazi – such is war."

After being treated in field hospitals in France, Allied soldiers were evacuated to England on troop transports and LSTs, often on a crowded deck. (Photo courtesy of U.S. Army Signal Corps)

Dr. Schwade's diary:

"Talked with a Jerry POW–sure glad to be out of the war. Guess they're fed up with it."

the patient and determined he had a badly mangled arm and several pieces of shrapnel just under the high of his back and shoulders. His arm was badly damaged in the elbow area. He didn't belong on our ward, so I just called some litter bearers and had him taken over to surgery. His name was Montgomery. I've forgotten his first name. It took as much as two or three days for most but they got Montgomery into surgery right away. When I got off duty the next morning I went to look him up and he had come through surgery all right. I don't know when they sent him back but I'm sure he was back across the channel very soon. I never did see him again over there. But I was sure that the war was over for him. When I got home I saw him. He now lives in Sanko."

It was not unusual for hospital personnel to rotate work shifts, working nights and sleeping during the day, which frequently presented problems in sleep patterns. Add to this the German shelling and bombing and it was not unusual for hospital personnel to be sleep-deprived.

Pvt. Jodie Harmon described such a situation:

"I was finally changed from the night shift to the day shift. I found it difficult sleeping for the first several nights after the change. You hear machine guns and artillery going off during the night. We were still in the same place one night when the ground began bouncing around me in my little foxhole. Artillery was firing all around. The Germans had made a counter attack and our artillery had also gone into full action. Sometimes I didn't get a whole lot of sleep, however I got to where I could sleep through most of it."

Hospital personnel caught naps when they could and on 29 June 1944, Lt. Hornback wrote home about the nursing duties that seemed never-ending:

"Things are rather quiet at our house tonight so the gals can get off for a little nap. I'm at present relieving Orie. She has abdominal section—twenty-nine patients tonight and six Wangensteens going, four of which are Miller Abbotts—two transfusions going and a couple of IVs not to mention the two-hour penicillin which are legion. In civilian nursing one could hardly manage all those and have time to write a letter. It's continually amazing what wonderful patients the GIs make. The Jerrys are good, too, once they're convinced we don't intend to torture them. With all the shots, IVs, etc., most anyone would wonder even if they understood the language. Orie is doing a grand job. I'm proud of her. Martin has pre-op shock and is doing OK. That's mostly mechanical though, a matter of pouring in blood and plasma. Me, I'm night supervisor. Guess I'll stay there for this setup.

"I help out where it's busy but mostly I seem to be stumbling around from ward to ward falling over tent ropes, etc., and making an estimate on the census.

Our clientele moves so fast, patients going back to communication zone as soon as they're able to travel—that's often as soon as they've had their wounds debrieded and recovered from anesthesia, so the turnover is enormous."

On 2 July, Lt. Hornback's letter home dealt with an entirely different subject. German forces in Cherbourg had surrendered to American and allied forces on 26 June, and by 2 July, the date of Hornback's letter, hospital personnel were caring for German prisoners of war:

"Life is peaceful with us now. The patients improving and being weeded out more each day to stand the trip back. Mostly they go to England, but some few go home. We have the cutest little German on Orie's ward. He's learned quite a little English since he came. Think he wants to get to America almost as bad as we. He's learned that the ambulances pull up to the ward door to take folks back to England. He's always saying, "Nix England, nix," so someone must stop and assure him that it isn't for him this time.

"He's a long lanky kid—must be about the size of Sneezie. He's twenty, but has no beard but long curly lashes. I always think of Sneezie when I look at him. They call us "fraulein" when they first come, but then learn to say "Sweetie" from the British.

"I wish all the world could work on our wards—British, French, Poles, Czechs, Germans and GIs—dressed alike, wounded alike and alike in heart, just homesick kids. God forgive us if we ever let this kind of a thing happen again."

Corpsmen were working just as hard as medical personnel and Jodie Harmon recalled those days and nights:

"About a month after the landings we had German prisoners assigned to help with the work. It was mostly outside work. They were quartered in a nearby laundry. The laundry stayed close to us throughout the rest of the war. It was a great help because we didn't have to wash our own clothes and the hospital linen anymore. It had been difficult to keep your clothes clean and pressed when you're washing them out in a helmet and trying to dry them into a shape that looked like they might have been ironed. We even got a shower stall where we could take a shower once in a while. It was a big improvement from what we had in North Africa."

The chief of the enlisted men was Technical Sgt. Larry Inderrieden. He was praised by all that worked for and with him. 1st Lt. Martha Cameron, nurse anesthesiologist, remembers Inderrieden as "super efficient." He would lead by example...when a crisis hit he never raised his voice but went to work with greater focus and fervor, leading those around him to do the same. 'Slick' knew how to do everything as a surgical technician, whether a chest or belly case."

Margaret Hornback wrote home about some nurses being in *Life* magazine:
"Some of our gang is in June 26 *Life* magazine – Vaughn Fisher and Margie Hart. Kinda nice I guess. I wouldn't be surprised if I didn't insult a few photographers

Dr. Schwade's diary: July 20, 1944:

Hitler almost assassinated:
"Lou Forman here for a visit today – he sure was railroaded. Heard news that Hitler was almost assassinated along with some generals by dynamite in a room – can't even kill the S.O.B."

July 24, 1944:
"James Findley left us tonight. He is off to England and home – lucky guy. Had meeting today, records show we saw and treated 6,800 patients in 31 working days while here. 3,800 surgical and the rest ordinary dressings..."

"Larry Inderrieden was the best natural leader, and we never heard him raise his voice."–Martha Cameron

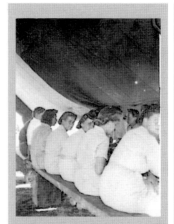

Nurses in the mess tent. (Photo courtesy of Dr. Edward Rosenbaum)

"I awoke to the wonderful smell of bacon. I got dressed in my uniform; you couldn't go out in your bathrobe (as if I had a bathrobe). We used the liners of our overcoats as bathrobes. You sat at the next place available and there was a bench you had to throw your leg over to sit down."
–Martha Cameron

Six weeks after the D-Day landings Dinah Shore entertained the troops in Normandy at a USO show. (Photo courtesy of Isabel Anthony)

about that stage of the game. It annoyed me to be always falling over them when I'm busy. It probably means a lot to the folks to see them, but they're always posed pictures and seem so stupid."

One of the things the *Life* magazine article did not mention was the 128th Evacs' use of German POW physicians to help care for wounded and ill German soldiers. In her letter of 24 July, Lt. Hornback addresses the topic:

"The Germans are excellent help. They take care of their own wounded under our supervision and it's amazing how readily they understand.

"The German patients believe we're equally as big liars as we think of them. We've two doctor prisoners, one Army and one Navy who take care of them. They are learning English (and quickly too). They live in officer's row, eat in officer's mess and are prisoners only in name. When they explained this to their patients, they refused to believe it—said they were Americans in German uniform—to try to get information out of them."

In addition to keeping track of things happening on the ground, personnel of the 128th Evac found a need to be concerned with enemy action in the air. In mid-July, the battle for St. Lo was fierce and German planes overflew the hospital area regularly. Jodie Harmon described the scene:

"We had been in Normandy for about seven weeks when in the middle of the afternoon large bombers began to circle overhead. They saturated the front line with heavy bombs. There were hundreds of four engine bombers involved in the raid on St. Lo. When they first appeared, the German anti-aircraft fire was heavy. The sky was filled with bursting shells that looked like black pepper. I didn't see any planes go down but it was only a matter of what seems like an hour until there was no more anti-aircraft fire."

On 24 July 1944, Operation Cobra began and one week later the 128th Evac packed up at Boutteville and moved to La Foret where they bivouacked for three days. Their journey through towns and along roads where soldiers had fought and died was not a pleasant one. Pvt. Jodie Harmon recalled an indelible memory of that time:

"The ground was plowed and cratered for miles. Buildings were pulverized. Some of the bombs fell short and killed many American soldiers and one of our generals. This attack opened the front and we started moving out of the beachhead. As we traveled through the bombed out area of St. Lo, the smell was so bad that I could hardly stand it. Body parts and animals were rotting everywhere. We moved thirty miles to another area and set up the unit."

After a brief rest, the 128th Evac moved to Tessy-sur-Vire and began to set up the hospital on 4 August in support of the American and allied troops engaged in combat east of St. Lo.

They commandeered a cow pasture and apple orchard which were littered with dead cattle, sheep, refuse and dead Germans. Intensive cleaning was required before the hospital could open. From 4 August to 13 August 1944, the 128th received 1800 wounded and ill soldiers and ran a daily census of between 300 and 450 patients.

On 15 August, Col. Wiley received orders to prepare the 128th Evac for a move east about 60 miles to Haleine in support of the American and allied soldiers who were engaged in a plan to encircle the German army. The new hospital site was a few miles south of Argantan, the city at the southern opening of the Falaise Pocket. The Germans were now locked in a desperate struggle to escape their entrapment and the fighting was fierce.

Pvt. Jodie Harmon recalled conditions at the new hospital site where they handled large numbers of German patients:

"The German anti-personnel bombs were getting dangerous to us. We dug foxholes and covered them with logs and dirt where the mortar shells wouldn't blow through it. We didn't stay there long. We had bodies stacked up in mattress covers and body bags like cord wood. The front then began moving very fast and we didn't stay in one area very long.

"On 31 August, 1944 we moved on towards Paris and stopped forty miles south near Senonches. We waited a short time and were ordered to move again. There were a number of patients that were too critical to move, so the commander asked the doctor that was leading our unit to stay behind with those until they were able to move. I was asked to stay behind. The doctor and I would make the rounds and check the wounds and dressings every morning. Then I didn't have too much to do the rest of the day. I'd go out and walk around down the roads. It was quite a change from what we had experienced. This peaceful time did not last long and we moved to the front again. When the front moved closer to Paris, they pulled us over in a pasture for some rest, recreation and resupply. Of course, there wasn't any recreation up there. It was breaking the monotony and giving us rest and time to get our equipment in shape."

During this rest period many personnel of the hospital were given passes and visited the recently liberated nearby city of Paris. One of those hospital members who went to Paris was Captain Ed Rosenbaum. When he returned from Paris, he learned that orders had arrived for him. He recalled that change in his army career:

"Just about at the fall of Paris, I'd had malaria, suffered the burn from the accident in Sicily, contracted hepatitis that left my blood out of whack, and they finally sent me home. So I came home and we spent a couple weeks in Little Rock, Arkansas in what they called a rehabilitation, recreation center. It was sort of a reward, a vacation. And then they sent me to a hospital in Lockney, Texas, which is 30 miles north of Dallas. I was a patient at that hospital for six months. Then they sent me back to Omaha for reassignment."

On 10 September 1944, the 128th Evacuation Hospital ended its bivouac and began their move to Belgium.

Dr. Schwade's diary, August 9, 1944:

"270 patients came in during the night and we have around 500 now altogether – what an outfit. Nuts."

August 14, 1944:
Dinah Shore USO show "Had USO show with Dinah Shore in person – good voice – but not such a good looker."

August 20, 1944:
"Falaise Pocket now closed and remains of Jerry Division trapped and being slaughtered. Got over 400 vehicles and 250 tanks by air corps in one day – wow. Patton's group crossed Seine River and are in outskirts of Paris. Sure wish they would end this mess once and for all already."

Next stop for the 128th after Normandy: Belgium, and the frigid winter that was the background for the Battle of the Bulge. (Photo courtesy of Jodie Harmon)

Chapter Seven
Closing in on the German Border—Belgium

THE MOVE INTO BELGIUM brought several changes to the 128th Evac. Those who thought they had seen mud before would revise their opinions and a new German weapon would rain terror from the skies. Pvt. Jodie Harmon recalled those days:

"The next time we stopped to set up the hospital we were in Belgium. We kind of bogged down there for a while. We then moved very close to the Belgium-

The mud of Belgium in the fall of 1944. (Photo courtesy of Vaughn Pulice)

Dr. Schwade's diary, Sept. 15, 1944:

"Left Ouffet 10:30 a.m. thru [Liege], Verviers, [Limburg] and bivouac area near Eupen. German and Belgium here – all German spoke here. Not such hot welcome in Eupen...We are to start work at 6:00 a.m. according to Col. Snyder, Ex. Officer 1st Army. Aachen only 16 [km] away."

German border, right up to the Siegfried line. The fall weather began to set in and we began to have a lot of cloudy, rainy weather. The conditions were extremely muddy. We had to haul material in to make streets in order to get vehicles between the hospital tents."

Lt. Margaret Hornback also commented on the mud in a letter home dated 28 September 1944:

"It was at this time that the Germans began using buzz bombs. These were unmanned rocket bombs that flew over us several times a day. We heard that when the motor died, they would come straight to the ground. The first one I saw, I stopped to watch it, and about the time it came over us, the engine cut off. I began to look for a place to hide. I hadn't dug a foxhole for several months and I didn't dig another one for the rest of the time I was in the army. Anyway, it just kept gliding ten or twelve miles past us before it came down. We were definitely in the path of the rocket launchers and they began coming over us all the time.

"About the first week in October the First army had advanced to the German border and was holding this section and building up supplies. They had to set a route for the supply trucks. It was tough going to the front and on a different road back to get supplies. They were ordered to run with full headlights at night. They used one road coming to us and one going away. It was quite a system."

In the midst of bad weather and war, the 128th Evac lost two of its nurses through transfer. Lt. Hornback wrote of this in a letter dated 14 October 1944:

"Two of our roommates, Vivian Sheridan "Sherry," and Helen Molony "Spats," left yesterday. They'd decided to go in a general hospital so there won't be so much moving, etc. We surely are losing the gang one by one."

With the battle for the German city of Aachen raging since 29 September 1944, and as October wore on, the 128th Evac had a good view of the destruction being rained down upon the city. Pvt. Jodie Harmon:

"The First army was attacking the city of Aachen located on the German-Belgium border. They had requested the city to surrender but they were turned down. The civilians were notified to leave because the city would be heavily bombed. We stood and watched those bombers destroy the city. I don't know how long they bombed it. There were still weeks of house-to-house fighting or pile-of-rubble to pile-of-rubble fighting. After weeks of fighting the remains of the city were captured on 21 October 1944."

With the fall of Aachen, hospital personnel had a little more leisure time and parties made their appearance again. In her letter dated 22 October 1944, Lt. Hornback described such an event:

"We had a nice party at John Roberts's (uncle John Kelly) last night. His is such a nice gang—we all just cut up and there's not a wolf in the bunch, I don't think. They had a charming chateau hidden away in the woods that some rich Nazi had used as a hunting lodge. It was elaborately furnished—rich mahogany but with heavy carving that looks overdone somehow. We spent the night and this morning picked late roses in the garden.

"It would have been lovely but the boys had to go back to work today. You hate so to see them go—guess the more people you know in this business, the more you have to hold your breath for."

November brought a steady rain to the area, and presented the hospital with a new problem. Rainwater began to pool on tent tops, pulling the canvas inward and exerting much stress on tent ropes. Some tents collapsed and had to be repitched, presenting hospital personnel with a decision regarding what they should do when the collapse of a tent seemed imminent. Lt. Margaret Hornback discussed the situation in a letter home dated 6 November 1944:

"The recommended procedure in this instance is to go outside and tighten the tent ropes but I haven't that kind of a brave spirit unless there are patients or someone inside who can't walk in case the tent falls down. As for my roommates, Genevieve and Orie are concerned; they'd look good climbing out in the rain."

"This morning's election day and it's mighty stormy here. One of the boys said even the Gods were weeping over the election."

As 1944 began to draw to a close, and the war in Europe seemed

Aachen, Germany; the destruction after being bombed in the fall of 1944. "I watched the P-47 dive bombers pound this city to almost complete destruction," said Jodie Harmon. (Photo courtesy of Jodie Harmon)

The hospital site in Heggin, Belgium, during the rainy, snowy winter, 1944. (Photo courtesy of Vaughn Pulice)

to be winding down, letters from the folks at home began to ask questions that pertained to more than just survival. Family and friends began to inquire about awards and decorations. The 128th Evac hospital had already won unit citations

along with the individual recognition of its personnel. In a letter dated 14 November 1944, Lt. Margaret Hornback answered some of her family's questions concerning awards:

"Now about the Bronze Star. No, I don't have one. They were awarded for our first performance on the beach. At that time I was nite supervisor and tho I did considerable scrambling about in the dark, setting up new wards, etc. it just wasn't the kind of a job that shows. That was a large number of Stars for a hospital and was really a unit citation. There wasn't anyone who didn't work really but for once the awards were quite fair and if any one did superior work, that gang did. We were sorry it couldn't have been given to departments, so the enlisted men too would be recognized,

Awarding of Bronze Stars, October 16, 1944. Right to left are Gladys Martin, Ora White, Genevieve Kruzic, and Amy Nickles.

but that's the way of the army, I suppose. Anyway, I don't think I'll ever get any decorations. Gen, Orie and I were recommended for Legion of Merit in Africa, but we were recognized before it went through. If you do deserve them, you know lots of other folks did equally too and you kinda feel bad. I'm sorry you all were disappointed but aside from that I truly wouldn't give much to have them. Awards like that are easy to win in the lines but it's pretty hard to do more than your duty in an outfit like this and you sorta feel guilty."

One week later, 23 November 1944, Hornback wrote home concerning the 1944 presidential elections:

"Got your Election Day letter today. Yes, I voted for FDR but it wasn't a very heated discussion with us. When you live with folks of such diverse ideas, you are convinced that one side can't be entirely right or entirely wrong. But if felt as most of the army that its not too good to change leaders in the middle of a battle."

When thanksgiving rolled around, roasted turkey was the order of the day. Whole turkeys were placed on mess hall tables and "the boys" were able to practice their carving techniques. All in all, there was a lot to be thankful for. Top at the list of blessings was the fact that the 128th Evac's patients did not seem as badly wounded or as seriously ill. In her letter of 29 November 1944, Lt. Hornback speaks to this issue:

"Our boys are not as sick as usual, lots of them being walking wounded. After a little washing, a good nights sleep and a hot meal or so, they're about as good as new and looking for mischief.

"They are the best old kids. No matter what happens after this is over, I'll be happy just thinking that they don't have to be out there killing and being killed."

At the beginning of December, the 128th Evac opened at a new site at Brandt, Germany about five miles south of Aachen. Pvt. Jodie Harmon commented on those days:

"We at last have a new home! It's an old German Army Post and will be a wonderful place when we ever get it clean. The old Wermacht eagle still stands guard over the door but we've about disposed of all likenesses of Adolph. It has been a nice place, quite as modern as at home and quite similar. It, of course, has been through the war and lastly it housed civilian refugees from an entire city and was it dirty. But the dirt is being moved out of our rooms. We hope to stay the winter here unless things move fast."

Housekeeping was only one of the things that personnel had to worry about. The Battle of the Heurtgen Forest was raging nearby. Although German planes were seen infrequently, when they appeared overhead, hospital personnel knew they could leave casualties and dead in their wake. Pvt. Jodie Harmon recalled those days:

"Our new hospital faced a main road with tall trees on the opposite side. I was on the second or third floor with four patients one who was scheduled to lose a leg or arm. Shortly, I heard the sound of an airplane and looked out the window. There had been heavy clouds for days and there was drizzle and mist this day. I glanced up the street and saw a German fighter plane coming at my eye level down the street. His wingtips were almost touching the building. If I had a rock, I could have hit him in the face. He passed our hospital, pulled up and disappeared into the clouds. We never saw him again.

"The fighting was very stiff in the Heurtgen Forest. I was told that they would fight three days and move forward three trees. The Germans were using a lot of air burst shells. They'd burst before hitting the ground and scatter the shrapnel down on the GIs. This type of shell was designed to wound many men at one time and overload the medical staff."

On 10 December, Lt. Margaret Hornback wrote home concerning the continuous flow of casualties:

"So senseless, it seems to go on and on with this wholesale murder; yet how can we stop?

"I have only one German now. A good-looking kid, eighteen, married and has a little curly-headed girl. Today he was crying because he doesn't know where his family is or if they're alive at all. He'd cover his face fiercely with his shirttail so the GIs wouldn't see him cry. And the "Dough Feet" who think they're enduring hell on earth, concluded it was even worse for the Germans. We, at least, know where and how our families are or labor under that delusion.

November 5, 1944: "Lots of buzz bombs over this a.m. One was shot down by P-51 and another landed about 1 mile from here –casualties–tough. Ginny left at 10:30 a.m. She sure felt badly for leaving us.

Big news today – our old nurses were given the opportunity of 1) Staying, 2) Transferring to fixed unit or 3) Going home. Golly – if they would only include us officers. I'd be so excited. Imagine! Going home. Well, they deserve it and perhaps our chance will come too.

I sure got a lump in my throat seeing this – my little dolly sending a letter already – Dear God why doesn't this mess end already so I can get back to my two darlings? I miss them so terribly."

German plane crash-landed near the Belgium perimeter.

Dr. Schwade's diary, December 20, 1944:

"Jerries broke thru into Belgium on Sunday, December 17. Every-one is quite worried. Buzz bombed several times. The 67th moved in–quite a mess. Things look pretty rough."

December 21, 1944:
"We were suddenly told we're moving in the a.m. – what a life."

December 22, 1944:
"Supposed to move today but roads are filled with our convoys – so we will move tomorrow."

December 24, 1944:
"Christmas Eve – 3rd one away from my darling. Time has sure flown by – great life. Got Christmas gifts tonight, Ormie Gold played Santa Claus. I got a fruitcake – sure have enough of these. Saw plenty of bomb-ers go over today – beautiful, clear, sunny day. I saw a couple of Jerries shot down."

"I lost one today—a big old sergeant almost the size of Johnnie. He had a complete paralysis of lower extremities with multiple abdominal wounds. He lived three days and survived all the precaution we presented in the way of IVs, penicillin and the like. At the end of the road, he had an overwhelming pulmonary edema. I held the mask of oxygen under pressure on his face to sorta hold the fluid back a bit. Conscious at times to the last, he told me he wasn't going to make it. I couldn't kid him; I said, is it all right, Sgt? He said yes. We said goodbye and that was that. Yes, there's much suffering. I'll write to his mother when enough time has passed."

THE BULGE

Mid-December brought blessings and hardships to the 128th Evacuation Hospital. Along with the elation personnel felt at being granted passes to Paris, came a surprise German counter-attack which was launched on 16 December 1944 and raged on into January 1945. Pvt. Jodie Harmon was one of the soldiers experiencing the mixed emotions that blessings and hardships brought with them:

"In mid-December I got an R&R leave to go to Paris. Seventy-two hours plus travel time. On December 16th I left the outfit and headed for Paris, riding in the back of a two and half ton truck before daylight. It was cloudy but I could see the heavy artillery flash behind us. I didn't know that this was the beginning of a huge battle.

"That was the morning the Battle of the Bulge started. But we didn't know at that time what was happening. I don't remember how far we traveled in the truck. It seemed like I caught a train somewhere on to Paris and spent my seventy-two hours down there, then headed back to the unit. I got back to my outfit and they were still there where I'd left them but they had just gotten orders to pull back into Belgium. So I got there in time to help move back."

The new German counter-offensive brought increasing air activity to the hospital. Personnel could hear anti-aircraft fire throughout the night and learned the next day that German paratroopers had been landed only miles away near Malmedy. Trucks from the 128th Evac were sent to the Malmedy area to move patients and personnel from other hospitals to safer positions behind the lines.

Despite the new German offensive, hospital personnel were making plans to celebrate Christmas. On 20 December 1944, Lt. Hornback wrote home:

"We're all working on Christmas plans. Such are a major undertaking but we're making candy and cookies for everyone, including our patients. We're planning to sing carols in town and we're getting small things for the children— as far as we can make it go."

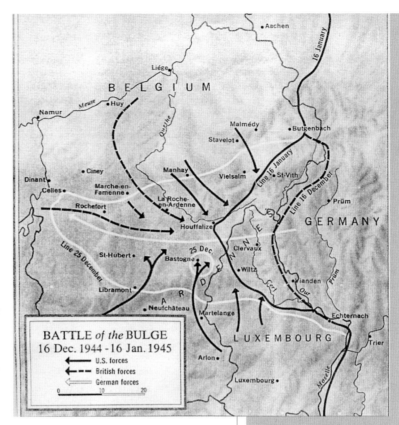

The Battle of the Bulge is the name given to a complex series of armor and infantry maneuvers over a month's time in very cold conditions.

Below, the hospital at Verviers, Belgium. (Photo courtesy of Vaughn Pulice)

On 23 December 1944, with German forces threatening their position, the 128th Evacuation Hospital moved to Verviers, Belgium and opened to receive casualties. Pvt. Jodie Harmon described that move:

"We moved back to this town called Verviers, Belgium. We set up in a building on the side of a hill at the edge of town on the main highway. We had a fairly good-sized open yard at the back. They set up the kitchen between there and some other building. The army had a lot of replacement, transient troops coming through. They would stop here to get food or wait for other transportation. The Germans starting shelling Verviers with a railroad gun. The first huge shells that came over made so much noise, I thought they were rockets. I was told that the size of the shell was 380 MM. We were on the opposite side of the hill from the direction that they were coming. They were trying to drop them beyond us on the railroad station. It was right down the hill in the bottom of the valley, in the middle of town. The new recruits were coming up after the ground was covered in snow and shells were still in the air landing in the snow like it was a featherbed or something. We had gotten used to the noise and didn't pay much attention. That went on for days, just off and on. We were taking many patients from the Battle of the Bulge, which included a lot of frostbite patients."

The 128th Evac opened its doors at

Dr. Schwade's diary, Christmas Day 1944:

Verviers, Belgium: "Plenty of patients coming in. Busy with terrific cases during the night; 13 bellies – what a night!"

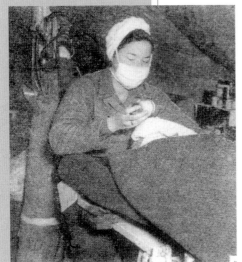

2nd Lt. Martha Cameron administers anesthetic to a wounded soldier in Belgium.

Verviers at 0800 on Christmas Day. That afternoon, a turkey dinner with all the trimmings was served to all personnel, including visitors from 97th Evac which had just moved into the area and had not yet set up their hospital. Christmas day proved to be relatively unbusy and the 128th Evac's nurses were able to carry out their plans for a Christmas dinner followed by a dance.

Nurse Anesthesiologist Martha Cameron remembers the importance of her trade at this time:

"Anesthesia was a necessary adjunct to surgery. General anesthesia was restricted to the use of sodium pentothal, nitrous oxide and ether. Nitrous oxide, oxygen and ether anesthesia, then popular, was deliverable only by the two field anesthesia machines which were used for special abdominal and all chest cases, one in each operating room tent. These cases were managed by M.D.s Kirby Schiffler, Chief of Anesthesia, Richard Stappenbeck and George M. Bogardus, who was sent to battalion Aid Station during the Battle of the Bulge and lost a leg due to a shrapnel wound. Those cases were long and hard.

"In addition to the two 'suitcases' that contained the breakdown Heidbrink Anesthesia machines, we had one five-by-two foot long boxes that contained syringes, needles, anesthetic agents, and various tools of the trade which when unpacked turned into our anesthesia worktable, one in each tent. We were responsible to evaluate each patient in turn, consult if necessary, and render the patient unconscious for surgery. I remember lining up the pins that accompanied each new syringe for pentothal on the chest pocket flap of my fatigues over a 12 hour duty tour. During the first Normandy day 20-25 pins were there, so that averages two or more cases per hour. We didn't try to count after that.

"Some cases were long with 3 or 4 specialty surgeons, particularly in face cases, which meant a long recovery period as well. We didn't have a recovery room set-up in those days so the anesthetist stayed with the patient until all reflexes were present and the patient talked. I got a new name after one such case. The patient 'McCarthy' and I were alone in surgery for an hour or two and I had resorted to repeating loudly, "Speak to me, McCarthy," not realizing I was being overheard. Finally McCarthy spoke and I called for help to take him to the post-op ward tent. To my surprise, the next day as I passed by a cluster of surgical techs on the way to mess I was greeted with a chorus of, 'Speak to Me McCarthy!' and that was not the end of it. It became my second name. Col. Proffitt called me by that name in the mess tent to step up to receive my promotion order to First Lieutenant. Corporal James G. Darsie was totally responsible for that and also for many pleasant memories of how excellent teamwork in the O.R. can be. He, Frances Farabough and Mike DeVito and I could turn out cases with unparalleled efficiency and speed."

Martha summarized, "Sodium Pentothal, not without its hazards, proved to be the answer to the challenge of caring for multiple surgical cases in the shortest time, keeping pace with the needs of war in the Forties, but we couldn't have done without ether. I never saw an explosion with ether even though once during the Bulge at Verviers the surgeon's hands were so cold they begged for the nearby stove to be lit. Dropping a few wet towels near the head of the patient, I relented and the surgeons appreciated it."

CHAPTER EIGHT
1945: THE YEAR THE WAR ENDED

ON 1 JANUARY 1945, THE OFFICERS and nurses of the 128th Evacuation Hospital attended an eggnog party given by the CO of the 97th Evacuation Hospital. It seemed an appropriate beginning for a month that could bring heavy snow and enemy artillery during its first two weeks. Their patient load was steady at about 300 patients a day. January would also bring the wedding of Lt. Gladys Martin to Lt. John Flynn. That wedding was the topic of Lt. Hornback's letter home on 14 January 1945:

"Today was a remarkable one. I was a bridesmaid and you'd never guess for whom—Martin, no less. She was so happy, and though I never have felt they were a perfect match, they should know their minds in two years. It was very quiet— they never announced it, and only the CO, the chief nurse and Orie composed the audience besides the Captain, and I who stood up with her. John is Catholic, so the Catholic padre who's a much better egg than the Protestant one, married them. We were going to a lovely little city down the river, but Jerry [the German Army], of course, decided to go there, so they just had it in the little town at the foot of our hill. They have an official 48-hour pass and are staying with a family we know.

"I'm so terribly sorry about Math [Gladys Martin's brother who was missing in action serving as an army Air Corps pilot in the ETO]. I told John and he will tell Martin while they're away. He stands a good chance of being a prisoner anyhow, and the eternal waiting is terrible, I know."

Following a brief move to Hannut, Belgium on 24-25 January 1945, the 128th Evac began its move to Banneux on 28 January, completed the move and reopened the hospital on 3 February 1945. February unfolded with warmer than usual weather and a steady but manageable flow of patients.

On 26 February 1945, Lt. Hornback wrote home and clarified several misunderstandings that have existed concerning Lt. Gladys Martin Flynn:

"It's a memorable morning, too. G. Martin leaves this AM on the long road home. Guess there's a few explanations needed to sorta set you all straight on some things.

"Martin hasn't been real well since Sicily when she had jaundice. So John, who is our adjutant and hence a quite dictatorial fellow, felt that she should go home. Now there is only one infallible way for an army nurse to get home from Foreign Service. Other methods work some but this one hasn't been known to fail. There's a catch though. After marriage, the pair are separated by army order to

St. Joseph Catholic Church in Verviers, Belgium, January 14, 1945. The Flynn's small wedding party includes, left to right, front row, Capt. Charles Ebbert, Lt. John J. Flynn, Lt. Gladys M. Flynn, and Lt. Margaret Hornback. Back row, Chaplain William E. Maher. (Photo courtesy of G. Jesse Flynn)

different outfits, often to different armies—another little practice to make folks as miserable as they can. So, sometimes, there's insufficient time to prepare a go for her army discharge. They got around that, too. They had a civilian priest marry them. Then they didn't ask permission to marry in the army until they were sure of all little details. Hence any little discrepancies in time which you may wonder about. We all sorta laughed up our sleeves, for that surely beats the army at its own game. She'll be transferred to a General Hospital [the 108th General Hospital] in Paris, where she'll turn in as a patient, and with a little luck, can fly home from there. We hope to arrive in time for the big event, but it will be a big surprise if we make it. Don't think we can."

With Lt. Gladys Flynn's departure from the 128th Evac, only 17 of the original 60 nurses who landed in North Africa on 8 November 1942 remained with the unit.

On 9 March 1945, the 128th Evacuation Hospital began its move to Euskirchen, Germany in order to be better positioned to support casualties from the battle for the Ludendorff Bridge at Remagen, Germany. The new hospital at Euskircen was set up in buildings that formerly housed a reform school. After nine days, the 128th Evac was moved again and this time their trip would take them across the Rhine River. Walter Larson recalled that journey:

"I went across the Remagen Bridge before it collapsed. I had a truckload of supplies and I don't know if anybody else in the outfit did, but I definitely remember going across that damn railroad bridge and getting on the other side and having a hell of a time to get off the tracks.

"The reason it collapsed was because it was over-loaded with heavy tanks and stuff. After it collapsed, then they built a pontoon bridge."

The pontoon bridge over the Rhine River at Remagen, Germany, March, 1945.

Right, the original Ludendorf Bridge at Remagen lies submerged in the Rhine River after its collapse.

The new hospital site was at Duenstekoven, Germany and operated under canvas. American and allied troops were moving rapidly toward the heart of Germany and, in just seven days, the 128th Evac was greeted with both beautiful scenery and almost total devastation existing in each other's shadows. Lt. Margaret Hornback addressed their surroundings in her letter of 21 March 1945:

"It's really spring now and, wonder of wonders, it doesn't rain all the time. You can see how the Germans would love their country. It is beautiful, and they're so thrifty and clean. You can see the difference in them and other countries we've known, and just as modern as anything we have. What you can't understand is why they couldn't be satisfied with what they have and not be always fishing fights.

They don't have much left, though, when we finally take a town. The ruins are unspeakable and poor people scrambling through what were their homes to see if anything remains. They know very little about being evacuees. When they leave, they carry pianos, pictures, china, etc., and leave clothes and food behind. I think they will probably starve unless we feed them, too. Wonder how long we can feed the whole world?"

Veteran members of the 128th were inwardly concerned about being sent to the conflict in the Pacific. Dr. Schwade made note in his diary March 19, 1945: "Discharged Col. Snyder. Col Wiley gave his farewell address to us at 1:15. Sorry to go–going to 48th in Paris. Said we vets of 128th wouldn't go to Pacific, but home after war in Germany is finished. Good news! Hope it's true."

The casualties were not the only ones needing the nurses' attention. It was spring, and mumps were making the rounds among hospital personnel. Lt. Hornback commented on the situation in her letter 27 March 1945:

"We've been awfully busy – Oh God, may it end soon. My boys have the mumps. In the army that spells 21 days in bed. We have only four trained to scrub and only one of the bunch has had it.

"This kid worked two days after having them and I didn't even notice until the swelling was notably marked. What a life!"

The fast pace of the final weeks of the war is described by Capt. Schwade in his diary:

March 24, 1945 – Across the Rhine

"Heard from auxiliary team today, all our 7th Army are across the Rhine – and nothing to do. Found news at noon – Montgomery crossed the Rhine last night in three places. Also 9th Army crossed – things going ok. Patients are starting to come in now that we are ready – great life – this army is nuts!

March 25, 1945:

"Worked all night till 8:00 a.m. 106 cases. I did around 25 – 30 myself – small staff. Sure am tired – slept till 12:30 and ate dinner."

Winifred Wagner Haus Hospital in Bayreuth, Germany, spring 1945.

March 28, 1945:

"Plenty of POW cases. Did 57 cases, arms, legs, and the usual – perforated rectums, did exploratory lap and colostomy – nurses wonderful. Armies on all fronts going like house on fire."

By 13 April, the 128th Evac had moved two more times and on 14 April 1945 the hospital was located at Kromback, Germany. Lt Hornback comments:

"It's now seven PM; I have only one patient. All is in order on the ward. My little Mexican boy is sleeping and my ward boys are popping the last of the popcorn down at the far end of the ward. How this little one continues to sleep I don't know, but soldiers are funny. They sleep through anything. This one isn't too sick, even though he does have a hole in his tummy. I sit by and watch his intravenous run and feel like I'm back home doing private duty.

"Usually we just connect them up and they run and if they don't run, we stick em again.

"We sorta live on easy street now. There are many Army hospitals, and casualties are light, so we take turns admitting. Surely makes it better, especially for patients who had to wait until we could get around to them when it's real busy.

With the war slowing to a close in Europe, cutup Walter Larson shows how he would like to pull guard duty. (Photo courtesy of Walter Larson)

"We have a real pretty place now. We look out our front door across a pretty little lake and far over to the mountains. It's real warm in daytime but awfully cold at night. The cold just crawls through your bones. Still our old five living together. Jen, Hobby, Zimmy, Orie and I. We've a kinda cute house. One school where we lived had checked gingham mattress covers, and we relieved them of a few. I acquired a wooly rug named Fido and the other gals have straw rugs. We've some beat-up lamps and bedside tables. It's quite homey really, and you're continually surprised at how much you can dress the place up out of a little bit of nothing. The boys never bother and their house looks like one junk heap.

"We got some more recovered prisoners but none knew Math or McKee. I don't think they were taken to this sector.

"Know how grieved you all were about the President. Maybe some were glad, too. It's astonishing how many doctors hated him—because of socialized medicine, of course. I don't think they can escape it though, no matter who or what's in power."

During the last week of April, the war in Europe was winding down and the number of American and Allied casualties decreased drastically. Lt. Margaret Hornback's letter dated 28 April 1945 reflects these facts:

"Had a fat letter from G. Martin today. Hope she's better now. Such matters make me fearful.

"Martin wrote today that she had a picture of Orie and me and a donkey, and that the resemblance was striking. Don't remember when such a picture was ever made, but she says its good. If it comes into my possession, I'll send it.

"At present, we sit around in the OR tent. The fellows are instructing the chief of surgical service in the fine arts of crap shooting. The teacher has just won around $300 in a friendly little game. I hate to see them do it, but there's not a thing on earth to do around here but sit and look at each other, so one can't altogether blame them.

"Well, the letter arrived and hostilities still haven't ceased. It's hard to find any place or time when peace can actually be. There's no one from whom we could accept surrender. One of these days maybe the armies will have covered the entire continent and then they'll say it's quits.

"We just received the first copy of another book by one of our first chief nurses, Theresa Archard, titled *G.I. Nightingale*."

Dr. Schwade reports to his diary the good news on the war fronts:

<u>April 28, 1945:</u>

"News excellent. Himmler says he will surrender to U.S. and Britain but not to the Russians – deal refused, all three must be surrendered to. Himmler also says Hitler's health is very poor – he may not last 48 hours – too bad. News that we were moving to Bayreuth near the Czechoslovakia border real soon – nuts! Well – time will tell – why and what's to be – and so it goes."

Members of the 128th were overjoyed at the news that the war in Europe was over.

On 30 April, the 128th Evac moved again, this time to Grafenwohr, Germany. By the first week in May, it was obvious to the personnel of the 128th Evac that the end of the war in Europe could not be far away. On 2 May 1945, Margaret Hornback wrote home and expressed her own opinion:

"At long last it does seem that it can't be much longer. How wonderful if the guns just stop—no matter how they do things afterwards. We're again hoping that we might get to come home together. How we'd love that. Did you read that business about people maybe getting out of the army after four years? Of course, they could just say you were essential and keep you anyhow."

On 7 May 1945, all of Germany's air, sea and land forces surrendered unconditionally and Admiral Doenitz signed the unconditional surrender of Germany at 0141 at Reims, France. All offensive operations were discontinued and 8 May 1945 was officially declared "V-E Day" – Victory in Europe Day.

The thoughts of the personnel of the 128th Evac turned almost exclusively to going home. Lt. Margaret Hornback's letter of 5 June 1945 reflects this sentiment:

"The papers say the discharged soldiers will be encouraged to go on the farms—likewise any that can be spared from war production. I wonder if that will help in our section? I doubt it, for I imagine the wheat out west and the cotton, etc., needed to feed and clothe the world will be first served.

"Must get packed for we'll move in the morning early before it gets hot. The roads are still crowded with poor people walking home. Some of the Russians, Poles, French, etc., have gone. Now it's the Germans walking home from the Sudetenland. Must seem funny to our master race to walk while we ride and we don't think much of the way we ride, either. But it just shows how much worse off one could be."

A happy nurse is packed and headed home.

Dr. Schwade makes an announcement in his diary:

"V.E. Day at last! Beautiful warm day. Heard Churchill, Truman, DeGaulle and Stalin on air at 3:00 announcing end of the war in Germany."

Going Home

The end of hostilities in Europe brought high expectations from members of the 128th. Going home was foremost in the minds of every soldier. Some of the doctors and nurses were already in the States. Dr. Rosenbaum had been assigned to the task of chief medical officer at a midwest post. Fully half of the original nurses had shipped home due to injury, pregnancy or request.

The war in the Pacific was still quite active with positions on the island of Okinawa still being contested and the home islands in firm control of the Japanese army. The troops not needed for occupation in Europe feard being sent to complete the battles in Japan.

It was in this atmosphere that a "point system" was instituted. A soldier was awarded points for time in the service, time in combat theaters and other factors. The more points accumulated, the closer one came to going home. Most of the cadre in the 128th was sent home between July 1 and December 1, 1945. They were transported by troop ships and bombers converted to troop transports.

Many came home and were married within weeks. George Willett, Gilbert Smith, Genevieve Kruzic, Vaughn Fisher and many others found spouses within weeks of their homecoming.

Walt Larson, Jodie Harmon, Leonard Schwade, Frank Burton and Ed Rosenbaum were among the group that had been separated from their wives for almost three years. The adjustment of returning was profound and required patience.

When it was all over, many soldiers collected souvenirs.

Leaving for home at the end of the war. (Photo courtesy of Jane Van Dyke)

There were certain indignities suffered by nurses traveling home on troop ships. An example of one remembered by Martha Cameron was: "As the ship passed the Statue of Liberty in New York harbor, the band struck up "Roll Me Over in the Clover." The men sang and cheered until the boat docked in the Brooklyn Navy Yard. Doris Brittingham agreed that "Stars and Stripes Forever" would have been more appropriate but understood the sentiment of the times.

To be married and separated for more than three years was a strain. The trip from Europe and homecoming is descibeed by Jodie Harmon:

"When night fell, and we were passed the Azores, I had gotten in my bunk, settling down just about half asleep and most everybody else was in his bunk, most of them asleep. All of a sudden it just felt like we'd run up against a wall. It kind of banged and ducked sideways. One soldier jumped out of his bunk and headed up the stairs. 'Where in the heck are you going?' I said. He just stopped and realized that there wasn't anywhere to go. It just meant that was indication of how edgy our nerves had become because of times spent in the war zones. Always in the back of your mind that there could be a floating mine out there somewhere the ship could hit. We had been hit by a tidal wave.

"The ship had been traveling smoothly until then but after that it was like a bucking bronco. We were bouncing and tossing from end to end and side to side. The next morning we all started lining up for breakfast. The serving table ran the width of the ship. We would line up all the way down one side, go across to get the food and leave down the other side. We were falling all over each other, spilling food and vomiting. One of my buddies broke an arm in a fall. I didn't go through the line again for the rest of the trip. Most of us just ate fruit.

Dr. Schwade's diary, July 9, 1945:

Coming Home: "Called to Gingles office at 11:00 a.m. Burton, Gordon, Rainey, Tropea, Predovitch and I – orders come thru to return to the States. I just couldn't believe it – we're leaving tomorrow."

July 10, 1945: "Up at 6:00 a.m. to be sure of being ready. Left 9:30 a.m. and drove to Frankfurt on Main and stayed overnight at hotel. To Luxemburg tomorrow. Hope we don't stay there too long."

"It was October 5, 1945, when we were greeted by the sound of artillery fire. We approached the port of Newport News, Virginia. The coastal guns were having practice but it unerved many of us onboard.

"The port authorities came aboard to check for any health problems before we were docked. We apparently passed inspection and were docked and unloaded into a huge auditorium.

"We were given a welcome speech and were offered exchange of foreign money for dollars. This surprised many of us because we understood that the money was worthless. One soldier had even burned his money.

"We were taken to a barracks and given access to a phone booth. I got in touch with Mary Jo and advised her that I would have a four-day troop train ride to San Antonio.

"She had been in San Antonio for over a month waiting for me. I was supposed to fly from France but was changed to a ship at the last minute. The reunion with her was strange. I had last seen her in July 1942. It was like meeting someone for the first time.

Eva Sacks, Mildred Harris, and Gladys Martin participate in a little communal knitting.
(Photo courtesy of G. Jesse Flynn)

"After a few weeks at Fort Sam Houston, I received a three-hundred dollar severance pay and headed out into the real world.

"I had the better of three months of leave time for which I was paid. I got the money and we caught a bus to Saint Angelo. Daddy met us at Saint Angelo bus station. He was driving a Hudson pickup. We got home late in the afternoon. I was getting out of the pickup and heard a couple of deep voices behind me. They walked up behind me while I was getting our bags out of the pickup. I was expecting to see my little brothers but they had grown up and were much taller than me."

Jodie continued explaining the time warp experience of the returning GI. He ponders some of the same questions that the soldiers of the Vietnam generation faced:

"The war was over and I was in civilian clothes. Now what am I gonna do? I expected to find things like it was when I left. But it wasn't quite that way. I found everything different. Everyone had just gotten a little older and changed their ways. I'm sure I had changed a lot more than they had . . . What did I expect? No one seemed to be interested in what I'd been doing all that time or interested in anything pertaining to the war. I guess probably they had heard all about it during the time and kept up with it through the news. But somehow, it seemed like there was something I needed to tell them but no one would ask me anything. It just occurred to me that they weren't interested. Of course, as time goes on I realized that they were just afraid of how it would affect me to have to talk about it. Whatever the reasons, though, I couldn't worry about it. Now I was out of the army where I now had to make decisions on what to do and where to go. They'd always been made for me in the army. I had to get a job and start making decisions and doing for myself to get Mary and me on track again. The first thing I had to do was get some wheels and then I had to check to see if I still had a job. I was supposed to have had a job when I came out, that was the law. They had to rehire you if you had a job when you left. The guy I worked for before I went into the service had sold his bulldozer and went into the oil drilling business. He wanted me to go work at that, which I did."

Jodie and Mary Jo made the adjustment after three years apart and were together for 57 more years. Mary Jo passed away in July, 2002.

Margaret Hornback, Gladys Martin and Ora White

Many difficult readjustments were made with wives and fiancées who were left stateside. An example of a relationship that didn't lose a step was George and Lucille Willett. George had met Lucille Laughary at a basketball game on a blind date about ten days before he went overseas. They wrote letters to each other daily for three years.

George returned home on October 12, 1945. On October 30 a Baptist preacher in the town of Madisonville, Kentucky tied the knot between Lucille and George. Today they live in Louisville, Kentucky and have been married for 58 years.

Dr. Leonard Schwade's diary chronicled his trip home beginning July 11, 1945. The last of over 1,000 diary entries summarizes his feelings and those of most returning soldiers:

July 11, 1945:
"At Luxembourg. Will travel by air to States – Yea Man!"

July 15, 1945:
"To Paris – stayed 11 days and left on green project by air from air field at 3:00 a.m. Stopped in Lisbon, Portugal, the Azores, Newfoundland and then Washington D.C. Too foggy to land in New York. Called Esther. On to Ft. Dix, New Jersey. Then Pullman train to Chicago to Ft. Sheridan. Saw Esther this night – 28 July – <u>Wonderful!</u>"

Conclusion

I HAVE READ ABOUT, INTERVIEWED and observed these special members of the "greatest generation." Several conclusions became obvious to me as I completed my work.

   The reason we, as their children, did not know much about what they did was simply that much of it was unexplainable, painful or personal. In addition, we must look over their shoulders and into the past to understand the "who" and the "where" that formed them and influenced their silence. It was Doris "Britt" Brittingham Simion who first pointed this out to me.

She felt Tom Brokaw had missed an important point in his book. It was on an earlier generation's shoulders that "the greatest" were perched when they answered the call to serve. For it was from an immigrant, pioneering people that the American 'can do' ethic sprung— from lives where hardship was met with hard work, where community cared for its own, where self-sufficiency was the norm. Theirs was a heritage of doers and achievers at all levels of society but many were from farming backgrounds. They were a people grounded in doing what was right, accomplishing what had to be done for the simple reason that that was what living was all about. "No sense chattering on about it!" They were in large part a people of God whose values and simple, straightforward love of their country led them to offer themselves as the bulwark against a political ideology that could not stand. Why should they have to explain that to us?

   They spoke with their fellow vets but they feared

glorifying the disturbing realities of war or creating nightmares for us. To a person, they all felt they had fought the "last war." Whatever their politics, the reason to fight, maim and kill became blurred as the thousands of wounded and dead came through their tents.

Further still, not until I donned my army uniform, after being drafted in 1971, did I begin to understand just how much anguish my mother and father had carried and hidden over the prospect of war for my generation.

There was a remote comparison in my life that had come to mind and helped me bridge the generation gap. I had been an orderly for a brief time at Brooke Army Hospital at Fort Sam Houston, Texas in 1971. After my first four hours of mopping, I found a table in the dining hall where I placed my tray for lunch. Moments later, a nineteen-year-old soldier seated himself across from me and introduced himself. I don't remember his name but he had no nose, ears, fingers or body hair and his skin was pink, brown and beige with scar tissue. I could eat very little and aged quite a lot in the ensuing twenty minutes. This was the face of war. It was this twenty minutes plus three years that the vets of the 128th could not or did not wish to discuss with "outsiders."

"Those who have seen war, never stop seeing it." These words were written by Joe Galloway about soldiers serving in Viet Nam but they could have been said about the soldiers and nurses of the 48th Surgical Hospital engaged in combat support over two decades before.

1st Lt. Margaret Hornback spoke for most in her letter from Normandy in July 1944: "I wish all the world could walk through our wards—British, French, Poles, Czechs, Germans and GIs—dressed alike, wounded alike, and alike in heart —just homesick kids. God forgive us if we ever let this kind of thing happen again."

APPENDICES

- The Formation of the 48th Surgical Hospital and 128th Evacuation Hospital

- A Capsule History of the Unit in Combat

- Members of the 48th/128th Evacuation Hospital August-September, 1942

- Members of the 48th/128th Evacuation Hospital Biographies

- Acknowledgements

- Index

THE FORMATION OF THE 48TH SURGICAL HOSPITAL AND 128TH EVACUATION HOSPITAL

Written by Dr. George G. McShatko, 1949

ON 30 JANUARY 1941, CAPT. GEORGE G. McSHATKO was assigned as commanding officer of the 48th Surgical Hospital at Fort Francis E. Warren, Wyoming. Upon arrival at Fort Warren, Capt. McShatko was given a cadre from the Station Hospital that consisted of six sergeants. Of those six sergeants, two were to leave the unit prior to our departure from the place. Two were to leave the organization in North Africa, and two remained with the unit—one became a Warrant Officer and the other a 2nd Lieutenant before the conflict was over. Those six—whom many remember as the first that they received Army commands from—are namely Sgt. Mario Silva, Sgt. Tom Dokken, Sgt. Wiley Roberts, Sgt. Ruben Shanks, Sgt. Tommy Thomas, and Sgt. Thomas Treece. These six sergeants joined Capt. McShatko and on the 10th February 1941 activated the 48th Surgical Hospital. Immediately they were assigned a group of infantry trained personnel from Camp Crook, Nebraska. With this group they basically organized the unit.

On 26 March 1941 one hundred men were assigned from Fort Snelling, Minnesota, with no previous military training. At this same time, Lt. Bruce B. Sutton, and Lt. William Gorishek were assigned to the unit. Within a very few days Lt. Samuel A. C. Grove was assigned to the organization. Some persons may think that this was the basis of the unit, but much more was to come. Throughout the early days of 1941 this group trained through the hills and sand piles, the barracks and old cavalry stables of the ancient Fort. In the spring the 74th Surgical Hospital was also activated, immediately adjoining our unit. In the summer of 1941 a large group of the 74th Surgical Hospital enlisted men were re-assigned to the 48th. This was to become the basic unit of our organization.

Many of our comrades and buddies in the enlisted ranks went for OCS or the Air Corps. When they did, they were never returned to our outfit. (Two of these people that I will always call friends were Ford Boock and Bill Kolen.) Throughout the fall of 1941 and the spring and summer of 1942 the unit sent men to the various medical and surgical schools over most of the western half of the nation. When these men completed their technical training, they were returned to the unit.

By June 1942 most of the command had been assembled. Major Merritt Ringer had replaced Capt. McShatko as commander on 15 September 1941. (Capt. McShatko was S-3 and CO of the Mobile Surgical unit until 15 June 1942, then was taken from the unit and appointed Medical Inspector for XI Corp, Chicago, Illinois). On 15 June 1942 Major Merritt Ringer was in Command of the organization; Capt. Wm. E. Proffitt, Sr., was Executive Officer; Major John M. Snyder was Commander of the Mobile Surgical Unit; Major Chester Mellies commanded the 2nd Hospitalization Unit; and Major Frederick C. Mackenbrock commanded the lst Hospitalization unit.

The unit under this command had a two week manuever in the Pole Mountain military range of the U.S. Army west of Fort Warren. This was, naturally, the only area that was available to the unit for any large-scale exercise. (Throughout later years, this reflected on the officers, especially in regards to the "Pole Mountain Boys.") Upon completion of this exercise in late June 1942, the unit retuxned to Fort Warren, and many furloughs and leaves were taken and contemplated. On 20 July 1942 most of the enlisted personnel were called back from their furloughs and many officers were instructed to return from their leave. As usual this brought on a certain amount of chaos. Many of the enlisted men had not been home in a long time and many of the officers had not been with their families. But as the inevitable always happens, everyone responded. And with this response, the old Army game of waiting taxed everyone of the command, On 26 July 1942, after a week of waiting and wondering what was to happen, at noon mess four sergeants were told to report to the office of the Commander immediately. There with Lt. William Gorishek, Sgt. Tom Dokken, Sgt. Phil Keyes, Sgt. Ed Kelly, and Sgt. Jay Matthews received orders to pack immediately and entrain. Only Lt. Gorishek knew where we were going. Thirty-six hours later we left the train at Indiantown Gap, Pennsylvania. This was the advance detail for overseas shipment. Upon arrival at Indiantown, one of the first things that happened was the assignment of 39 nurses under the supervision of Capt. L. A. Salter, ANC. Needless to say, the nurses remained in their quarters. One hour later 77 enlisted men were assigned to the unit. Sgt. Dokken requisitioned four of the 77 that could type; Sgt. Kelly took 15 that could work, cleaning the mess hall for the main party; Sgt. Keyes employed four; and the remainder, 54 men, were the subjects of Sgt. Matthews to clean the barracks, and equip them for the main party that arrived late on the night of 1 August 1942. After several days of shots, pictures, B-bag inspection, and practice loadings, the unit boarded the *U.S.S. Wakefield* for wherever she was going. On 6 August 1942 the 48th was at sea with a good sized convoy. It then pulled into the harbor at Halifax N.F. and there was joined by many more ships and left there almost immediately with, at that time, the largest convoy attempted, with the destination being the ETO.

16 August 1942 the unit arrived at Greenock, Scotland, and immediately entrained for the south of England. We arrived there the following day and were stationed east of Tidworth Barracks at a place remembered as Shipton-Ballanger. There the unit stayed, with training hikes and practice foxholes until the rainy season set in and then we moved to the west of Tidworth to a place known as Kangaroo Corners. The unit was to remain there until 20 October 1942 when it, fully equipped and personal compliment full, returned to Greenock Scotland for loading on the ancient *Orbita* for sail to destinations unknown.

THE 48TH SURGICAL HOSPITAL/128TH EVACUATION HOSPITAL
A Capsule History of the Unit in Combat

Compiled and written by Col. William E. Proffitt

The 48th Surgical Hospital, which became the 128th Evacuation Hospital, was a prototype (the first of its kind) MASH unit that was in combat situations from November 8, 1942 through May 8, 1945. They had a six-month training and rest period spent in England from late 1943 to June 6, 1944.

Many times the unit was split into two or more sections, prime examples being the landings in Algeria and the battles for Southern Tunisia. The southern section was actually overrun by the German Army. A brief summary of the time the 48th/128th spent in combat, written by Col. Proffitt in 1945, follows:

During the invasion of North Africa (Operation Torch), one surgical unit was attached to the 26th Infantry Division for the assault on the west of the city of Oran, Algeria, and the remainder of the 48th accompanied the 16th and 18th Infantry divisions on the assault through the village of Arzew. This entire operation was known as the Center Task Force. The 48th Surgical Unit was then under the Command of Col. Merritt G. Ringer, and had a strength of 48 officers, 47 nurses, and 273 enlisted men.

The trip from Greenock, Scotland, to the African shore was uneventful, with the usual cleaning and general details that accompany any trip. After landing on the beaches just north of Arzew, with the assault waves of infantry, the main body of the unit moved into the city proper and began operating a clearing station. The First Hospitalization Unit and the Mobile Surgical Unit took over the old military barracks, and after cleaning it as thoroughly as possible, began operating four surgical tables. The Second Hospitalization Unit took over the old Infirmary two blocks away. Both units continued to operate in these places until four days later when hostilities ceased. This was accomplished by using some captured, outdated instruments, operating with

bare hands, without drapes, using alcohol-burning sterilizers and Lysol cold sterilization and using ethyl chloride and chloroform for general anesthesia. These conditions prevailed for the first thirty-six hours because the only instruments available were those of the clearing station. The infantry moved on a few miles and the port refused to unload even one of the trucks of the unit, all combat loaded, and the hospital was forced to work almost empty-handed. Notwithstanding, over 300 patients were operated on in the three-day period, with only three post-operative or operative deaths. In the group there were twelve abdominal laporatomies with only a single death (and he seven weeks later), some major amputations performed by flashlight, and many wounds surgically treated. During the period there was constant sniper fire between the barracks buildings as well as sniper fire into the courtyard of the Infirmary.

The following day the sea shipment was transported to the unit and the 48th moved out intact to the vicinity of Tebessa and set up camp in the wooded hills eleven miles north of the city. On 24 January the First Hospitalization Unit was ordered to set up a hospital near Thala, Tunisia. On 27 January the Second Hospital Unit with the Mobile Surgical Unit were ordered to Ferianna, Tunisia, to set up a hospital in the old French outpost barracks. These barracks were of the one-story type and were in an advanced state of disrepair. Large holes in the roofs, windows out, and no doors were the rule, not the exception. These were repaired with cardboard, canvas, and any materials available. GI pot-bellied stoves were erected in each ward. Tents were erected for the mess and supply tents. On 1 February the First unit closed down at Thala and rejoined the Second and mobile units. After three days it was ordered again to Thala and to reopen. By 10 February 1943, organization day, all units were operating. While the units of this organization were supposed to function in a coordinated way, the army was short of field units at this time and this forced the 48th to serve as two independent hospitals. Later, after the period of trial and error had been completed, the army developed the Mobile Evacuation Hospital, which the 48th became.

On 15 February 1943 German forces under the command of Field Marshall Erwin Rommel launched his counter-offensive against the American sector. The second unit and the Mobile Unit with Headquarters were ordered to evacuate and clear the area immediately. Orders were received at 2030 hours and by 2400 were closed, packed and moved. The Second Unit moved back and set up at Bou Chebka, Algeria, and before patients could be received, were forced to move again, this time back to Youks les Bains, Algeria. The First Unit was forced out of their area at Thala and went to El Kef, Tunisia. Two days later the First Unit moved to La Meskiana, Algeria. After handling patients from the large Evacuation Hospitals so that they might retreat further back, the Second Unit closed the hospital and went to Montisquieu, Algeria, and set up a hospital. On March 8, 1943 the Second unit, with the Mobile Unit and Headquarters detachment moved to an area near Bou Chebka.

At this time another change was made in the organization. Lt. Col. Chester A. Mellies was relieved of command and Col. Norman H. Wiley became the fourth commanding officer on 15 March 1943. On 19 March First Unit was ordered to set up in the old French Barracks at Feriana. The Mobile Unit and Headquarters accompanied them on this mission. On 27 March 1943 the Second Unit was ordered to Gafsa to set up near this highly important battlefront. The Mobile Surgical Unit and Headquarters joined the Second immediately. During this period Ivan (Cy) Peterman, war correspondent, was brought to the hospital as a patient and eventually wrote about the organization in an article that appeared in *Liberty* magazine under the heading, "The Medics Also Fought." On 15 April 1943 both units shut down and reassembled at Feriana. The following day the entire organization moved on the long trip to the north of Tunisia. The unit was again supposed to set up in an old French barracks, but they were so dusty and dirty that Col. Wiley found a very nice location alongside a cork grove, and there the old 48th Surgical Hospital set up for the last time on the 19th

April, 1943, near Tarbarka.

In this location and pursuant to CG #34, HQ II Corps, dated 30 April 1943, the organization became the 128th Evacuation Hospital (Semi-Mobile). The strength of the command of the old 48th was at this time 48 officers, 56 nurses and 275 enlisted men. The new T O/E did not allow this number. A certain number had to be transferred; in some instances normal attrition took care of excess personnel.

The new 128th Evacuation Hospital moved on 4 May 1943 to the little station by famous Hill 609, called Sidi Nisir. Here the unit remained through the cease-fire order of 18 May 1943, and on 13 June 1943 moved to the area on Lac Bizerte east of Ferryville. Here the Unit opened as a medical hospital, with malaria and dysentery the chief foes. On 19 July the unit moved to a staging area near Bizerte to prepare for shipment to support the invasion of Sicily.

During the days spent in North Africa there were no casualties. Many narrow escapes were accomplished. The strafing of "Stuka Alley" and "Messmerschmidt Lane" by the enemy had kept all of the motor personnel constantly on the alert. During an air raid while encamped at Lac Bizerte, 4.5 shells were landing in the area but none found a mark on the personnel. This history is not designed to recount personal triumphs. This is for the unit in general.

The 128th set sail for Sicily 20 July 1943 in many different serials and many arriving dates. The first group landed at Licata, Sicily, and as they slowly gained more serials they moved across the island and set up the hospital five miles west of Cefalu. More serials continued to join and on 14 August moved to San Stefano. After the island was captured the unit was sent to an area west of Palermo called Castellammare de Golfo. Here the unit set up on a bluff overlooking the sea. The area had about six inches of red soil over solid rock. The entire tentage was erected with the help of army engineers, who would drill holes in the rock and insert steel pegs. And in many instances they went so far as to use a powder charge to get into the rock. On the early morning (0700 British Double Summer Time) of 2 October 1943 a very strong hurricane struck the 128th. Approximately 195 patients were then on the wards of the hospital. Within a five-minute period every tent in the organization had been completely torn down by the force of the storm. Tent poles were broken, canvas ripped, the X-Ray equipment and laboratory equipment lay broken on the ground and ruined. Rain was cascading down, personnel drenched and their personal equipment soaked. As quickly as the storm had struck, it abated. But the damage was substantial. This equipment had been in use in the field, with all the packing and unpacking of two invasions, and countless moves in the field, for almost a year. Yet with 195 patients, the unit in two hours time had them all back in tents, all dry and without any losses. The seriously sick were sent to other hospitals, the less sick were made as comfortable as possible, and soon other tents were located about 50 yards from the original site in an olive grove and set up. The unit remained in this area until 9 October 1943 when the 128th set up in a school building in the town of Alcamo. The enlisted men, nurses, and officers were billeted in three different locations around the town. On 29 October the unit closed down and prepared for movement to embarkation area. On 8 November 1943, exactly one year from the landing at Arzew, the unit was loaded onto the USAT *Santa Paula*, again for destination unknown. The ship was packed to the very limit. Many more units were boarded than were originally scheduled due to the loss of another ship. On 25 November 1943 the unit disembarked at Newport, England, and marched, or rode, to Tortworth Court, a large old castle near Bristol. Arriving there at about 0330 the unit had hot coffee and light lunch and found a bunk anyplace possible. The following day the unit organized in its new home, a place that was to be home for a longer period than any other place since leaving Fort Warren.

To sum up the first year of treating combat troops: this organization had handled 21,305 patients. Of these, 2500 malaria cases were treated without one death. 4000 patients had been treated on the surgical service, and of these 2586 operated upon with a post-operative mortality rate of 1.7 percent. The unit had made over 30 moves, including special units and the unit as a whole. Many lessons had been learned in this period of combat support, and many new procedures and methods had been developed. The assignment to the U.S. First Army of this organization seemed to support the pride that the members of this unit had in themselves—pride in knowing that they had done a job well. Throughout the encampment at Tortworth Court, the unit had a complete hospital set up in the field adjacent, and this was used as a demonstration center for the new Evacs coming from the States. Many conferences and meetings were held at our location. Lecture groups were sent out from the 128th to other units. Many officers went to the various schools in London and elsewhere to find new and improved methods or techniques. Nurses were attending schools and conferences and visiting other hospital units. Enlisted men were continuing with their usual routine—working, getting out of work, locating the best pubs, pursuing what other entertainment that suited their fancy, and training when ordered.

This order of business continued until 6 June 1944 (D-Day Normandy, France) when part of the unit personnel departed Tortworth Court by motor convoy with all equipment combat loaded. The remaining personnel entrained at Charfield. The entire unit loaded on the liberty ship *William Pendleton* in Falmouth harbor and very early on the morning of 8 June left the port. On 10 June 1944 at 1530 hours the unit landed at Utah Red Beach. All vehicles of the unit were unloaded by the enlisted personnel of this unit. In addition they had to unload all engineer equipment with their 40 tons of land mines and TNT. By 11 June the unit was set up and again operating a hospital in the combat zone. Location this time was Boutteville, France. 30 July the 128th moved to a field 1.5 miles east of La Foret and remained there until 4 August when it moved to the Tessy sur Vire area (Battle of the Falaise Pocket). Here the men had to remove dead cattle, sheep and Germans before setting up the hospital. The 128th remained at this location until 17 August and then moved to Haleine near the sight of the Falaise Gap. Here there was a great influx of German prisoners. Over 1800 of them passed through the hospital. Many of them were not treated or recorded. 402 received emergency treatment, 123 received as patients. The remainder were sent to P.O.W. enclosures further to the rear. The unit remained active at this location until 30 August and then moved to Senouches. September 14-16 were spent moving on the long trip to Dolphin, Belgium. This was completed with

Col. William Proffitt

a stopover at Ouffet, Belgium of one night. At 0600 on 16 September, the 128th was again ready to accept patients. A move of over 360 miles was completed for the unit in its entirety, involving 61 trucks. This was one of the unit's longest periods of single emplacement in all combat locations. The unit remained in this spot until 1 December 1944. During this time many problems arose. It was the rainy season in Belgium. The streets and roads throughout the hospital area were a sea of mud. The 1110th Engineers were ordered to help the unit in this hazard. They came to the rescue by building roads and streets of rock and covered them with gravel. The Buzz Bombs were a daily menace. They were not aimed at the unit but the organization was in the direct line of travel for these implements of destruction. It is common knowledge that 128 of these weapons passed over the installation during the daylight hours during certain periods in November, and daylight was not long at that time of year. Many exploded in the vicinity but the luck of the 128th held out and none ever hit the unit. During this time there was one remarkable incident that happened immediately over the unit that everyone remembered; the dogfight in which an enemy aircraft was dropped almost in the area of the hospital.

On December 1, 1944 the unit was moved to the old German Army Barracks immediately south of Brandt, Germany (the battle of Aachen). During the

period of the operation in this location, many robot bombs and much enemy air activity was in the immediate area of the hospital. A considerable number of patients were handled at this spot. The normal activity continued until 18 December 1944 (the Battle of the Bulge) when the unit was ordered to remove the hospital back to Verviers, Belgium. By 24 December the unit was completely moved to the rear and operating again as a hospital. Robot bombs were plentiful, and activity on the combat front was at a high pitch. The Battle of the Bulge was at its peak. Patients were many, the weather cold. The work was more than hectic. This continued until 24 January 1945 when the unit moved again to Banneux, but not until 5 February 1945 did the remaining part of the hospital—which had been left in Verviers with patients—join the main body of the unit in Banneux. During the period of location in this area, from 5 Feb to 9 March, there started a transfer of personnel. Many personnel began moving back. Naturally when they were sent to the rear, new faces began to take their places. It is certain that many of the people who read this will realize that they may be the ones that are referred to here.

On 9 March 1945 the organization moved a mile northeast of Euskirchen, Germany, and set up in a former reformatory. It was there that the unit first came in contact with displaced persons. The unit remained there until 18 March 1945. It then moved to Irlich, Germany and on 21 March 1945 welcomed a new Commander. Col Charles H. Gingles relieved Col. Norman H. Wiley on this date. Col. Gingles was to remain with the unit for the remainder of the war. The unit stayed in Irlich, in tents, until 10 April and then moved to Kromback, Germany in support of troops reducing the Ruhr pocket. On 30 April the unit was moved to Grafenwohr, Germany, where it remained until all members of the original unit were transferred to either the U.S. or to another unit. The German army formally surrendered on May 8, 1945.

The unit's history ends on 1 June 1945. The 128th remained active for some time after this. On 19 September 1945 Col. Gingles was relieved. It is not known if at this time the 128th was inactivated or not, but it is known that the 128th Evacuation Hospital was reactivated. On 19 January 1955 at Landstuhl, Germany, the unit again began functioning as the 128th.

The 48th/128th in 31 months of combat duty had, from all available records, handled in excess of 70,000 patients. Of this number over 52,000 received hospital care from the unit. Over 21,200 of these were admitted on the surgical service. The post-operative mortality rate of 1.08 is something of which every member can be proud.

MEMBERS OF THE 48TH/128TH EVACUATION HOSPITAL
AUGUST-SEPTEMBER, 1942

NURSES

Archard, Theresa
Atkins, Edna
Ayers, Ginny

Becke, Ann
Boden, Leola M.
Boyd, Ann
Bringham, Amy
Brittingham, Doris
Browning, Edna Marie
Burke, Emily V.

Cameron, Martha
Carl, Maude M.
Coates, Elizabeth G.
Cooney, Annie
Coty, Emma I.
Cox, Dorothy
Cunningham, Catherine

Davidson, Gertrude
Devine, Rosemary
Dickie, Aldra
Dorton, Maribel E.
Ducibella, Carolyn T.
Duer, Agatha

English, Helen M.

Farabough, Frances
Ferree, Ella J.
Fisher, Evelyn Vaughn
Flippo, Helen C.
Forbes, Thelma B.
Francis, Mary E.
French, Evelyn
Friedlund, Doris H.

Gecke, Annie G.
Gerhard, Dorothy E.
Greene, Betty J.

Grier, Etoyl
Grimes, Florence M.

Hale, Allison
Hall, Ursula
Hamaker, Mary
Harris, Mildred H.
Hart, Margaret
Haskell, Ruth
Hatcher, Mary
Helm, Kathlyn
Hilton, Esther
Hobson, Helen W.
Hodges, Edith M.
Hodges, Evelyn
Hornback, Margaret R.
Howard, Lula J.

Kahle, Maybelle
Kaelin, Mildred H.
Karban, Beryl
Kavanaugh, Billie
Kelly, Marie
Kemer, Evelyn
Kenny, Margaret F.
Kirkwood, Doris
Knight, Kathleen
Kruzic, Genevive F.
Kunst, Margaret

Leible, Hilda
Littlefield, Edith F.

MacDonald, Phyllis
MacKay, Margaret
Madigan, Margaret
Martin, Gladys
Martin, Maureen J.
McNeive, Rosemary
Meyers, Mary
Miller, Agnes
Miller, Margaret
Miller, Violet

Molony, Helen M.

Nichols, Beatrice E.
Nickerson, Emily
Nickles, Amy L.

Parker, Edna M.
Parks, Ruth
Pettingill, Janet
Pridham, Dorothy
Purnell, Carrie E.

Rickman, Marie H.
Rinehart, Elma L.
Rogers, Kate
Romohr, Gladys

Sacks, Eva
Self, Gladys
Sheridan, Vivian
Smith, Carrie
Spears, Lois A.
Sramcik, Margaret
Standley, Hazel C.
Stanfill, Margaret B.
Sullivan, Mary Ann
Swaney, Edith M.

Taylor, Kathryn R.
Thompson, Julia D.
Tonzes, Berneice A.
Tyler, Eunice C.

Vogler, Vilma E.

Wheeler, Ruth E.
Wheeler, Sarah P.
White, Ora
Williams, Nell
Willis, Luella

Zimmerman, Marieta

CHAPLAINS

Arsenault, Frank (Chaplain's Assistant)
Father Paniera
Grove, Samuel A.C. "Chappie"
Power, John J.

OFFICERS

1st Lt. George Bogardus
Capt. Henry J. Borgmeyer
Dr. Thomas W. Burgess
Maj. Frank M. Burton

Capt. Art Carney
Maj. Richard H. Clark
Capt. Harry J. Connelly

Capt. Michael P. DeVito
WOJG Thomas N. Dooken
Capt. Frank K. Duffy

Capt. Charles A. Ebbert

Capt. John G. Fast
Capt. James W. Findley
1st Lt. John J. Flynn
2nd Lt. John M. Ford, Jr.

Capt. Louis H. Forman

Capt. Frederick D. Geist
Col. Charles H. Gingles
Capt. John H. Gordon
Dr. William M. Gorishek
Dr. Ellis V. Grabau

Capt. Hyman Katzovitz
Dr. Henry Kavitt
Capt. Richard S. King
Capt. Louis C. Kingston
2nd Lt. Vincent J. Klein
Dr. Harold Klockseim

Capt. Arthur LeeRoy
Capt. John H. Leimbach

Maj. Frederick C. Mackenbrock
Capt. Max R. Mansfield
Dr. Milton J. Marmer
Capt. George J. McDonald
Dr. Russell B. McIntosh
Lt. Col. George G. McShatko
2nd Lt. Rupert Meier, Jr.
Dr. Chester A. Mellies
1st Lt. Ray J. Moore

Col. Ben Peake
Dr. Milan Predovitch
Lt. Col. Wm. E. Proffitt, Sr.

Maj. Harry C. Rainey
Capt. Samuel Rifkin
Col. Merritt G. Ringer
Capt. Ed L. Rohlf
Asst. Chief Maj. Edw. E. Rosenbaum
Capt. Harold S. Rosencrans
Capt. Samuel H. Rutledge, Jr.

Lt. Col. A. L. Salter
Dr. W. B. Schafer
Capt. Leonard J. Schwade
Capt. Harry Kirby Shiffler
Lt. Col. John M. Snyder
Capt. David Solomon
Dr. Richard Stappenbeck
Capt. Bruce B. Sutton

Dr. Rocko Tello
Capt. Frank Tropea, Jr.

Capt. Robert H. Wahl
Dr. Howard Weinberger
Dr. Wilson Weisel
Capt. William H. Wheeler
Col. Norman H. Wiley

ENLISTED MEN

Aasheim, Oscar E.
Adamek, James
Albright, Delbert
Alwine, Francis
Anawaush, Howard P.
Arbeit, Joseph
Arnold, Lee W.
August, Maurice

Bair, Cecile "Teddy"
Baker, Melvin H.
Bakken, Lionel S.
Banitt, Myles W.
Baumhardt, V. E.
Baxa, Leonard J.
Beckman, Walter J.
Bellanger, Benjamin
Bellcourt, Paul L.
Bellrichard, Howard H.
Benson, Clarence E.
Bernhardt, Rubin
Beyers, Shorty
Bissen, Raymond J.
Blackburn, Theodore
Blanchard, Thomas E.
Bohman, Alex J.
Boock, William A.
Boswell, Robert
Breuer, Julies R.
Brewer, Aaron
Brizzolara, George
Brookman, Hunter
Brown, Bertle J.
Bryngleson, Leslie D.
Budziak, Alex J.
Burrack, Alvin W.
Bursey, John A.
Butts, Loren E.

Calcaterra, Mario
Cantu, Edward R.
Carter, Deloy O.
Catania, Anthony
Cetola, Joseph P.
Chadwick, Kenneth H.
Chalfant, James R.
Chapa, Joe
Chinn, Donald
Clausen, Arlid
Cloud, L. J.
Cohen, Ben F.
Cohen, Jerome
Conner, Dexter
Coronado, Francisco J.
Craig, Robert F.
Czuyper, John

D'Aloia, Peter
Daniele, Joseph
Darsie, James C.
Dauzat, Robert
Davidson, Kenneth
Davidson, Roy G.
Davis, Al
Dennis, John E. "Jack"
Diamond, Charles S.
Dick, James
Dickie, Aldra
Dirkson, Henry
Doolin, Alfred E.
Douglas, Joseph
Drime, Alfred A.
Drost, Maynard
Duensing, Francis E.
Dunbar, Elmer J.
Duxbury, Marcus W.
Duzat, Robert

Eden, William G.

Fagerlund, Maurice W.
Farnham, Robert W.
Felcyn, Roman D.
Flaugh, Marvin O.

Foy, Hugh D.

Gacke, Walter W.
Glade, Gerald E.
Gold, Ormie
Goodman, George "Goody"
Gray, Lester A.
Gregory, Michael L.
Gregory, Michael P.
Griebel, Alvin C. "Fritz"
Groves, Joseph Everett
Gunderman, Clarence L.
Gustafson, Ervin J.

Hagan, Gordon J.
Halverson, Maurice E.
Hamm, William E.
Hanson, Donald M.
Harden, Robert Lee
Harmon, Jodie D.
Harms, Wilbur C.
Harris, Marshall
Hartigan, John P.
Hartman, Robert D.
Hartmann, Joseph N.
Hartson, Clifford C.
Harwell, Earl
Harwell, Hilliard E.
Heinke, John P.
Helle, Arnold F.
Herbolsheimer, Gerhardt
Hetland, Henry L.
Hoctor, John A.
Hogan, Ray
Holeck, Fred H.
Hourican, Donald
Howe, George R.
Hudson, Harold J.
Huelsman, Lester J.
Hughes, Lonnie N.
Hurley, Burton F.

Inderrieden, Lawrence

James, Joseph F.

Jenkins, Dolcie
Jensen, Raymond H.
Jerdet, R.L.
Johnson, Elmer C.
Jones, Leslie A.
Justice, Graham

Kalb, Clifford J.
Katzen, Murray
Kaufmann, Edward A.
Kelly, Edward T.
Kelly, John
Kessler, George W.
Keyes, Joseph P.
Kircher, Theo
Klinsing, Raymond
Knott, Elton H.
Koloen, Wilbur B.
Kopan, Christ T.
Krist, Frank J.
Krokos, Louis E.
Kruger, Robert E.
Kubet, Frank
Kuhl, Don
Kukowski, Frank W.
Kuyper, Glen

Lail, Paul
Lakes, George A.
Lanning, Max L.
Lansing, Thomas
Larson, Walter F.
LaRoque, Jean F.
Laurenson, Clarence W.
La Varnway, Jack
Lentz, Harley U.
Leudecke, Hilton
Lucchese, Tony

Malecha, Joseph A.
Malfa, Sol A.
Malfa, Vincent
Mapes, Albert E. "Shorty"
Marshbanks, James
Mathistad, John

Matthews, Jay W.
McBride, Robert W.
McCafferty, John J.
McCullough, Earl L.
McGinley, Robert S.
McHenry, James P.
Meinders, Marvin H.
Meinen, Otmer M.
Meyers, Joseph C.
Michel, Arnold A.
Miller, Mark B.
Moll, Garnet E.
Morgan, George
Morgan, John
Mudge, James P.
Murphy, George R.
Murphy, James E.
Murphy, Owen B.
Murphy, Sayler B.

Nath, Raymond B.
Nefstead, Raymond B.
Nelson, Leo F.
Noland, George S.
Nowakowski, Mitchell

Ochocki, Stanley S.
Olson, Melfred J.
Oppek, Florian J.

Pagano, Samuel
Pagoria, Joseph
Pappas, Paul C.
Patton, John W.
Paustis, Edward E.
Payan, Jose E.
Peterson, Stanley
Peterson, Theodore C.
Pewitt, Robert
Pigoni, Wino
Platt, Harold W.
Popeck, Jr., Robert
Power, Allen R.

Rascop, Felix H.

Rasmussen, Floyd T.
Reinier, Hugh W.
Renninger, George F.
Rhoades, Dixon F.
Riesenberg, Paul A.
Ritter, D.R.
Roberts, Wiley L.
Rollins, Wm. R.
Rourk, Alva C.
Rousu, Ruben A.
Ruddy, E. J.
Ryan, Ernest J.

Sagan, Julian W.
Salisbury, Elmer G.
Salmon, Arnold L.
Sampson, Lawrence
Sanders, Harm D.
Sanders, Willard
Sapienza, Rocco
Scannel, Raymond
Scheiber, Frederick H.
Schmitt, Joseph
Schulz, Harold F.
Shanks, Hunter W.
Silva, Torivio
Silverberg, Maurice A.
Simion, Frank A.
Skiver, Herman I.
Smith, Delmer I.
Smith, Edward J.
Smith, George
Smith, Gilbert
Smith, John
Sorlie, Arnum L.
Sorlye, Oliver A.
Steinmetz, John E.
Stephens, Frank E.
Stephenson, Russell
Stevenson, Paul W.
Stone, James O.
Stratton, Harold H.
Straub, Paul R.
Strode, J. R.
Stubbs, Howard W.

Sturdevant, Richard H.
Sundby, Karnes
Surmeyer, Orville J.
Sutton, Ralph E.
Svec, James
Swan, Wesley
Swanson, Jack
Swezey, John P.

Tall, Vernon
Tarr, Oliver W.
Taylor, Edward
Taylor, Gerald C.
Taylor, R. T.
Thoeny, Ralph H.
Thomas, Leonard
Thorson, Charles
Tisler, Joseph
Toschi, Aldo
Treece, Thomas J.

Urbanski, Joseph L.

Van Delinder, Scott
Van Woert, Dwight E.
Veres, Charles J.

Wagner, Robert L.
Wain, Albert E.
Waller, James A.
Warner, Wilfred E.
Watson, William
Weathers, B. P.
Weaver, James A.
Weber, Clarence F.
Weber, Leo D.
Weiss, Leon
Wertz, Donald
West, Woodrow W.
Whitman, James
Wildman, James D.
Willett, George
Willis, Kenneth E.
Winzeler, Edwin C.
Wood, Walter S.

Woodruff, Melvin S.
Woodyard, Marion M.

Zeichner, Edward
Zetterlund, Lawrence
Zlataritz, Felix

BIOGRAPHIES

[I have attempted to compile information on all former soldiers in the 48th/128th. Unfortunately there were many people I was unable to contact and many bios are incomplete. To those who are not included or contain little or no information, I apologize.]

Oscar Aasheim

Aasheim, Oscar E.
Oscar Aasheim was born September 14, 1919 in Canton, South Dakota. He entered the United States Army March 19, 1941 from Fort Snelling, Minnesota, he then was assigned to Ft. Francis E. Warren, Wyoming. Technician-4th Aasheim served with the 48th/128th as a truck driver. He was honorably discharged September 15, 1945.

Upon returning home, Oscar resumed farming, he never married. Through the ensuing years, Oscar gained a reputation as a welder, repairing machinery for anyone who asked, at no cost, simply because he considered it the neighborly thing to do. His hobbies included restoration work (an old Packard, a Rumley tractor), collecting gas engines and also developed a penchant for skeet shooting. That interest eventually led to Oscar's New Years Day trap shoot, where he entertained up to 50 friends and neighbors, treating them to his special recipe chili when the shoot was completed.

Fellow 48th/128th vets Charles Thorson and Oliver Sorlye remained close friends, visiting frequently until the day he died, December 28, 1998 while under the care of his sister, Elsie Severson.

Adamek, James
James was from Illinois.

Albright, Delbert
Delbert was from Iowa.

Alwine, Francis
Francis was from Ohio.

Anawaush, Howard P.
Howard entered the United States Army in 1941. Howard was one of the original group ordered to Ft. Francis E. Warren, Wyoming where the 48th Surgical Hospital was established.

Arbeit, Joseph
Joseph was from Illinois.

Archard, Theresa
Captain Archard was the chief nurse in Unit 2. She returned to the states due to illness following the Sicilian campaign. Theresa wrote a book entitled *G.I. Nightingale* about her experiences with the unit during the war. Theresa was from Massachusetts.

Arnold, Lee W.
Lee entered the United States Army in 1941. Lee was one of the original group ordered to Ft. Francis E. Warren, Wyoming where the 48th Surgical Hospital was established.

Arsenault, Frank
Frank was an assistant to the chaplains.

Atkins, Edna
Edna was a nurse with the 48th/128th Evacuation Hospital, originally from Wisconsin.

August, Maurice
Maurice was from Ohio. Maurice passed away in 1980.

Edna Atkins

Ayers, Virginia 'Ginny'
Ginny was a nurse with the 48th/128th Evacuation Hospital. She married William Jamison. Ginny passed away in 1991.

Bair, Cecile 'Teddy'
Cecile was from Colorado.

Baker, Melvin H.
Melvin entered the United States Army in 1941. Melvin was one of the original group ordered to Ft. Francis E. Warren, Wyoming.

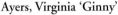

Lionel Bakken

Bakken, Lionel S.
Lionel entered the United States Army in 1941. He was one of the original group ordered to Ft. Francis E. Warren, Wyoming. Lionel was from Minnesota.

Banitt, Myles W.
Myles entered the United States Army in 1941. He was one of the original group ordered to Ft. Francis E. Warren, Wyoming. Myles was from Minnesota.

Baumhardt, Vernon E.
Vernon was from Wisconsin.

Baxa, Leonard J.
Leonard entered the United States Army in 1941. Leonard was one of the original group ordered to Ft. Francis E. Warren, Wyoming.

Becke, Ann
Ann was a nurse with the 48th/128th Evacuation Hospital. Ann was from Florida.

Beckman, Walter J.
Walter entered the United States Army in 1941. He was one of the original group ordered to Ft. Francis E. Warren, Wyoming. Walter was from Minnesota.

Bellanger, Benjamin
Banjamin entered the United States Army in 1941. Benjamin was one of the original group ordered to Ft. Francis E. Warren, Wyoming.

Bellcourt, Paul L.
Paul entered the United States Army in 1941. He was one of the original group ordered to Ft. Francis E. Warren, Wyoming. Paul was from Minnesota.

Bellrichard, Howard
Howard Bellrichard was born August 2, 1915 in Prairie Du Chien, Wisconsin. Howard entered the United States Army March 20, 1941 and was honorably discharged September 15, 1945. Tec/3 Bellrichard served with the 48th/128th as a pharmacist. Howard married his high school sweetheart, Gertrude Wagner October 2, 1945. Gertrude died May 24, 1972. He married Veronica (Lastine) Bissen December 14, 1974. Veronica was the sister of Ray Bissen who also served with the unit. Howard and Ray were good friends. Veronica died November 5, 1995. Howard passed away August 1, 2001.

Howard Bellrichard

Benson, Clarence E.
Clarence was from Ohio.

Bernhardt, Rubin
Rubin was from Wisconsin.

Beyers, Shorty
Shorty was from Wisconsin.

Bissen, Raymond J.
Raymond Bissen was born December 15, 1918 in Rose Creek, Minnesota. Raymond entered the United States Army March 20, 1941 from Fort Snelling, Minnesota and was assigned to Ft. Francis E. Warren, Wyoming. While assigned to the 48th/128th, Corporal Bissen assisted with patients, by feeding, bathing and helping with whatever needed to be done. He was honorably discharged September 16, 1945 at Camp Mc Coy, Wisconsin.

Raymond met Elaine Dooley (100% Irish, she is) at the VFW club in Austin, Minnesota. Her uncle was the bartender at the club and Ray was there with several of his buddies and as Elaine says, the rest is history. They were married January 8, 1947 at Queen of Angels church in Austin Minnesota. The Bissen's had six children, two boys and four girls. Elaine recalls how proud he was of his service in WWII and his love for his outfit and all his buddies. Raymond died February 14, 1977, at the early age of fifty-eight. Elaine resides in Austin, Minnesota.

Blackburn, Theodore
Theodore was from Alabama.

Blanchard, Thomas E.
Thomas entered the United States Army in 1941. He was one of the original group ordered to Ft. Francis E. Warren, Wyoming. Thomas was from Minnesota.

Boden, Leola M.
Leola was a nurse with the 48th/128th Evacuation Hospital.

Bogardus, 1st Lt. George M.
George was ward officer with the unit.

Bohman, Alex J.
Alex entered the United States Army in 1941. Alex was one of the original group ordered to Ft. Francis E. Warren, Wyoming.

Boock, William Alvin
William entered the United States Army in 1941. He was one of the original group ordered to Ft. Francis E. Warren, Wyoming. William was from South Dakota. William passed away August 11, 1985.

Borgmeyer, Capt. Henry J.
Henry was an assisting operating surgeon.

Henry Borgmeyer

Boswell, Robert
Robert was from Oklahoma.

Boyd, Ann
Ann was a nurse with the 48th/128th Evacuation Hospital. Ann was from Maryland.

Breuer, Julies R.
Julies was from Wisconsin.

Brewer, Aaron
Aaron entered the United States Army in 1941 from Camp Robinson, Little Rock, Arkansas. He was one of the original group ordered to Ft. Francis E. Warren, Wyoming. Aaron was from Franklin, Kentucky.

Brigham, Amy I.
Amy was a nurse with the 48th/128th Evacuation Hospital. Amy was from Tamora, Nebraska.

Brittingham, Doris H.
Doris "Britt" (Brittingham) Simion was born August 13, 1920 in Whitesville, Delaware. Her mother was 41, her dad 45, at the time of her birth. Mr. Brittingham was a prosperous farmer who owned and operated a canning factory but later lost it all. The family, which included a sister 18 and a brother 16 years her senior, moved to a farm near Delmar, Delaware where Doris grew up and attended school. She described her parents as hard-working people who dealt with their setbacks by simply working harder. As a child, Doris read the story of Clara Barton and the Red Cross and was filled with admiration. This childhood awe led her into the field of nursing. She graduated with fellow member of the 48th, Emily Nickerson from Wilmington General Hospital School of Nursing in June 1941.

Doris was busy with general duty nursing at Wilmington General in Wilmington, Delaware when the United States entered the war. Doris states it took little more than the suggestion from her friend, Emily, for her to respond to the call to serve in the armed forces. After

Doris Brittingham

getting her affairs in order, she and Emily entered the army at Fort Slocum, New Rochell, New York on February 16, 1942. While waiting assignment to a unit, Doris received special training to prepare her for the demands of neurosurgery. Postoperative neurosurgery would become her job while serving with the 48th/128. According to Doris's recollections, she was one of six nurses from Ft. Slocum who received orders in mid-August 1942 to report to a specific location in New York City in preparation for deployment. Doris remembers the staging area where they repacked their belongings and then being directed on board ship. She states it was on board that they were informed of their assignment to the 48th Mobile Army Surgical Hospital. The destination of their ship remained a mystery. On board there was much conjecture about the route they were taking. After learning they were skirting Ireland, it was no tremendous surprise to disembark in Scotland.

From late August 1942 to approximately the first of October Doris found herself assigned to a hospital in Salisbury, England. Her contingent traveled there by train and were greeted by an American major with "You are that bastard outfit!" which set Doris back on her heels but briefly. He went on to observe that he'd never seen anything like it, with enlisted men from states out west, nurses from military installations all over the place and doctors quite the same. In conversation with Doris, she reflected on her time with the 48th , returning to Scotland where she found the emphasis turned to training for disembarking from a naval vessel with a fully packed bag on her back, to the first taste of war on November 8, 1942 upon coming ashore in North Africa as the battle raged, to the wonder and amazement of the wounded when real live American women appeared bedside the next day, to the Christmas celebration in Arzew where tin cans, emptied of their contents, were transformed into Christmas ornaments that lifted the spirits of patient and staff alike, to the rush of hours spent working without rest to treat the gravely wounded and those who would ultimately not survive, to the interminable waiting in the heat of Sicily or the cold of Belgium, the packing and the unpacking and staging of a hospital as each new battle, each new campaign unfolded. Doris emphasizes, it was the bond of trust and friendship within the 48th/128th that sustained them. She described an unspoken understanding that each would give their all for the men coming off the front line. This bond held fast through the heart-stopping clash of artillery as they fought to save shattered men and made the dark hours, the lonely moments, bearable.

Doris experienced an unfolding sense of family within the 48th/128th. Through their service, she and many others were bound fast in what would become lifelong friendships. Departing the European Theater and the army in mid-August 1945, Doris married another member of the unit, T/Sgt. Frank Simion, a surgical assistant from Pittsburg, Kansas. The couple was introduced by nurse, Jane Ferree in Tabaka, Algeria.

Upon Frank's return to the states he went to work for Chrysler in Detroit. Doris noted that Frank was always a good provider, which allowed her to retire from nursing to stay home with their daughter, Ester, as a fulltime mother and homemaker. Frank and Doris lost their only child in 1983. Ester left behind her husband and three young daughters. In 1993 the Simion's son-in-law passed away. The granddaughters have scattered to California, Arizona and Illinois. Frank passed away on January 1, 1996. Doris now finds herself residing in Dearborn where her faith in God and friends sustain her. She remains a spirited, charming, out-going woman who states she would do it all again. Doris (Brittingham) Simion does not waiver in her positive, fiercely patriotic belief in this nation, the one she served so well.

Brizzolara, George
George was from Illinois.

Brookman, Hunter
Hunter was from Peterstown, West Virginia.

Brown, Bertle J.
Bertle was born May 8, 1918 in Mentor, Minnesota. He was drafted into the army on March 19, 1941, sent to Ft. Francis E. Warren, Wyoming along with about one hundred others from Ft. Snelling, Minnesota to start the very nucleus of the 48th Surgical and remained with the unit until mid May 1945 when he was one of the first five enlisted men to go home while the 128th was still functioning in Germany.

One of Bertle's favorite memories of the war was the time General Patton pined a medal on him, shook his hand and exchanged salutes. Bertle was the sergeant in charge of receiving and evacuation. In the evacuation process his job was going to the ward tents to recover the patients designated for evacuation. The primary function that he remembers most is in the receiving tent. "The wounded came to us directly from the battle field, some still bleeding, some almost dead, and some were German soldiers. Many wounded were reloaded and sent further back."

Bertle was responsible for keeping all their records and personal belongings. He also oversaw the loading and correct destination for each patient. In unloading and loading he handled hundreds of patients. He recalls handling so many wounded and near death soldiers that when he returned home from the war he wanted to forget it all. He thus never kept in touch with the organization except to pay the yearly dues. Bertle met his wife, Bernice Paulson, at the Rural Farm Community Center of Polk County, near Mentor. They were married August 25, 1946. He spent all of his post war working years in the telephone industry. His beloved wife died in 1990. The Brown's had two children, a daughter, Julie and a son, James who live nearby. Bertle now resides in Erskine, Minnesota.

Browning, Edna Marie

Edna was born May 3, 1920 in Cumberland, Maryland. Edna shared musings she recalled forty-six years after the end of WW II. "I took a jaunt down memory lane forty-six years ago to WW II: Invasion of Normandy with nurses crawling over shipside and down rope ladders to landing crafts.

Alvin Burrack

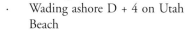

Edna Marie Browning

· Wading ashore D + 4 on Utah Beach
· Working in wet fatigues until midnight
· The masses of casualties
· The blackout restrictions
· Sleeping in a field artillery just over the hedgerow
· The beauty of daybreak and sunrise and <u>thanking God</u> for watching over us the night
· Then into the twelve, fourteen and sixteen hour days caring for wounded

<u>Memories of the fields of Germany</u>

· The cold fear on hearing buzz bombs approaching
· Sometimes the explosion not far away
· Sighs of relief when sounds were in faint distance
· Our hasty retreat (Germany to Belgium) during the Battle of the Bulge

<u>Aftermath:</u>

· Fears and excessive dreams inside a nightmare
· Screaming in sleep . . . . awaking tired
· Cold shiver during thunderstorm noise
· Backfire of a vehicle . . . heart pounding; You see, we had no time to cry!

Then memories jumping ahead two decades to training and equipping a 400-bed Evacuation Hospital for service in Vietnam:

· Field maneuvers with simulated casualty triage
· Ambulance and helicopter evacuation."

Edna passed away January 13, 2002.

Leslie Bryngleson

Bryngleson, Leslie D.

Leslie entered the United States Army in 1941. He was one of the original group ordered to Ft. Francis E. Warren, Wyoming. He was from Minnesota.

Budziak, Alex J.

Alex was from Chicago, Illinois.

Burgess, Dr. Thomas W.

Thomas was from Rhode Island.

Burke, Emily V.

Emily was a nurse with the 48th/128th Evacuation Hospital.

Burrack, Alvin W.

Alvin was born August 4, 1908 in Fayette, Iowa. He entered the United State Army June 2, 1942 and was honorably discharged November 19, 1945. He worked as staff in the headquarters. Alvin was the oldest enlisted member of the 48th/128th Evacuation Hospital unit. Alvin met Charlene Croyle at a party in Iowa before the war broke out. They corresponded while Alvin was stationed overseas and were married November 19, 1945 upon his return to the states. They had one child, a son named Lea. Alvin now resides at the home of his son and daughter in law, Linda.

Bursey, John A.

John entered the United States Army in 1941. He was one of the original group ordered to Ft. Francis E. Warren, Wyoming. He was from Minnesota.

Burton, Maj. Frank

Dr. Burton was born November 18, 1907 in Hot Springs, Arkansas. He entered the U.S. Army Reserves in 1932 as a first lieutenant and

Frank Burton (far right)

was promoted to captain in the U.S. Army Medical Corps in 1935. Dr. Burton began active duty on December 12, 1940, at Camp Joseph T. Robinson, North Little Rock, Arkansas, promoted to the rank of major, he then was assigned to Ft. Francis E. Warren, Wyoming. He departed for Europe and was operating surgeon in North Africa, Sicily, France, Belgium and Germany with the 48th Surgical Hospital that became the 128th Evacuation Hospital.

On June 10, four days after D-Day, Burton landed on Utah Beach as chief of surgery for the U.S. Army. Later, he would recall that he'd worked twelve hours without pause, estimating that in ten days he performed 1,500 procedures. When he stepped off the plane in New Brunswick, Nova Scotia, at the end of the war, the first leg of his trip home, he kissed the ground. Back home in Hot Springs, Burton worked around the clock. The nurses who worked for him were sometimes frightened of his stern demeanor, but patients could recall only his kindness. One woman, alone on Christmas Day, her sick husband entering his second week at the hospital, recalled a knock on her door. On the porch stood Burton, personally escorting her husband, his patient, home for the holidays.

He met his wife, LaRue (Williams), when he was a young doctor. She came in for a checkup and it was love at first sight. The large wedding they planned in Hot Springs had to be postponed; instead, they married in Denver, on the way to his station at Cheyenne, Wyoming. Dr. Burton died May 5, 2000. He was married fifty-nine years and had two children, Dr. James F. Burton and Isabel Burton Anthony. LaRue resides in Hot Springs, Arkansas.

Loren Butts (left)

Butts, Loren E.

Loren Butts was born August 19, 1919 in Terre Haute, Indiana. He was sworn in the army January 30, 1942, at Ft. Benjamin Harrison, just outside of Indianapolis, Indiana, he completed basic training at Camp Robinson, North Little Rock, Arkansas, and was assigned to Ft. Francis E. Warren, Wyoming with the original group of the 48th Surgical Hospital. He was honorably discharged September 25, 1945. Loren became a M/Sgt. in charge of communication in the headquarters. Captain Sutton told Loren that he had the best job in the army, working next to the colonel. Loren received a Bronze Star for meritorious action in Belgium in 1944.

I had several discussions with Loren about interesting times in the unit. The first is regarding the Germans breakthrough at Kasserine Pass in Tunisia: "We were operating out of French barracks at Feriana, Tunisia. Late afternoon I noticed an unusual amount of traffic on the blacktop in front of our organization, all of it going the wrong way. There were hundreds of tanks and vehicles moving back.

"About 5:00 p.m. the phone rang and it was Lt. Col. Anspacher of 1st Army Hdqts. wanting to know if we were all packed and ready to go? When I informed him that we had not received any information about a move, he almost panicked. He talked to our CO and told him how urgent it was to move immediately as the Germans had broken thru the Kasserine Pass. We broke a record in packing and moving, most of it in the dark. We had to travel with 'cat eyes.' I was driving the CO's command car with both Col's aboard. Tanks were moving forward, coming right down the middle of the road. Once the moon went behind a cloud and I couldn't see anything. I flashed my lights on for an instant and we were about to go over the edge of a cliff. We aged ten years that night but we finally made it to a location outside Youks les Bains."

Other incidents went as follows:

"Our commanding officer, Col. Wiley, would have made a great supply sergeant. He was quite a "scrounger" and never failed to surprise us in headquarters. In North Africa he came home with an amphibious jeep. Right away he had to try it out. So we headed for the Mediterranean. When we got there we saw a lot of Arabs watching something interesting—GI's swimming. Arabs are not too fond of water. But they quickly turned their attention to these two crazy guys who drove down the beach and right into the sea. It was my first attempt at walking on water. But it worked. Everyone enjoyed it.

"Col. Wiley appeared one day with a brand new flight jacket. It was too large for him, so he gave it to me. I wore it for at least a year. I'll bet all our visitors wondered what I was doing with a flight jacket.

"Another time he came back with a Thompson submachine gun. Lt. Ford and I decided to try it out. We went out in the desert and Lt. Ford shot it several times on single shot and repeat. Then it was my turn. Somehow he or I turned it on "constant" and it carried me around in a circle. If Ford hadn't jumped on my back, he wouldn't be here.

"After the landing in Normandy we didn't think we would ever get paid. But finally the day came; our troops had gone in about fifty miles, and we were informed that we could pick up our payroll at Caen. It was about forty miles inland. I don't remember how I got selected to make this trip, but I know I wasn't too happy about it. Gus, the CO's driver, and I made it to Caen without incident. But on the way back we saw a German strafer coming over the horizon toward us. Gus jumped in the left gully and I jumped in the right gully.

"I got the worst of it. It was deep and full of ancient blackberry bushes. The trunks were an inch or better thick and the thorns were like small daggers. I really was cut up and my cloths were ruined. When we got back to the outfit everyone thought it was very funny. I wasn't even mentioned for a Purple Heart." Loren was away from home for four years without a furlough. He was due for a leave when news arrived that his unit was going overseas. He was assigned to the African/European Theatre for three years and one month.

I asked Loren what the greatest lesson WWII taught him. He said, "It made you grow up in a hurry; you go from a boy to a man real fast."

When asked what memory stands out the most regarding wounded soldiers he said, "I remember one day when twelve black boys came in to the hospital. I asked someone what were they here for? I was told that they had all drank V2 juice (unknown to these guys, very lethal stuff). The next thing Loren recalls is all twelve of them were out side pitching a baseball to each other, having a good time. Within the next 24 – 36 hours they were all dead from the lethal juice. V2 juice was 190 proof alcohol. If it had color added to it, the guys were to stay away from it, and if it was clear in color, it was ok to drink. V2 juice had color, but the twelve boys drank it anyway, costing them their lives. When asked what the most difficult part of his job was, he said, "Boredom." Same old thing day in and day out. The best part of his job was getting to meet a lot of "brass" such as General Patton. Loren said Patton loved to be around the nurses, and every chance he got he would be there to have dinner with them. Like most enlisted men, Loren spoke highly of Ernie Pyle. He and Ernie became good friends. Ernie was from Dana, Indiana (thirty miles from Loren's hometown.) When Loren was stationed in England, he was at Tortworth Castle one day when Ernie Pyle walked in. Loren said, "Your Ernie Pyle, aren't you?" Ernie said, "Yes." Loren said, "I got a message for you from your buddy Curt Bridwell (a news reporter Ernie worked with at a Evansville, Indiana paper.) Curt said for you to keep your head down." The irony of this was that a sniper killed Ernie Pyle when he raised his head from a foxhole near Le Shima on April 18, 1945.

Loren tells of a time when word got out that there was going to be a quadruple amputation done on an American pilot who was shot down. Loren said he and others went to witness this procedure because it was history being made. He said he did ok until they started sawing and then he got physically sick and had to leave. The horrors of war sunk in that day. He never knew what happened to the pilot who had all four limbs amputated, and wondered what kind of a life he had after such a horrific ordeal. Loren met his wife, Luella "Lou" Cribelar when his best friend who was a mail carrier told Loren about this girl he delivered mail to that Loren just had to meet. Loren worked as a clerk at the post office. His buddy arranged a double date (his friend was married) with Loren and Luella and he and his wife. When it came time for the date, his friend and his kids came down with the chickenpox. Loren was left to go pick Luella up on his own, and as they say, the rest is history. They were married June 11, 1949 in Terre Haute, Indiana. They have one child, a son named Mark.

Calcaterra, Mario
Mario was from Michigan.

Cameron, Martha M.
— by G. Jesse Flynn

Martha Cameron, known as Marte to her fellow vets, traveled from her home in Tampa, Florida to attend the 1999 Convention of the 48th/128th in Louisville, Kentucky where I first had the pleasure of making her acquaintance. Retired but not retiring, Martha impressed me with her easy charm and zest for life as we discussed the various activities that were currently filling her calendar.

Martha Cameron

From time devoted to issues concerning her condominium association to her interest in the arts, Martha exuded an energy and enthusiasm that would shame many of my contemporaries. It was Martha Cameron who had long expressed a desire to chronicle the 48th/128th's years of service in the European Theater of World War II. She had begun to collect information many years earlier but hadn't yet addressed putting it into a publishable form. Born September 5, 1918, in City Point, Virginia, Martha was residing with her family in Nutley, New Jersey when she became that city's first nurse to join the armed forces in March 1942. She was accepted into the U.S. Army Nurses Corps. at Fort DuPont, Delaware. Martha was trained as a nurse anesthetist after being sent to England in July 1942. The then Lt. Cameron with the 151st was transferred to Oran, Algeria that same November two days after D-Day. She served eleven months there before receiving a requested transfer to "the Front" – the 128th Evacuation Hospital. Martha joined the unit in Sicily in October 1943 where she was assigned as tent mate with Parks, English, Cunningham, and Miller, (Margaret.)

Throughout her service with the 128th she continued to perform as a nurse anesthetist. In off hours, she kept busy as the resident hair stylist for the 128th, trimming locks for other nurses in the unit. Following her service with the 128th, Martha returned to the United States to England General Hospital in Atlantic City, New Jersey, and then went on to see service in the Philippines and Okinawa, where she met her husband and was separated from the Army. At Tyndall Air Force Base in Panama City, Florida, Martha was wed to Charles

McCaskey, a medical administrative officer in the newly formed Air Force, which Martha also joined when the rules changed, and married people could be stationed together. Entering in the rank of Captain, Martha retired a Lt. Colonel, after a total of twenty-three years service. After twenty-eight years, the marriage ended in divorce in 1978 with Martha returning to her maiden name at that time. In the early '70's Martha met Col. William Proffitt another 128th vet, at a meeting of the American Hospital Association/American Association of Nurse Anesthetists in Atlantic City. It was on this occasion that he presented her with a history of the 128th. Anxious to investigate other sources for data on the 128th, Martha found herself in Washington shortly before the 50th anniversary of D-Day, visiting the National Archives. The information she retrieved was combined with Col. Proffitt's and Martha independently worked to disseminate the history, to former members of the 128th. Along with Helen Moloney Reichert and her husband, Hugh, Martha sailed on the Cunard S.S. *Vistafiord* as part of its 50th anniversary of D-Day tour. They visited the Normandy beaches, including Utah Beach where they landed, and the town of Boutteville where they saw the site of the 128th Evacuation's first encampment and met members of the Groult family who owned the land. In Cherbourg the D-Day veterans were honored by the mayor. Helen and Martha were the only women veterans of the Normandy invasion present. When the mayor pinned on their medals they were the only veterans kissed on both cheeks.

Martha and James and Florence Dick joined Elaine and me for dinner the evening after the '99 Reunion broke up. We dined at Louisville's Zephyr Cove, at which time Martha graciously 'passed the torch' to me. I was humbled but committed to recording their story.

Cantu, Edward R.
Edward was from Chicago, Illinois.

Carl, Maude M.
Maude was a nurse with the 48th/1228th Evacuation Hospital.

Capt. Art Carney

Carter, Deloy O.
Deloy was from Arkansas.

Catania, Anthony
Anthony was from New York.

Cetola, Joseph P.
Joseph entered the United States Army in 1941. He was one of the original group ordered to Ft. Francis E. Warren, Wyoming.

Chadwick, Kenneth H.
Kenneth entered the United States Army in 1941. He was one of the original group ordered to Ft. Francis E. Warren, Wyoming. He was from Marshall, Minnesota.

Chalfant, James R.
James entered the United States Army in 1941. He was one of the

original group ordered to Ft. Francis E. Warren, Wyoming.

Chapa, Joe
Joe was from Texas.

Chinn, Donald
Donald was from Michigan.

Clausen, Arlid
Arlid entered the United States Army in 1941. He was one of the original group ordered to Ft. Francis E. Warren, Wyoming. Techinician-4th Arlid served with the 48th/128th in the orthopedic ward. He was from Minnesota.

Clark, Maj. Richard H.
Richard was an oral surgeon for the unit.

Cloud, L. J.
L.J. entered the United States Army in 1941 from Camp Robinson, Little Rock, Arkansas. He was one of the original group ordered to Ft. Francis E. Warren, Wyoming. L.J. served with the 48th/128th as a cook. He was from Benton, Kentucky.

Coates, Elizabeth G.
Elizabeth was a nurse with the 48th/128th Evacuation Hospital. She was from Pennsylvania.

Cohen, Ben F.
Ben entered the United States Army in 1941. He was one of the original group ordered to Ft. Francis E. Warren, Wyoming.

Connelly, Capt. Harry J.
Harry was an assistant operating surgeon with the unit. He was from Baltimore, Maryland.

Conner, Dexter
Dexter was from Indiana.

Cooney, Annie
Annie was a nurse with the 48th/128th Evacuation Hospital. She was from Massachusetts.

Harry Connolly

Coronado, Francisco J.
Francisco entered the United States Army in 1941. He was one of the original group ordered to Ft. Francis E. Warren, Wyoming.

Coty, Emma I.
Emma was a nurse with the 48th/128th Evacuation Hospital.

Cox, Dorothy
Dorothy was a nurse with the 48th/128th Evacuation Hospital. She was from Illinois.

Craig, Robert F.
Robert entered the United States Army in 1941. He was one of the original group ordered to Ft. Francis E. Warren, Wyoming. He was from Lincoln, Missouri.

Cunningham, Catherine
Catherine was a nurse with the 48th/128th Evacuation Hospital. She was from White Plains, New York.

Czuyper, John
John was from Wisconsin.

D'Aloia, Peter
Peter was from Illinois

Daniele, Joseph
Joseph was from Illinois.

Darsie, James C.
James was from Pennsylvania.

Dauzat, Robert
Robert was from Louisiana.

Davidson, Gertrude
Gertrude was a nurse with the 48th/128th Evacuation Hospital. She was from Oklahoma.

Davidson, Kenneth
Kenneth was from Forsyth, Missouri.

Davidson, Roy G.
Roy entered the United States Army in 1941. He was one of the original group ordered to Ft. Francis E. Warren, Wyoming.

Davis, Al
Al was from Michigan.

Dennis, John 'Jack' E.
John entered the United States Army in 1941. He was one of the original group ordered to Ft. Francis E. Warren, Wyoming. He was from Ellendale, Minnesota.

Devine, Rosemary
Rosemary was a nurse with the 48th/128th Evacuation Hospital.

DeVito, Capt. Michael P.
Michael was a surgeon specializing in Facio-Maxillary with the unit.

Diamond, Charles S.
Charles entered the United States Army in 1941. He was one of the original group ordered to Ft. Francis E. Warren, Wyoming. He served with the 48th/128th as a surgery technician. He was from Wyoming. His wife, Eva lives in Denver.

Dick, James F.

James Dick was born December 29, 1924 in Los Angeles, California. James graduated from high school June 10, 1943 and the very next day his draft notice arrived in the mail. At the young age of eighteen, he entered the United States Army July 6, 1943. He had basic training at Camp Barkley, Texas followed by active service at Presido of Monterey, California July 12 thru November 18, 1943. He went home on a ten-day furlough, November 19 – 28, and immediately after returning was sent to Camp Reynolds in Pennsylvania for five days and then on to Camp Shanks in Newark, New Jersey for overseas preparations. On December 14 Dick, along with 15,000 other soldiers in New York harbor boarded the ship Queen Elizabeth, and sailed for Glasgow, Scotland arriving December 20. About six days later Dick became part of the 128th Evac. Hospital at Tortworth Court, England. Tech.-5 Dick was assigned to ward duty and cooking.

James Dick

When asked how the war changed his way of looking at life, James said, "Letting go of my desires, realizing that life can be short and letting God take control of my life." He said the greatest lessen WWII taught him was to do what he was told to do and not ask any questions. His most vivid WWII memory was waiting to get off the ship at Normandy (Utah) Beach while being shelled continuously. The most difficult part of his job was assisting with soldiers who were burned severely when their tanks wre hit by mortar fire and not being able to do more for them. The best part of his job was being part of the 128th Evacuation Hospital and experiencing the sense of being 'family' as the doctors, nurses and enlisted men worked together to ease pain and save lives.

On November 28, 1945 he sailed home on a Liberty ship to Boston, Massachusetts. Flying home on a C-47 from New York to Sacramento, California, he was honorably discharged on December 19, 1945 at Camp Beale, California. Dick mentioned how honored he still feels, to have been a part of the 128th Evac. Hospital unit. He stated that being so young, he had no concept of the magnitude of what was happening during the preparations for Normandy. However he did know the experienced personnel he joined at Tortworth Castle and the unit's record of service in Africa and Sicily, did much to provide the 19 year old James Dick with a sense of security when they were finally deployed in June, 1944 for the Invasion of Europe.

Dick met Florence Bartell in Fresno California while visiting his brother in college. They were married September 12, 1947 in Bakersfield, California. They were blessed with two children, a boy and a girl. James and Florence reside in Bakersfield, California.

Dickie, Aldra

Aldra was a nurse with the 48th/128th Evacuation Hospital. She was from Brookline, Massachusetts.

Dirkson, Henry

Henry was from West Liberty, Iowa. He died in January 1984.

Dooken, WOJG Thomas N.

Thomas was an assistant registrar with the unit.

Doolin, Alfred E.

Alfred entered the United States Army in 1941. He was one of the original group ordered to Ft. Francis E. Warren, Wyoming.

Dorton, Maribel E.

Maribel was a nurse with the 48th/128th Evacuation Hospital.

Douglas, Joe Tom

—by Patricia Douglas, his daughter:

Joe Tom Douglas was born December 20, 1917 into a family of five boys and a girl. He was the son of Abe and Maude Douglas of Wewoka, Oklahoma. He enjoyed the arts, especially acting and music. He sang and played the piano quite well. For a short time before and after his time in the service, Joe even pursued a professional acting career. He did some print ads in the late 1930s and spent time studying at the Pasadena Playhouse in California.

The lack of theatrical opportunities in Wewoka and the need of a job led him to become an undertaker at Key Funeral Home. He enlisted in the Army in April of 1942 and was assigned to the 48th Evac Unit (later the 128th), remaining with that unit until October 1945. He initially served as a medic and later worked his way up to a T-5 Surgical Technician. He met his future wife, Ruth Ellen Wheeler, in October of 1944 and they were married July 18, 1945 in Bayreuth, Germany.

After the war, Joe and Ruth returned to Joe's hometown of Wewoka, Oklahoma and he returned to Stout-Sarber Funeral Home as an undertaker and ambulance driver. He also tried his hand at sales, working for Filson Motors and Smart Insurance Agency, eventually returning to Stout-Sarber. Joe and Ruth had two children—Michael born in 1946 and Patricia born in 1952. In 1961 he and Ruth divorced and Joe remained in Wewoka. Though he had a steady girlfriend, he never remarried.

Joe suffered a severe back injury forcing the fusing of five vertebrae in the base of his spine as the result of a fall in 1965. He remained disabled for the rest of his life. He died of cardiac arrest November 4, 1987. Throughout his life, he treasured the friends and the memories of his time with the 48th/128th and was proud to have had the honor of serving his country.

Though my father and I were not very close, I thank him for passing on his talents in acting and singing. I'm grateful for the time I've been able to spend with his friends of the 48th/128th Evac. Hospital, for giving me a chance to learn that my dad was remembered as a very kind and honorable man.

Drime, Alfred A.

Alfred entered the United States Army in 1941. He was one of the original group ordered to Ft. Warren, WY. Alfred was from Minnesota.

Drost, Maynard
Maynard entered the United States Army in 1941. He was one of the original group ordered to Ft. Francis E. Warren, Wyoming. He was from Iowa.

Ducibella, Carolyn T.
Carolyn was a nurse with the 48th/128th Evacuation Hospital.

Alfred Drime

Duensing, Francis E.
Francis entered the United States Army in 1941. He was one of the original group ordered to Ft. Francis E. Warren, Wyoming.

Duer, Agatha
Agatha Duer was born June 14, 1920 in Akron, Ohio. Agatha entered the service October 1942, did her basic training at Fort Knox, Kentucky and worked at the Ft. Knox General Hospital for a while. She volunteered for overseas duty and departed from Louisville, Kentucky and was assigned to the 128th Evacuation Hospital December 13, 1944.

1st Lt. Agatha Duer met corporal Alvin Griebel in Aachen, Germany. The corpsman lived in a café where beer was sold on the second floor. The nurses lived in a convent behind the café. When asked what was her most vivid memory of WWII, Agatha said, "The Battle of the Bulge," as she watched the troops moving back waiting for the trucks in order to evacuate. The most difficult part of her nursing job in the war was when the soldiers died; just boys, calling for their mothers. Her best part of the war, as I am sure is echoed by most, was the end of the war.

Agatha was discharged from the army December 22, 1945. Agatha and Alvin were married in Pipestone, Minnesota, December 1, 1945. Leslie Jones (enlisted man), and Margaret Madigan (fellow nurse), stood up for them at their wedding.

The Griebel's had five children, two girls and three boys. Alvin passed away September 28, 2000 at the age of 81.

Duffy, Capt. Frank K.
Frank was an eye surgeon with the unit. He was from Palmer, Massachusetts.

Dunbar, Elmer J.
Elmer was from Akron, Ohio.

Duxbury, Marcus W.
Marcus was born April 8, 1919, in Canova, South Dakota. He volunteered for service in March of 1941. He was part of a group of fourteen young men from Salem in McCook County, South Dakota that were ordered to Ft. Francis E. Warren, Wyoming where the 48th Surgical Hospital was established. Marcus served for four and a half years with the 48th/128th, three of them overseas, before he was honorably discharged on September 19, 1945.

Frank Duffy (far left)

Corporal Duxbury (Dux to most) was the "Radar" of the 48th/128th MASH (a focal character in the 1970 hit movie and subsequent TV series MASH). He too served as "mail order clerk, telephone pusher

Marcus Duxbury

and chaplains assistant." No reports on whether he carried a teddy bear as "Radar O'Reilly" did! Dux has reflected often on the war years. By far, the best part of his job was mail delivery. He relished the joy and sincere happiness reflected in the faces of servicemen and women upon receipt of letters or packages from home. Dux's service in WWII left him with an incredible appreciation for simply having survived while surrounded by so much death. While his memory blazed with images of caring for the wounded, understandably, Dux found the most difficult part of his job was being the chaplain's assistant, burying the dead. Upon his return home, Marcus renewed his acquaintance with Floreine Schulte. They were married on June 11, 1951 and are the parents of four sons, Roger, Terry, Tom, and Mike Duxbury.

Dux worked primarily in the concrete industry after the war years. Marcus Duxbury and his wife Floreine were steadfast supporters of the 48th/128th reunions in recent years, acting on numerous occasions as both planners and hosts. Dux succumbed after a long battle with cancer, January 31, 2003. He is laid to rest in Salem, South Dakota where Floreine, still resides.

Duzat, Robert

Ebbert, Capt. Charles A.
Charles was a supply officer with the unit.

Eden, William G.
William entered the United States Army in 1941. He was one of the original group ordered to Ft. Francis E. Warren, Wyoming.

Charles Ebbert

English, Helen M.
Helen was a nurse with the 48th/128th Evacuation Hospital. She was from Florida.

Fagerlund, Maurice W.
Maurice entered the United States Army in 1941. He was one of the original group ordered to Ft. Francis E. Warren, Wyoming. He was from Colorado.

Maurice Fagerlund

Farabough, Frances
Frances was a nurse with the 48th/128th Evacuation Hospital.

Farnham, Robert W.
Robert entered the United States Army in 1941. He was one of the original group ordered to Ft. Francis E. Warren, Wyoming.

Fast, Capt. John G.
John was a Med. Inspector and ward surgeon with the unit. He was from Wisconsin.

Felcyn, Roman D.
Roman entered the United States Army in 1941. He was one of the original group ordered to Ft. Francis E. Warren, Wyoming.

Ferree, Ella J.
Ella was a nurse with the 48th/128th Evacuation Hospital.

Findley, Capt. James W.
James was a ward surgeon, EMT with the unit. He was from Kansas City, Missouri.

Jim Findley (second from right)

Fisher, Evelyn Vaughn
—by G. Jesse Flynn
January 5, 2002, Elaine and I drove five and one half hours from Louisville, Kentucky to Clarksburg, West Virginia. About one mile off I-79 at the corner of Chestnut and Main we located an imposing three story brick home at 530 W. Main. It was located next to the Main Street Grocery which Vaughn and her husband, Joe Pulice operated until 1984, the year of his death. The home is now encroached upon by commercial development, but it speaks loudly of a neighborhood that in an earlier day had rows of impressive homes. We were met by Christine, Vaughn's daughter who ushered us into the large kitchen where Vaughn sat in her wheelchair. We introduced ourselves and over coffee and sweets, small talk eventually led us to a discussion of her life story.

Vaughn Fisher was born March 19, 1918, and raised on a farm 25 miles from Clarksburg. She attended Weston High School and graduated in 1935. She traveled to Clarksburg attending St. Mary's Hospital School of Nursing, graduating in 1939. Vaughn then traveled to St. Petersburg, Florida and worked two years private duty before

Vaughn Fisher Pulice

joining the Red Cross, December 1, 1941. When the war broke out six days later she was sent to Fort Knox and worked general duty at Ireland Army Hospital. In the next few weeks she was joined by Margaret Hornback, Gladys Martin, Genevieve Kruzic, Ora White, Ursula Hall, Beryl Karban, Carrie Smith, Phyllis MacDonald, Margaret Madigan, Doris Friedlund, Mildred H. Kaelin and Ella J. Ferree. This group would report enmass for duty overseas with the 48th Surgical Hospital some eight months later and they would be climbing down rope ladders going ashore in the invasion of North Africa in less than a year.

Within the unit, Vaughn worked as a surgical nurse. Vaughn's one encounter with General George Patton was late at night during a sandstorm in the surgical ward tents in Tunisia. As she worked over a badly wounded infantry captain, a voice boomed from behind her. "Girlie, how is he?" She turned to face him and her jaw dropped. She does not recall her reply. It was her first and last personal encounter

with the general. Vaughn returned home in 1945 and renewed a relationship with Joseph Pulchi, a former mechanic in the 13th Air Force in the Pacific Theatre. The renewed relationship was difficult due to the four-year separation and both being "set in their ways."

However on January 31, 1946, after a two-month courtship Vaughn and Joe obtained a license to get married. They were taking a ride through the Kentucky countryside when they noticed a small chapel in Catlettsburg, and stopped to take a look. Finding the door unlocked, they discovered the church was decorated for a wedding to be held later in the day. As luck would have it, they bumped into the minister who identified himself as the Reverend Smith. Impetuously they told him of their plans to marry in the very near future. In a matter of minutes, after producing their license, they found themselves pronouncing their vows in front of Reverend Smith with the church maintenance man and his wife serving as witnesses. Vaughn's memories are of a small wedding party, in a beautiful setting followed by a two-day honeymoon in Cincinnati and thirty-eight years of marriage. After returning to Clarksburg they found that Italians were persona non grata in most areas of town, so they changed their name from Pulchi to Pulice. Vaughn and Joe worked together in the store for thirty-eight years, until its closing.

Flaugh, Marvin O.
Marvin entered the United States Army in 1941. He was one of the original group ordered to Ft. Francis E. Warren, Wyoming. He was from Nebraska.

Flippo, Helen C.
Helen was a nurse with the 48th/128th Evacuation Hospital.

Marvin Flaugh (right)

Flynn, 1st Lt. John J.
Born November 17, 1912, in Waltham, Massachusetts, John was one of five children born to George and Mary Flynn. He graduated St. Mary's High school in 1930 and received a degree in pre-dental from Boston College in 1934.

He worked several jobs after graduation, saving money to continue his studies. He partnered in a small café that apparently failed, worked filling prescriptions in a drugstore and finally sold electrical products and accessories along the east coast. He called on manufacturers, hotels, churches and business establishments.

John was drafted into the army for a one-year term in March 1941. The war caused the term to become five. He served initially as a surgical technician in an artillery regiment.

Just prior to being drafted, John was one of twenty men selected to train for a Massachusetts State Police position. He was chosen from over 600 applicants. Four and a half years later he was over the age limit and followed another

John Flynn

profession.

He attended officer training school at Camp Barkley, Texas in 1942 and joined the 48th Surgical Hospital in Tunisia in March 1943 as Supply/Motor Transportation Officer. He remained with the 48th/128th through July 1, 1945 and was assigned to the 100th Evacuation Hospital until September 19, 1945, when he was sent home.

Forbes, Thelma B.
Thelma was a nurse with the 48th/128th Evacuation Hospital.

Ford, Jr., 2nd Lt. John M.
John was a registrar with the unit.

Forman, Capt. Louis H.
Louis was chief of lab service with the unit. He was from Kansas.

Foy, Hugh D.
Hugh entered the United States Army in 1941. He was one of the original group ordered to Ft. Francis E. Warren, Wyoming.

Louis Forman

Francis, Mary E.
Mary E. Francis was born September 25, 1912 in Waynesville, North Carolina. Mary served as a nurse with the 48th/128th from May 1, 1942 through February 13, 1946. She came to the hospital with specialized training in neurosurgery. When not on duty, she assisted with typing for the unit. Mary's memories of her service include training for field hospital operations after the unit's arrival in Scotland in August of 1942, going ashore with the main force at Arzew during the Invasion of North Africa, the numbers of their own personnel who succumbed to malaria and hepatitis while in Sicily and the overwhelming numbers of casualties that marked the Battle of the Bulge where they fought the odds to save the wounded in incredible cold and snow. But her most vivid memory is of wading ashore on Utah Beach with artillery firing overhead. Mary's sorrow, working to save men who were mained for life, if they survived their wounds, was muted by the sense of humor and positive attitude those brave men exhibited in their suffering. During her time with the 48th/128th, Mary developed more tolerance for other nationalities and discovered she could 'get along with a lot less' than she thought she could. Mary lives in Asheville, North Carolina.

French, Evelyn
Evelyn was a nurse with the 48th/128th Evacuation Hospital. She was from Monroe, Louisiana.

Friedlund, Doris H.
Doris Friedlund was born April 13, 1907 in Gary, Indiana. Lt. Friedlund enlisted September 15, 1941, when Uncle Sam called for RNs to give one year of service. Lt. Friedlund and Miss Genevieve Kruzic (Thompson) were "tentmates" for three years of overseas service. She received eight battle stars serving the three years in the African

theater of war, Sicilian invasion, then a stay of recuperation and rest in England until the European invasion, landing under fire off the LSTs, D-Day Plus 4 at Utah Beach. She continued in all the battles, seeing the concentration camp at Dachau, Germany. Her closing days of the war were spent at Hitler's secret hideout in his mountain retreat in Bavaria. She returned home to Gary, Indiana in September 1945. Doris continued helping GIs, but this only prolonged the war and its memories for her so she worked as staff nurse at Gary Methodist Hospital for a number of years. Doris never married. She died July 16, 1984.

Gacke, Walter W.
Walter entered the United States Army in 1941. He was one of the original group ordered to Ft. Francis E. Warren, Wyoming. He was from Arco, Minnesota.

Gecke, Annie G.
Annie was a nurse with the 48th/128th Evacuation Hospital. She was from Rhode Island.

Geist, Capt. Frederick D.
Frederick was from Wisconsin.

Walter Gacke

Frederick Geist (center)

Gerhard, Dorothy E.
Dorothy was a nurse with the 48th/128th Evacuation Hospital.

Gingles, Col. Charles H.
Charles was from San Francisco, California.

Glade, Gerald E.
Gerald was from Culver City, California.

Gold, Ormie
Ormie was from Minnesota.

Goodman, George 'Goody'
George was from New York.

Gordon, Capt. John H.
John was an orthopedist with the unit. He was from Missouri.

Goody Goodman

Gorishek, Dr. William M.
William resides in Price Utah.

Grabau, Dr. Ellis V.
Ellis was from New Jersey.

Gray, Lester A.
Lester was from Skokie, Illinois.

John Gordon

Greene, Betty J.
Betty was a nurse with the 48th/128th Evacuation Hospital.

Gregory, Michael L.
Michael entered the United States Army in 1941. He was one of the original group ordered to Ft. Francis E. Warren, Wyoming.

Griebel, Alvin C. "Fritz"
Alvin was born November 17, 1918 in Pipestone, Minnesota. He entered the service March 19, 1941 and was discharged September 15, 1945. Corporal Griebel served with the 48th/128th in Algeria, Tunisia, Sicily, Normandy, Northern France, Rhineland, Ardennes, and Central Europe.

Michael Gregory

He married Agatha Duer who was a nurse with the 48th/128th. They had five children. Alvin retired in 1979 from Duer Construction as vice president and bricklayer. Alvin died September 28, 2000 at the age of 81.

Grier, Etoyl
Etoyl was a nurse with the 48th/128th Evacuation Hospital. She was from Georgia.

Grimes, Florence M.
Florence was a nurse with the 48th/128th Evacuation Hospital.

Grove, Capt. Samuel A. C. "Chappie"
Captain Samuel Grove "Chappie" was the chaplain of the 48th Surgical 128th Evacuation unit. Samuel was born February 22, 1906. He was the sixth of seven sons. His father died when he was four, and his

Chappie Grove (left)

mother and all the boys scrambled to support themselves. Only he was able to get an education.

He earned two Bronze Stars, but what he recalled vividly was a seriously injured soldier who asked only that someone blow smoke in his face. "That was the only time I ever smoked a cigarette," he said. He and his wife, Marjorie Glotfelty, had two sons, Lynn and Larry, and a daughter, Trudy. His Christmas message December 25, 1942 to the troops was as follows:

Merry Christmas
"What strange words. They seem so queer to us this year, above every year that we have ever known. Yet the first Christmas was such a one as this.

Joseph and Mary couldn't be home and we are told that they had to pick up shortly after the birth of Jesus and run to a far away country. Christmas has been wrapped in packages —gifts instead of the Spirit of Peace and Good Will. May we not only try to win that peace with this war, but with our living try to keep that peace." Samuel treasured the years spent with the men of the 48th/128th. He kept in contact with several of them after the war.

Marjorie passed away February 23, 1993. Rev. Grove passed away December 13, 2000.

Groves, Joseph Everett
Joseph was from Cherokee, Iowa.

Gunderman, Clarence L.
Clarence entered the United States Army in 1941. He was one of the original group ordered to Ft. Francis E. Warren, Wyoming. He was from Fulda, Minnesota.

Clarence Gunderman

Gustafson, Ervin J.
Ervin entered the United States Army in 1941. He was one of the original group ordered to Ft. Francis E. Warren, Wyoming. He was from Nebraska. Ervin passed away in 1984.

Ervin Gustafson

Hagan, Gordon J.
Gordon was from Iowa.

Hale, Allison
Allison was a nurse with the 48th/128th Evacuation Hospital.

Hall, Ursula
Ursula was a nurse with the 48th/128th Evacuation Hospital. She was from Sardinia, Ohio.

Halverson, Maurice E.
Maurice was born February 4, 1918. There were two draft boards in the town he lived in. When you registered you were given a number and his was #9 – so he volunteered. He left by train for Ft. Snelling in St. Paul, Minnesota and later on to Ft. Francis E. Warren, Wyoming. He joined the service March 1941. He was only supposed to be in the service for one year and then discharged – but Hitler changed all that. After basic training in Cheyenne, Wyoming he was attached to the 48th/128th. He was stationed in England – took part in the Normandy Invasion, Scotland, Algeria, Africa, Sicily and back to England. He was honorably discharged September 1945 with a rating of technical sergeant. Maurice said he had a lot of memories of the war – some good and some bad. He said he is thankful that he came home again safely. He shared three stores with me. They are as follows.

#1: When he returned to England the second time he was housed

Maurice Halverson (back left)

in an old castle at Tortworth. There were about six men to a room and they had to do their own "house-cleaning." The fellows thought that the more water used to scrub the floors (old wood) the cleaner they would be, until the water started soaking through and the ceiling in the kitchen below them fell down.

#2: They had a very efficient "motor pool." When they went for gasoline – they came back with 50 gallons of gas and 100 gallons of wine!

#3: When they headed for Africa aboard an old WW I ship resurrected from mothballs in South America, it was loaded with tanks and gas in the bottom and 250 enlisted men in upper level. They slept in hammocks or on tables or wherever they could. Their food was British rations of fish and stale bread. It was a very rough ride and most of the men became ill and the "bucket brigade" became a necessity. A doctor (Captain Schwade) came out with pills – but they didn't seem to help and it finally caught up with him too, to the point where he covered nearby men with his bucket contribution. He also was going to take the clip from his revolver and it accidentally discharged. The bullet ricocheted around the floor and room, but luckily no one was hit! Maurice and his wife, Isabelle reside in Rose Creek, Minnesota.

Hamaker, Mary

Mary was a nurse with the 48th/128th Evacuation Hospital. She was from Pennsylvania.

Hamm, William E.

William entered the United States Army in 1941. He was one of the original group ordered to Ft. Francis E. Warren, Wyoming. He was from Ohio.

Hanson, Donald M.

Donald entered the United States Army in 1941. He was one of the original group ordered to Ft. Francis E. Warren, Wyoming. He was from South Dakota.

Harden, Robert Lee

Robert L. Harden was born July 15, 1919 in Jacksonville, Arkansas. Robert entered the service November 25, 1940. He was a cook with the 48th/Surgical 128th Evacuation Hospital and was with the unit four years, ten months and eighteen days. When asked how she and Robert met, Lucille (Ray) said that her family owned the only restaurant in Jacksonville, Arkansas, and Robert would come there to eat. As Lucille tells it, "he was the best looking thing in town and I got him."

After surviving the horrors of WWII, Robert was killed in an accident June 23, 1952, while on his job six years after returning home from the war.

Lucille not only lost her husband but also was left to raise three small children on her own. Robert would be proud of how Lucille

managed through much sacrificing on her own to raise their children well. They have a son and two daughters. Lucille said that Robert would not talk about the war. Like many who returned home, the memories were too painful to talk about.

Lucille lives in Jacksonville, Arkansas.

Harmon, Jodie D.
—by G. Jesse Flynn
January 10, 2002 I landed at the Odessa/Midland airport in west Texas. A stop

Robert Lee Harden

at the car rental counter and one hundred twenty miles later, I entered Robert Lee, Texas (population 1,174). I drove to a ridgeline at the edge of town to find a deceptively large ranch style house, which was the home of Jodie and Mary Jo Harmon. Jodie greeted me and gave me a tour of the house that he and Mary Jo had built in the 1960's. It had a large living room with large exposed wooden beams in the ceilings. There were two bedrooms and a bath at one end of the house and a very large multi purpose room at the other. We talked for a while and then went to the only restaurant in Robert Lee to eat. It was called the Cracker Barrel. I had vegetable stew, fried steak fingers with gravy and salad. Jodie had the same except half portions. Mary Jo had been in the local nursing home for some time and Jodie normally stayed with her from 4:00 to 6:00 p.m. each day. It was now 5:30 as we entered the lobby. As we entered the room she had her back to us seated in a wheelchair. "Is that you honey?" she said. Jodie put his hand on her shoulder and apologized for being late. Mary Jo was a very handsome woman with multiple physical problems that included eyesight and balance. I talked to them together for an hour before Jodie and I went back to his house for a seven-hour interview.

Sometime after 2:00 a.m. I told him I needed to get an early start to the airport because I had a 1:00 p.m. flight to Portland, Oregon. I asked him what time he normally got up and he replied 5:30 a.m. Well, we were at the Cracker Barrel at 6:00 a.m. being greeted by dozens of men who all seemed to know "J.D." The waitress without asking brought J.D. two scrambled eggs, sausage, dry toast and coffee. I ordered the same. We visited his former business, drove to a huge lake with a tremendous panoramic view and went back to see Mary Jo. She was radiant! Dressed in a pink pantsuit, hair fixed to perfection, sitting in the lobby waiting for us. We chatted, took pictures, said goodbye and I started the one hundred twenty mile trek to Odessa.

Jodie Harmon was born June 21, 1917 in Robert Lee, Texas. He joined the United States Army April 14, 1942 and served with the 48th/128th Evacuation Hospital in Algeria, Tunisia, Sicily, Normandy, Northern France, Central Europe and the Rhineland in Germany. He worked alongside Doris Brittingham and Leonard Thomas in the head and spine ward. He was honorably discharged from service October 11, 1945.

Jodie Harmon

Jodie married Mary Jo Caston February 14, 1942 in Ballenger, Texas. They have a daughter Amanda "Mandy" and three grandchildren, Damon, Erin and Brandon. Mary Jo passed away July 31, 2002, after being his wife for more than sixty years.

Harms, Wilbur C.
Wilbur entered the United States Army in 1941. He was one of the original group ordered to Ft. Francis E. Warren, Wyoming.

Harris, Marshall

Harris, Mildred H.
Mildred was a nurse with the 48th/128th Evacuation Hospital. She was from Georgia.

Hart, Margaret
Margaret was a nurse with the 48th/128th Evacuation Hospital.

Mildred Harris

Hartigan, John P.
John entered the United States Army in 1941. He was one of the original group ordered to Ft. Francis E. Warren, Wyoming. He was from Toledo, Ohio.

Hartman, Robert D.
Robert entered the United States Army in 1941. He was one of the original group ordered to Ft. Francis E. Warren, Wyoming. He was from New Jersey.

Hartmann, Joseph N.
Joseph entered the United States Army in 1941. He was one of the original group ordered to Ft. Francis E. Warren, Wyoming. He was from Ohio.

Hartson, Clifford C.
Clifford entered the United States Army in 1941. He was one of the original group ordered to Ft. Francis E. Warren, Wyoming. He was from South Dakota.

Harwell, Earl
Earl Harwell was born August 21, 1918 in Camden, Arkansas. He entered the United States Army November 25, 1940 at Little Rock Arkansas. He was honorably discharged August 8, 1945 at Jefferson Barracks, Missouri. Tec – 3 Harwell served with the 48th/128th as a surgical technician. He worked in the hospital keeping equipment sterilized and helped out in the operating room.

Earl met Ida Nell Poole in 1945 after his return home from the war. Ida was manager of a Western Union Telegraph office in Smackover, Arkansas. Earl started working as manager of the Natural Gas office after a few weeks training in El Dorado, Arkansas. They dated off and on for about two years and were married June 28, 1947 in Smackover, Arkansas. The Harwell's had two sons, Gregory Earl and Max H. Harwell. Nell mentioned that Earl did not talk much about the war. She said that when Earl and R.L. Harden got together they would talk

mostly about their fun times during the war. Nell remembers Earl telling of a time when he and Robert Harden traded candy and cigarettes to some young boys in Arzew for fresh eggs. Then they went back to their quarters and Robert (being the cook of the unit) made them some corn bread. Earl served in the Algeria, Tunisia, Normandy, Northern France, Rhineland, Ardennes, and Central

Earl Harwell (left)

Europe campaigns. Earl was awarded eight Bronze Stars for the above named campaigns and a good conduct medal. Nell recalls the thirty-four good years of marriage they shared. She said they had lots of plans for the future. He was 62 years old and she was 56 when Earl had his heart attack. He was planning to retire at 63 so they could travel and have some fun times. Earl passed away April 21, 1981.

Haskell, Ruth G.
Ruth was a nurse with the 48th/128th Evacuation Hospital. Ruth wrote a book entitled 'Helmets and Lipstick.' The book is about her experiences during WWII.

Hatcher, Mary
Mary Hatcher was born June 4, 1911 in Mt. Airy, North Carolina. Mary entered the service March 20, 1941. She was a nurse anesthetist with the 48th/128th during WWII. She was trained in Camp Lee, Virginia. She was billeted 1A with Lt. Hall, Lt. Karban and Lt. Smith. Captain Hatcher served in England, North Africa, Sicily and France. Mary met Lewis Myers just after discharge from the army. They were married June 1, 1946. Mary's most vivid WWII memory is going in on D-Day, 6 June 1944. The wounded soldier that stood out most in her memory is when she helped Dr. Tropea remove a live round from the chest cavity of a soldier. The most difficult part of her job was exhaustion and getting caught in the "Battle of the Bulge," ending with frozen feet and evacuation. The best part of her job was her friends. Her husband, Lewis wrote to tell me that Mary passed away January 31, 1997.

Heinke, John P.

Helle, Arnold F.
Arnold entered the United States Army in 1941. He was one of the original group ordered to Ft. Francis E. Warren, Wyoming. He was from Michigan.

Arnold Helle (left)

Helm, Kathlyn
Kathlyn was a nurse with the 48th/128th Evacuation Hospital. She married W. T. Turner. She was from New Jersey.

Herbolsheimer, Gerhardt W.
Gerhardt was born September 16, 1916 in Pierce, Nebraska. He was from a family of ten children. After graduation from the eighth grade

Gerhardt Herbolsheimer

he worked as a farm hand in the neighborhood and later as a highway maintenance man until leaving for the Army. Gerhardt was inducted in the Army from Pierce County, Nebraska May 21, 1942 and sent to Fort Leavenworth, Kansas, then to Camp Great, Illinois for seven weeks of basic training. The group left the USA from New York Harbor. Gerhardt spent three and one half years overseas. He served with the 48th/128th in Algeria, Tunisia, Sicily, Normandy, Northern France, Central Europe and the Rhineland in Germany. He worked as a medical aide in the field tent hospital attending the wounded after they were stabilized. He kept records on patients, cared for and fed them. He reloaded patients onto ambulances and sent them to general hospitals. Gary returned to the states on Thanksgiving Day in November of 1945. He earned four medals and four battle stars including Good Conduct, Army of Occupation, Victory WWII and World War II. After returning home from the war he worked for his brother in law attending a gas station. He later moved to Sioux City, Iowa and was a truck driver for Blue Bunny Ice Cream Company. Gerhardt married Beverly Rasmussen in 1947. They had two daughters, the youngest died at the age of four and a half. He owned and operated a construction business for over forty years. He enjoys golf and spending time visiting his daughter and her family in Texas.

Hetland, Henry L.
Henry entered the United States Army in 1941. He was one of the original group ordered to Ft. Francis E. Warren, Wyoming. He was from Minnesota.

Hilton, Esther
Esther was a nurse with the 48th/128th Evacuation Hospital. She was from Texas. Esther passed away November 18, 1984.

Hobson, Helen W.
Helen was a nurse with the 48th/128th Evacuation Hospital. She was from Delaware.

Hoctor, John A.
John entered the United States Army in 1941. He was one of the original group ordered to Ft. Francis E. Warren, Wyoming. John was from Ohio.

Hodges, Edith M.
Edith was a nurse with the 48th/128th Evacuation Hospital.

Hodges, Evelyn
Evelyn was a nurse with the 48th/128th Evacuation Hospital. She married Ben Mixon.

Hogan, Ray
Ray was from New Haven, Connecticut.

Holeck, Fred H.
Fred entered the United States Army in 1941. He was one of the original ordered to Ft. Francis E. Warren, Wyoming. He was from Forest Park, Illinois.

Hornback, Margaret
Margaret Hornback was born December 10, 1918 in Anderson County, Kentucky. Margaret graduated from nursing school in the midst of the Great Depression. She went to work as a nurse at the old King's Daughters Hospital in Shelbyville, Kentucky. When the U.S. entered World War II, she enlisted in the army and found herself serving as a first lieutenant general-duty nurse in the European Theater, setting up tent hospitals in Morocco, Tunisia, Sicily, France and parts of Central Europe. Miss Hornback received EAME Theater Ribbon W/1 Silver Battle Star, three Bronze Battle Stars and six Overseas Service Bars.

Fear was not in Hornbacks' vocabulary. "I have never been too afraid," she said. "I know the Lord can take care of me so I don't worry much about it." Upon arriving in North Africa in a town called Arzew, she recalled that the people were very poor and the town was dirty. "We set up a hospital as best we could in the barracks that belonged to the French Legion," she said. There were bugs in the walls that would crawl out at night and get on the people's skin. Miss Hornback said that army nurse life was challenging. She was quick to point out the war was terrible and there were hardships. She enjoyed caring for the soldiers, who she said were appreciative. She remembers one particular outfit of soldiers in North Africa, of which many had malaria. She fell in love with one of the soldiers, Captain W. J. Anderson (Andy) from this unit. When Andy started recovering, he was shipped with his unit to Sicily ahead of her while the 48th was sent back to England. They wrote letters and called, but they knew each

Margaret Hornback

other for such a short time. After the invasion of Normandy in June 1944 and subsequent advance past Paris the 10th FA Bn Infantry was to invade Southern France. A meeting of the two was to occur in Paris in the fall of 1944. Andy never arrived. She would have known him for about a year when a chaplain informed her that he had died from malaria.

After the war, Miss Hornback returned to Shelbyville, Kentucky and began working with the local health department as a public health nurse. She held this job for a little over eighteen months. In September 1947 she returned to King's Daughters Hospital to work. She remained there as director of nursing for the next 27 years. She became a volunteer nurse in the Gaza Strip in Israel.

Margaret passed away April 2, 1998. She never married.

Hourican, Donald J.

Howard, Lula J.
Lula was a nurse with the 48th/128th Evacuation Hospital.

Howe, George R.

George R. Howe was born May 23, 1918 in Chicago, Illinois. George entered the service August 6, 1942. He was a Private 1st Class Field Medic. It was his job to recover the wounded and bring them back to the hospital. He was honorably discharged October 14, 1945. He was quoted as saying, "Not all of the memories of that time were comfortable to recollect." But, he said, the human spirit survived under the dreadful conditions of war. George met Betty Deibler at a dance party. They were married February 27, 1949 in Milwaukee, Wisconsin. The Howe's had two sons. George died January 12, 2002. Betty wrote that this was her first Christmas without George and that she misses him dearly.

Hudson, Harold J.

Harold entered the United States Army in 1941. He was one of the original group ordered to Ft. Francis E. Warren, Wyoming.

Huelsman, Lester J.

Lester entered the United States Army in 1941. He was one of the original group ordered to Ft. Francis E. Warren, Wyoming. He was from Ohio.

Hughes, Lonnie

Lonnie entered the United States Army in 1941. He was one of the original group ordered to Ft. Francis E. Warren, Wyoming.

Hurley, Burton F.

Burton entered the United States Army in 1941. He was one of the original group ordered to Ft. Francis E. Warren, Wyoming. He was from South Dakota.

Inderrieden, Lawrence N.

Lawrence was born July 24, 1918 in Cincinnati, Ohio. After basic training in Texas, beginning in March 1941, he joined the Surgical Hospital unit at Fort Francis E. Warren, Wyoming. He went to England with that unit as Staff Sergeant in charge of the operating room, and saw service in the invasion of North Africa. Tech Sgt./5 Inderrieden was honorably discharged September 4, 1951.

For "service far beyond the call of duty," during the Southern Tunisian Campaign, Lawrence was decorated by General Patton in Palermo, Sicily on September 20, 1943. At that time he was wearing the Legion of Merit ribbon. How Larry installed and maintained the operating room of the 48th Surgical Hospital under fire, was recorded in an affidavit from his commanding officer, Lt. Col. John M. Snyder, which is as follows:

AFFIDAVIT / Dated 26 April 1943

Lawrence N. Inderrieden, Technician Grade III, 35122502, 48th Surgical Hospital, is recommended for the degree of Officer of the Legion of Merit. I have personally witnessed his work and recommend him unqualifiedly. The hospital of which he is a member is designed to support one division of troops or at most two, in combat. During the recent Southern Tunisian Campaign it supported four divisions, attached corps troops and neighboring air corps installations. The influx of patients for the period March 19th to 27th at Feriana and

Lawrence Inderrieden

again March 28th to April 9th at Gafsa, where this unit functioned was thereby greatly abnormal. Technician Grade III Inderrieden was in charge of the maintenance of equipment and supplies and the transportation and erection of the operating room. He quickly installed the operating room and had it ready to function. The leaded gas, which it has been necessary to use, has interfered with the efficient use of the gasoline stoves under the autoclaves and he has been responsible for their maintenance. In the six-day period at Feriana he sacrificed many hours of sleep in order to be constantly at hand to insure the proper maintenance of equipment. When the demand grew even heavier, he found additional supplies, erected more operating tables and as we were short of anesthetists, further aided by giving intravenous anesthesia. When orders to move forward came, he quickly struck the operating room and packed it, being exemplary in his action, and upon arrival at Gafsa, installed the operating room under tentage erected at night in the blackout despite the hum of enemy planes overhead and the fire of tracer bullets around him. Here again he continued to work night after night without sufficient rest, and his calm, quiet efficiency under all conditions – the bombing of the ammunition dump one mile away at Gafsa, the dogfights at night overhead, have marked him as outstanding in service far beyond the call of duty. Without his constant attention, the operating room might well have failed because of breakdown in equipment and supplies. His exemplary conduct was outstanding and served to spur on those who though will power did not lack but physically were hard pressed.

—*John M. Snyder, Lt. Col., Medical Corps, Commanding*

Lawrence met Carol Yorke in Charfield, England after the units return from Sicily, November 1943. They were married June 16, 1945 in Charfield, England. The Inderrieden's had two children, a girl and a boy. Lawrence and Carol reside in Dayton, Ohio.

James, Joseph F.

Joseph was born July 10, 1915 in Oakland, Minnesota. Joseph joined the United States Army March 20, 1941. He served with the 48th/128th as surgical technician. He was honorably discharged from the army August 22, 1945. He met Mildred Perkins Watt at the VFW Club in Austin, Minnesota and they married October 19, 1974. Joseph passed away February 14, 2002. His wife, Mildred resides in Austin, Minnesota.

Joseph James

Jenkins, Dolcie

Dolcie was from Garden City, Missouri.

Jensen, Raymond H.
Raymond entered the United States Army in 1941. He was one of the original group ordered to Ft. Francis E. Warren, Wyoming. He was from Illinois.

Jerdet, R. L.
R. L. was from Minnesota.

Johnson, Elmer C.
Elmer was born May 31, 1917. He joined the service March 18, 1941. Elmer was awarded the "Bronze Star" for meritorious service beyond the call of duty in ground operations against the enemy. Having a creative mind he was able to improvise and make instruments for doctors as well as other innovative things to better the operation of the hospital. Elmer met his wife, Joan at Tortworth, England January 1944, while his unit was readying for the big invasion. Joan had lived

Elmer Johnson

in that area, north of Bristol for most of her life, and Elmer became quite well acquainted with the area and was a frequent visitor to her home, and got to know her family. When D-Day approached, she promised Elmer that she would write to him and did so daily until he left Europe to return home in July 1945. By 1946, Elmer had returned to his business of house-moving and general contracting. He invited Joan to move to the United States. Joan said it was a very difficult decision for her to leave her loving family and homeland, but as love won out, in November 1946 she boarded the "Queen Elizabeth" at Southampton and came to Minnesota. She and Elmer were married December 3, 1946 and have spent many happy years together. They have three children. Elmer passed away February 20, 2003. Joan resides in Warren, Minnesota.

Jones, Leslie A.
Leslie entered the United States Army in 1941. He was one of the original group ordered to Ft. Francis E. Warren, Wyoming. Leslie was married to Margaret Madigan, a nurse from the unit. He was from Pipestone, Minnesota. Leslie passed away in 1975.

Justice, Graham
Graham was from Oklahoma.

Kahle, Maybelle
Maybelle was a nurse with the 48th/128th Evacuation Hospital. She was from Wisconsin.

Leslie Jones

Kalb, Clifford J.
Clifford entered the United States Army in 1941. He was one of the original group ordered to Ft. Francis E. Warren, Wyoming.

Kaelin, Mildred H.
Mildred was a nurse with the 48th/128th Evacuation Hospital. She was from Louisville, Kentucky.

Karban, Beryl
Beryl was a nurse with the 48th/128th Evacuation Hospital.

Katzen, Murray

Katzovitz, Capt. Hyman
Hyman was a shock officer with the unit.

Kaufmann, Edward A.
Edward Kaufmann was born June 12, 1918 in Fairview, Montana. He entered the service December 9th, 1940 and was one of the original members of the 48th Surgical Hospital in Ft. Francis E. Warren, Wyoming. He was honorably discharged August 17, 1945. T/sgt.

Hyman Katzovitz

Kaufmann served as clerical helper and driver with the 48th/128th Evacuation Hospital. Kaufmann was awarded eight battle stars and six medals for his services during WWII. He was involved in three major invasions. He served in North Africa, Tunisia, Sicily, Normandy, Northern France, Ardennes, and the Rhineland in Germany. Ed married Beatrice James July 27, 1942 in Cheyenne, Wyoming. They had two children, a daughter, Janice Lynn and a son, James Anthony. Beatrice passed away February 3, 1996. Edward passed away October 19, 2000.

Kavanaugh, Billie
Billie was a nurse with the 48th/128th Evacuation Hospital. She was from New York.

Kavitt, Dr. Henry
Henry and his wife, Margaret reside in Portland, Oregon.

Kelly, Edward T.
Edward entered the United States Army in 1941. He was one of the original group ordered to Ft. Francis E. Warren, Wyoming. He is from Nebraska.

Kelly, John

Kelly, Marie
Marie was a nurse with the 48th/128th Evacuation Hospital. She was from Delaware.

Edward Kelly (far left)

Kemer, Evelyn
Evelyn Frances Kemer was born November 3, 1919 in Cleveland, Ohio. Evelyn entered the service April 6, 1942 and was honorably discharged July 3, 1945. Evelyn served with the 48th/128th Evacuation Hospital. She was awarded four battle stars for her work in Algeria, Tunisia, Sicily and Rome-Arno. When asked how the war changed her outlook

on life, she said, "I am thankful for every day and for living in the United States of America". She said the greatest lessen the war taught her was that war is a waste, and that we have to find a better way. Her most vivid WW II memory is the time she opened the wrong door and the room was being used as a temporary morgue. The most difficult part of her job was seeing all the young men (just boys) hurt. But being able to care for them was the best part of her job.

After she left the 48th/128th she met Ward Master Anthony "Tony" Slotwinski in Oran, Algeria. They were married October 4, 1944 in Vatican City, Italy. The Slotwinski's had seven children, four boys and three girls. Tony died August 2, 2000. Evelyn resides in Westlake, Ohio.

Kenny, Margaret F.
Margaret was a nurse with the 48th/128th Evacuation Hospital.

Kessler, George W.
George entered the United States Army in 1941. He was one of the original group ordered to Ft. Francis E. Warren, Wyoming. He was from Ohio.

Keyes, Joseph Phillip
Joseph entered the United States Army in 1941. He was one of the original group ordered to Ft. Francis E. Warren, Wyoming. He was from Pipestone, Minnesota. Phillip passed away October 24, 1985.

King, Capt. Richard S.

Kingston, Capt. Louis C.
Louis was from Vermont.

Joseph Keyes (far right)

Kircher, Theo. E. J.

Kirkwood, Doris
Doris was a nurse with the 48th/128th Evacuation Hospital. She was from Ohio.

Klein, 2nd Lt. Vincent J.
Vincent was acting adjutant with the unit.

Klinsing, Raymond
Raymond was from Pipestone, Minnesota.

Vincent Klein (left)

Klockseim, Dr. Harold

Knight, Kathleen
Kathleen was a nurse with the 48th/128th Evacuation Hospital.

Knott, Elton H.
Elton Knott was born in Kettle Falls, Washington January 7, 1920. Elton did his basic training in Texas and went overseas from there. Corporal T/5 Knott served with the 48th/128th Evacuation Hospital in Algeria, French Morocco, Tunisia, Sicily, Normandy, Northern France, Central Europe and the Rhineland in Germany. He was a cook with the unit. He entered the service in October 1942 and was honorably discharged in 1945. Elton did not want to talk about the war. He said he was not happy when he was drafted and getting out was his best memory. He and his wife, Lillian live in Everett, Wisconsin.

Koloen, Wilbur B.
Wilbur entered the United States Army in 1941. He was one of the original group ordered to Ft. Francis E. Warren, Wyoming.

Kopan, Christ T.
Christ entered the United States Army in 1941. He was one of the original group ordered to Ft. Francis E. Warren, Wyoming. He was from Illinois.

Krist, Frank J.
Frank entered the United States Army in 1941. He was one of the original group ordered to Ft. Francis E. Warren, Wyoming. He was from Illinois.

Krokos, Louis E.
Louis entered the United States Army in 1941. He was one of the original group ordered to Ft. Francis E. Warren, Wyoming. He was from Minnesota.

Kruger, Robert E.
Robert entered the United States Army in 1941. He was one of the original group ordered to Ft. Francis E. Warren, Wyoming. Robert served as a cook for the unit. While stationed at Tortworth Court, England, he would sneak snacks from the kitchen to his roommates. He was from Minnesota.

Kruzic, Genevieve F.
Genevieve Kruzic was born October 23, 1915 in Moses Lake, Washington. From Camp Shelby, Mississippi she was transferred to the 48th Surgical Hospital disembarking at Gourak, Scotland to Tidworth Barracks, England where she did basic training and surgery preparation. November 8, 1942, Genevieve along with fifty-six other nurses, forty-eight officers, and two hundred seventy-three enlisted men came ashore at Arzew, Algeria. Genevieve served with the 48th/128th in Algeria, Tunisia, Sicily, Normandy, Northern France, Central Europe and the Rhineland in Germany. She was issued a Bronze Star for meritorious services as an Operating Tent Supervisor. She left the 48th/128th April 11, 1945 and was discharged from service December 31, 1945. Some of her memories of the war were the horrific chest and head injuries at the Battle of the Bulge to the beautiful sky in North Africa. She said one could almost reach up and touch the stars. The best part of her job was knowing the group. "What workers! When one sees a tent (portable) work from sunrise to night – then

work another round. The effort was unbeatable." Genevieve married Murray Thompson in 1945 after her return from the war. Murray had two children by his first marriage. He and Genevieve had a daughter, Barbara and a son, John Charles "Jay." Genevieve lives in Moses Lake, Washington.

Kubet, Frank

Frank was from Nebraska.

Kuhl, Don

Don entered the United States Army in 1941. He was one of the original group ordered to Ft. Francis E. Warren, Wyoming. He was from Minnesota.

Kukowski, Frank W.

Frank entered the United States Army in 1941. He was one of the original group ordered to Ft. Francis E. Warren, Wyoming. He was from Ohio.

Kunst, Margaret

Margaret was a nurse with the 48th/128th Evacuation Hospital.

Kuyper, Glen

Lail, Paul

Lakes, George A.

George entered the United States Army in 1941. He was one of the original group ordered to Ft. Francis E. Warren, Wyoming.

Lanning, Max Leroy

Max Lanning was born August 17, 1914 in Melbourne, Iowa, the son of Earl and Bertha (Halter) Lanning. Raised and educated in Melbourne, he graduated from Melbourne High School. He was one of the first men in Marshall County to enlist during WWII. Max entered the United State Army December 5, 1940, and was one of the original members of the 48th Surgical Hospital in Fort Francis E. Warren, Wyoming.

He served with the 48th/128th Evacuation Hospital in Algeria, Tunisia, Sicily, Normandy, Northern France, Central Europe and the Rhineland in Germany. His duties were helping out with patients and wherever else he was needed. Max recalls his dislike for the Arabs while in Africa. He said they were very dirty and scroungy. Max was awarded the Good Conduct medal, American Defense Service ribbon, European African Middle Eastern Theater ribbon with one Silver, and three Bronze Battle Stars. Sergeant Lanning was honorably discharged August 8, 1945 at Ft. Sheridan, Illinois. His sister, Jane Van Dyke said whenever Max talked of the war, he had tears in his eyes. He said that war was hell and the memories, good and bad stay with you. At the

end of the war, Max had enough points earned to leave for home. Several other guys were already on a boxcar of the train that was leaving. They yelled, "Come on Max," and grabbed him up on the boxcar with them just in time. If he had missed that train, he would have had to stay another month or two before he would have another chance to head home. Max was very thankful to be able to return to the United States, where so many of us take it for granted. He had an all-new "respect" for his freedoms. He was so thankful to be alive, unlike so many of the boys that never returned home.

On December 27, 1974 Max married Helen Robinson. They never had children. Max died January 12, 2003. His wife, Helen, preceded him in death.

Lansing, Thomas

Thomas was from Danville, Kentucky.

Larson, Walter F.
— by G. Jesse Flynn

I first remember meeting Walt when I was nine or ten years old. Walt, Mayme and their children visited our farm in Lawrenceburg, Kentucky on their way to a vacation in the south. This would have been 1959/1960. My next encounter with Walt was 1998 in Sioux Falls, South Dakota. Walt comes across to the unsuspecting person as the "devils advocate." He is always controlling the conversation by the fact that everyone knows that he will state an opposing opinion. It was easy to imagine Walt in charge of supply. Going to him requesting a new pair of boots or jacket must have been interesting for a newcomer. After a day or two of knowing him, you see through the bluster and realize what a pussycat he really is. Walt was born September 5, 1917, in Grenora, North Dakota and lived there until he was twelve. His parents separated in 1929 and he moved with his mother and five brothers and sisters to Minneapolis, Minnesota. He quit school after the eighth grade to get a job and help feed the family. He worked as a dishwasher, busboy, then began working in a bakery where he got work as a delivery truck driver when he was old enough.

In his early twenties, Walt purchased a Harley Davidson motorcycle, which became his obsession. He and a good friend would ride together every spare hour. As fate would have it, his friend was in a serious accident and hospitalized in a nearby city. Walt visited on a regular basis and became enamored with his friends nurse, Mayme Goky. He convinced her to go riding on the Harley behind him and a few months later they went to Mason City, Iowa and got married. The year was 1939. The minister made his best argument that they were too young, hadn't known each other long enough etc. Well, as Walt put it "she climbed on the Harley behind me and she's been on my back ever since." He will always follow up this joke by saying "she's the best thing that ever happened to me." It was 1942 when Walt reported to the draft board. Following basic training, he was transferred to Ft.

Warren, Wyoming where he was assigned to the 48th Surgical Hospital. He shipped overseas with the unit in August 1942 and was assigned to be in charge of supply. My father worked with Walt quite often and they became good friends. A letter written home to Mayme in October 1944 describes an eight-hour trip in a two and a half ton truck with Lt. Flynn to Brussels, Belgium for supplies. They were to go into the city, get a room for the night, obtain the supplies and come back the next day. "Lt. Flynn and I arrived about dark, checked into a small hotel and went to a bar for a drink. We sat down, got a drink and two girls sat down with us. We didn't want the girls, so we finished our drinks and left to go to another bar where we ordered more drinks. More girls tried to sit with us so we finished our drinks and went back to the hotel for the night. Can you send me some of those great

Walter Larson

cookies you make? That would be great! Love, Walt." Walt and a partner bought a silk-screen business in 1950. They had operated it for a few years, when his partner died. Walt bought the balance of the business from his partners estate and continued to run it for another thirty-eight years. Walt and Mayme have three children, two boys and a girl.

LaRoque, Jean F.
Jean entered the United States Army in 1941. He was one of the original group ordered to Ft. Francis E. Warren, Wyoming.

Laurenson, Clarence W.
Clarence entered the United States Army in 1941. He was one of the original group ordered to Ft. Francis E. Warren, Wyoming. He was from South Dakota.

La Varnway, Jack

LeeRoy, Capt. Arthur
Arthur was an anesthetist with the unit.

Leible, Hilda
Hilda was a nurse with the 48th/128th Evacuation Hospital.

Leimbach, Jr. Capt. John H.
John was a shock officer with the unit.

Arthur LeeRoy (right)

Lentz, Harley U.
Harley entered the United States Army in 1941. He was one of the original group ordered to Ft. Francis E. Warren, Wyoming.

Leudecke, Hilton
Hilton was from Texas.

Littlefield, Edith F.
Edith was a nurse with the 48th/128th Evacuation Hospital.

Lucchese, Tony
Tony was from Illinois. He passed away in October, 1984.

Hilton Leudecke

MacDonald, Phyllis
Phyllis was a nurse with the 48th/128th Evacuation Hospital.

MacKay, Margaret
Margaret was a nurse with the 48th/128th Evacuation Hospital.

Mackenbrock, Maj. Frederick C.
Dr. Frederick C. Mackenbrock was a graduate of Creighton University School of Medicine, majoring in Internal Medicine. He joined the 48th at Fort Francis E. Warren, Wyoming where the hospital was first activated in February 1941. On June 15, 1942 records indicate Major Frederick C. Mackenbrock commanded the 1st Hospitalization Unit of the 48th Mobile Army Surgical Hospital.

When Dr. Mackenbrock departed for Europe, he left behind his wife, Jen and nine-month old son, Freddy in Omaha, Nebraska. Excerpts from his letters home from North Africa in November 1942 were featured in a December 1942 article in the World-Herald in Omaha, the first information the paper had received directly from the North African Theater of war. He couldn't be specific about his whereabouts in North Africa but he could describe the fear and trepidation felt waiting to go ashore during the invasion, his first nights sleep in North Africa spent in his overcoat in a sandy foxhole on the beach, covered with a gas cape as rain began to fall. He described endless hours of surgery performed with bare hands and practically no supplies, tending the wounded under sniper fire. He spoke of the pride felt backing up "a very famous division of the United States Army . . . They were well pleased with our work." He went on to ask Jen to, ". . . tell Freddy

Frederick Mackenbrock (second from right)

that he has no need to be ashamed of his dad . . . I am sending Freddy a small American flag worn by his daddy the first time he went into action as a medical officer in the United States Army and as a member of one of the first American task forces in action in this war. It is dirty and soiled but was worn honorably." Further he stated, ". . . I guess I am only a family man at heart. I don't even want to cross the Missouri river when I return."

Madigan, Margaret
Margaret was a nurse with the 48th/128th Evacuation Hospital. She

met and married Leslie Jones, a member of the unit.

Malecha, Joseph A.
Joseph entered the United States Army in 1941. He was one of the original group ordered to Ft. Frances E. Warren, Wyoming.

Malfa, Sol A.
Sol was from New York.

Malfa, Vincent
Vincent was from New York.

Mansfield, Capt. Max R.
Max was in charge of receiving and evacuation with the unit.

Mapes, Albert E. 'Shorty'
Albert entered the United States Army in 1941. He was one of the original group ordered to Ft. Francis E. Warren, Wyoming. He was from Ponca, Nebraska.

Milton Marmer

Marmer, Dr. Milton J.
Milton was from New York.

Marshbanks, James
James entered the United States Army in 1941. He was one of the original group ordered to Ft. Francis E. Warren, Wyoming.

Martin, Gladys
Gladys Martin was born October 4, 1918 in Shelby County, Kentucky to A.J. and Mary Martin. She was raised on a farm with her four brothers and two sisters. She lost her mother to an accident when she was five. Gladys attended a one-room school in Mt. Eden, Kentucky and graduated from high school in 1937.

She attended nursing school at Baptist Hospital in Louisville, Kentucky and became a Registered Nurse in 1940. She worked at King's Daughter Hospital in Shelbyville, Kentucky for 18 months before moving to Fort Knox's Ireland Hospital in early 1942.

Gladys was commissioned a 2nd Lt. in the ANC in the summer of 1942 and served primarily as a pre-operative shock ward nurse in the 48th Surgical/128th Evacuation Hospital in WWII.

She married 1st Lt. John Flynn of Massachusetts in January 1945. They raised eleven children. John died October 9, 1990 and she passed away January 20, 2000.

Gladys Martin

Martin, Maureen J.
Maureen was a nurse with the 48th/128th Evacuation Hospital. She was

from Florida.

Mathistad, John
John was from Watford City, North Dakota.

Jay Matthews (left)

Matthews, Jay W.
Jay entered the United States Army in 1941. He was one of the original group ordered to Ft. Francis E. Warren, Wyoming. He was from Minnesota.

McBride, Robert W.
Robert entered the United States Army in 1941. He was one of the original group ordered to Ft. Francis E. Warren, Wyoming.

McCafferty, John J.
John entered the United States Army in 1941. He was one of the original group ordered to Ft. Francis E. Warren, Wyoming.

McCullough, Earl
Earl McCullough was born November 27, 1918 in Salem, South Dakota. He joined the United States Army March 1941 and served with the 48th/128th as a medical technician.

Cpl. McCullough was honorably discharged September 19, 1945. Earl met Esther Gossel after his return home from the war. They were married May 3, 1947 in Long Beach, California. They spent several years in California, and then moved back to South Dakota where they spent most of their married years farming. Before retirement they both worked at the public school in Salem, South Dakota. Earl was their custodian and Esther managed the food service. Esther mentioned the many very special trips they enjoyed together before their retirement, and

Earl McCullough (second from right)

the many army reunions attended with the Duxbury's. She said the joys and happiness they shared were many.

The Mc Cullough's had two daughters who are married and are in the teaching profession. They have five grandchildren who have given them much happiness. Earl passed away March 24, 1989.

McDonald, Capt. George J.
George was a urologist with the unit. He was from Pennsylvania.

McGinley, Robert S.
Robert entered the United States Army in 1941. He was one of the original group ordered to Ft.

George McDonald

Francis E. Warren, Wyoming.

McHenry, James P.
James entered the United States Army in 1941. He was one of the original group ordered to Ft. Francis E. Warren, Wyoming.

James McHenry (left)

McIntosh, Dr. Russell B.
Russell was from Michigan.

McNeive, Rosemary
Rosemary was a nurse with the 48th/128th Evacuation Hospital. She married James Mahoney.

McShatko, Lt. Col. George G.

Meier, Jr., 2nd Lt. Rupert
Rupert was assistant Det. Commander with the unit.

Meinders, Marvin H.
Marvin entered the United States Army in 1941. He was one of the original group ordered to Ft. Francis E. Warren, Wyoming. He is from Iowa.

Meinen, Otmer M.
Otmer entered the United States Army in 1941. He was one of the original group ordered to Ft. Francis E. Warren, Wyoming. He was from South Dakota.

Mellies, Dr. Chester A.
Chester was from Missouri.

Meyers, Joseph C.
Joseph entered the United States Army in 1941. He was one of the original group ordered to Ft. Francis E. Warren, Wyoming. He was from Minnesota.

Meyers, Mary
Mary was a nurse with the 48th/128th Evacuation Hospital. She married William De Cindis.

Michel, Arnold A.
Arnold entered the United States Army in 1941. He was one of the original group ordered to Ft. Francis E. Warren, Wyoming. He was from South Dakota. Arnold passed away in 1983.

Miller, Agnes
Agnes was a nurse with the 48th/128th Evacuation Hospital. She was from Alabama.

Miller, Margaret
Margaret was a nurse with the 48th/128th Evacuation Hospital.

Miller, Mark B.
Mark entered the United States Army in 1941. He was one of the original group ordered to Ft. Francis E. Warren, Wyoming. He was from Salem, South Dakota.

Miller, Violet
Violet was a nurse with the 48th/128th Evacuation Hospital.

Moll, Garnet
Garnet Moll was born November 1, 1913 in Sikeston, Missouri. He entered the United States Army April 7, 1941. Tech 4 Sgt. Moll served with the 48th/128th as X-Ray Technician. Garnet said that the war taught him that all his friends had rights same as he did. So he respected their wishes same as his. He said we all get along much better.

When asked what his most vivid WWII memory was, Garnet said, "I broke my ankle sliding into 2nd base while playing baseball. A cast was put on and I had to decide to go back or stay and work with a cast on my leg. I stayed." When asked which wounded soldier stood out most in his memory, he replied, "A soldier came to his x-ray tent. He had a foot of shrapnel sticking out his front and a foot sticking out of his back. He was shipped back". Garnet said the most difficult part of his job was moving at night and setting up the equipment in the dark. Garnet met Helen Smolecki in the elevator at the La Salle Hotel in downtown Chicago, Illinois. Helen was an elevator operator and Garnet was a bellboy at the same hotel. They were married July 9, 1949 in Chicago, Illinois. The Moll's had four children, three boys and one girl. Helen passed away July 31, 2002.

Moloney, Helen M.
Helen served as a nurse with the 48th/128th. Her field of special training was psychiatry. She received her training at Ft. Slocum, New Rochelle, New York before joining the unit in February 1942. Like many other nurses in the unit, she went ashore at Arzew with the Rangers, dealt with the large number of casualties at the Battle of the Bulge, and waded ashore on Utah Beach with guns shooting overhead. Helen met

Helen Moloney

and married Hugh "Rick" Reichert after the war was over. Helen passed away December 2, 2002.

Moore, 1st Lt. Ray J.
Ray was mess officer and Det. C. O. with the unit.

Morgan, George

Morgan, John

Mudge, James P.
James entered the United States Army in 1941. He was one of the original group ordered to Ft. Francis E. Warren, Wyoming.

Murphy, George R.
George entered the United States Army in 1941. He was one of the

original group ordered to Ft. Francis E. Warren, Wyoming.

Murphy, James E.

James entered the United States Army in 1941. He was one of the original group ordered to Ft. Francis E. Warren, Wyoming.

Murphy, Owen B.

Murphy, Sayler B.

Sayler entered the United States Army in 1941. He was one of the original group ordered to Ft. Francis E. Warren, Wyoming.

Nath, Raymond B.

Raymond entered the United States Army in 1941. He was one of the original group ordered to Ft. Francis E. Warren, Wyoming. He was from Sandusky, Ohio.

Nefstead, Raymond B.

Raymond entered the United States Army in 1941. He was one of the original group ordered to Ft. Francis E. Warren, Wyoming. He was from Minnesota.

Nelson, Leo F.

Leo entered the United States Army in 1941. He was one of the original group ordered to Ft. Francis E. Warren, Wyoming. He was from Minnesota.

Nichols, Beatrice E.

Beatrice was a nurse with the 48th/128th Evacuation Hospital.

Nickerson, Emily

Emily was a nurse with the 48th/128th Evacuation Hospital. She met and married R. T. Taylor, who was also with the unit. They had a daughter, Debbie, who lives in Michigan.

Emily Nickerson

Nickles, Amy L.

Amy was a nurse with the 48th/128th Evacuation Hospital. She was from Georgia.

Amy Nickles

Noland, George S.

George entered the United States Army in 1941. He was one of the original group ordered to Ft. Francis E. Warren, Wyoming. He was from Columbus, Ohio.

Nowakowski, Mitchell

Mitchell entered the United State Army in 1941. He was one of the original group ordered to Ft. Francis E. Warren, Wyoming. He was from Ohio.

Ochocki, Stanley S.

Stanley entered the United States Army in 1941. He was one of the

original group ordered to Ft. Francis E. Warren, Wyoming. He was from Hendricks, Minnesota. He passed away in September 1983.

Olson, Melfred J.

Melfred entered the United States Army in 1941. He was one of the original group ordered to Ft. Francis E. Warren, Wyoming. He was from Iowa.

Oppek, Florian J.

Florian entered the United States Army in 1941. He was one of the original group ordered to Ft. Francis E. Warren, Wyoming. He was from Minnesota. He passed away in 1980.

Pagano, Samuel

Pagoria, Joseph

Joseph entered the United States Army in 1941. He was one of the original group ordered to Ft. Francis E. Warren, Wyoming.

Joseph Pagoria (right)

Paniera, Father

Father Paniera was a chaplain with the unit.

Pappas, Paul C.

Paul entered the United States Army in 1941. He was one of the original group ordered to Ft. Francis E. Warren, Wyoming. He was from Morton Grove, Illinois.

Parker, Edna M.

Edna was a nurse with the 48th/128th Evacuation Hospital.

Parks, Ruth

Ruth was a nurse with the 48th/128th Evacuation Hospital.

Patton, John W.

John entered the United States Army in 1941. He was one of the original group ordered to Ft. Francis E. Warren, Wyoming. He was from Ohio.

Paustis, Edward E.

Edward entered the United States Army in 1941. He was one of the original group ordered to Ft. Francis E. Warren, Wyoming. He was from Illinois.

Payan, Jose E.

Peake, Col. Ben

Peterson, Stanley

Peterson, Theodore C.

Theodore entered the United States Army in 1941. He was one of the original group ordered to Ft. Francis E. Warren, Wyoming.

Pettingill, Janet
Janet was a nurse with the 48ᵗʰ/128ᵗʰ Evacuation Hospital. She was from Maine.

Pewitt, Robert

Pigoni, Wino

Platt, Harold W.
Harold entered the United States Army in 1941. He was one of the original group ordered to Ft. Francis E. Warren, Wyoming.

Popeck, Jr., Robert
Robert entered the United States Army in 1941. He was one of the original group ordered to Ft. Francis E. Warren, Wyoming. He was from Michigan.

Power, Allen R.

Power, John J.
John was a chaplain with the unit.

Predovitch, Dr. Milan
Milan was from Colorado.

Chaplain John Power (center)

Pridham, Dorothy
Dorothy was a nurse with the 48ᵗʰ/128ᵗʰ Evacuation Hospital.

Proffitt, Sr., Lt. Col. William E.
William was executive officer of the unit.

Purnell, Carrie E.
Carrie was a nurse with the 48ᵗʰ/128ᵗʰ Evacuation Hospital.

Rainey, Maj. Harry C.
Harry was a neuropsychiatrist with the unit.

Rascop, Felix H.
Felix entered the United States Army in 1941. He was one of the original group ordered to Ft. Francis E. Warren, Wyoming. He was from Illinois.

William Proffitt (right)

Rasmussen, Floyd T.
Floyd entered the United States Army in 1941. He was one of the original group ordered to Ft. Francis E. Warren, Wyoming. He was from South Dakota.

Reinier, Hugh Willis
Hugh was born September 11, 1912 in

Felix Rascop

Packwood, Iowa. He was called to active duty March 3, 1942 and served with the 48ᵗʰ/128ᵗʰ Evacuation Hospital during WW II as an X-Ray technician. His campaign credits during WW II included, Algeria, Tunisia, Sicily, Normandy, Northern France, Rhineland, Ardennes-Alsace and Central Europe. He was honorably discharged July 28, 1945. Hugh met Margaret A. Bittle in 1946 and married her June 15, 1947. They had one daughter, Linda. He was employed as journeyman electrician both before and after serving in the army. He also worked as an X-ray technician/inspector. He retired in 1978 at the age of sixty-six. His main hobbies were hunting and fishing. After retirement, he and Margaret purchased a motor home and did extensive traveling across the United States and flew to San Salvador and Guatemala and several Scandinavian countries. He died January 15, 1997.

Hugh Reinier

Renninger, George F.
George entered the United States Army in 1941. He was one of the original group ordered to Ft. Francis E. Warren, Wyoming. He was from Ohio.

Rhoades, Dixon
Dixon entered the United States Army in 1941. He was one of the original group ordered to Ft. Francis E. Warren, Wyoming.

Rickman, Marie H.
Marie was a nurse with the 48ᵗʰ/128ᵗʰ Evacuation Hospital.

Riesenberg, Paul A.
Paul entered the United States Army in 1941. He was one of the original group ordered to Ft. Francis E. Warren, Wyoming. He was from Reading, Ohio.

Rifkin, Capt. Samuel

Rinehart, Elma L.
Elma was a nurse with the 48ᵗʰ/128ᵗʰ Evacuation Hospital.

Ringer, Col. Meritt G.

Samuel Rifkin (left)

Ritter, D. R.
D. R. was from Oklahoma.

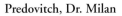
Paul Riesenberg

Roberts, Wiley L.
Wiley entered the United States Army in 1941. He was one of the

Wiley Roberts (far right)

original group ordered to Ft. Francis E. Warren, Wyoming.

Rodgers, Kate
Kate was a nurse with the 48th/128th Evacuation Hospital. She was from Houston, Texas.

Rohlf, Capt. Edward L.
Edward was a operating surgeon with the unit.

Rollins, William R.
William entered the United States Army in 1941. He was one of the original group ordered to Ft. Francis E. Warren, Wyoming.

Romohr, Gladys
Gladys was a nurse with the 48th/128th Evacuation Hospital.

Rosenbaum, Maj. Edward E.
— by G. Jesse Flynn

Edward Rosenbaum was instrumental in encouraging me and assisting with his vast knowledge of the 48th/128th. I spent several weekends in Portland with the Rosenbaums and had quite an enjoyable visit.

A biography of Ed would probably take a volume, so I chose an article written in 2001 about a Chair at Oregon Health and Science University in his name. It reads as follows:

"Oregon Health and Science University...is committing $1 million to establish the Edward E, Rosenbaum chair for the study of inflammatory diseases in honor of a pioneering Oregon physician and his family.

"One of Rosenbaum's books, A Taste of My Own medicine, is about his experiences as a patient. The book was made into the movie The Doctor....[It] is now required viewing for new employees at several major medical centers such as the MD Anderson Hospital in Houston. Rosenbaum, who wrote about his own experience as a patient with laryngeal cancer, lectured internationally while in his 70s about humanitarian issues in medicine.

"[Rosenbaum] began the private practice of rheumatology in Portland in 1948, having trained at the Mayo Clinic with a future Nobel laureate, Philip Hench. He had served five years in the armed forces and earned a Bronze Star in World War II for his role in trauma care for five divisions during the invasion of Normandy, June and July, 1944. He was part of one of the first MASH units.

"He established the division for Arthritis and Rheumatic Diseases at OHSU's medical school in 1950. For more than 30 years he donaated his time each week to supervise a clinic at the medical school for patients with rheumatoid arthritis and other inflammatory conditions. Seven full-time physicians and five Ph.D. researchers now make up this division.

"Rosenbaum was also a pioneer in exploring the potential role of DMSO in treating arthritic diseases. His collaboration with Dr. Stanley Jacob was featured in photo essays in Life and the Saturday Evening Post. He edited a book on the chemical properties of DMSO.

"Now [December 2001] 86 years old, Rosenbaum lives with his wife of 59 years, Davida, in a West Hills home they purchased in 1949....Ed and Dee have four sons, including three physicians and an attorney." —*Article courtesy of The Scribe, a publication of the Portland Medical Society*

Rosencrans, Capt. Harold S.
Harold specialized in dentistry with the unit.

Rourk, Alva C.

Rousu, Ruben A.
Ruben entered the United States Army in 1941. He was one of the original group ordered to Ft. Francis E. Warren, Wyoming. He was from Minnesota.

Ruddy, E. J.
E. J. was from Iowa.

Rutledge, Capt. Samuel H., Jr.
Samuel was in charge of receiving and evacuation with the unit.

Ryan, Ernest J.
Ernest entered the United States rmy in 1941. He was one of the original group ordered to Ft. Francis E. Warren, Wyoming.

Sacks, Eva R.
—by G. Jesse Flynn
Eva Sacks was born in Philadelphia, Pennsylvania. She was a supervisor of nurses at Jewish Hospital in

Ernest Ryan (left)

Dr. Ed Rosenbaum and sons, 2001.

Eva Sacks

Philadelphia before she entered the United States Army. Eva, along with fifty-six other nurses, was assigned to the 48th/128th Evacuation Hospital. Her job in a tent hospital near the lines included not only nursing but directing hard-working enlisted men to heat water on pot-bellied stoves, feed, bathe, shave, and bandage the patients. Eva never felt in danger. She had great faith in our American Airforces to take care of them and not let any Germans strafe them. She gave high praise for General Patton whom, she said, everyone is "crazy about."

A personal remembrance by the author: "Eva Lebby was known as Aunt Eva to the Flynn children. She lived with her husband, Bill Lebby, in Philadelphia and visited our home in Massachusetts in the 1950s on a regular basis. She and "Uncle Bill" would come to Kentucky during the summers in the 1960s. I had an opportunity to go with them to Philadelphia in 1966 and spend a week. She also hosted my oldest sister, Mary, in her nursing education at Einstein Medical Center in Philadelphia. Mom (Gladys Martin Flynn) remained as close to Eva over the years as any friend with whom she served."

Sagan, Julian W.
Julian entered the United States Army in 1941. He was one of the original group ordered to Ft. Francis E. Warren, Wyoming. He was from Michigan.

Salisbury, Elmer G.
Elmer entered the United States Army in 1941. He was one of the original group ordered to Ft. Francis E. Warren, Wyoming. He was from Michigan.

Salmon, Arnold L.
Arnold entered the United States Army in 1941. He was one of the original group ordered to Ft. Francis E. Warren, Wyoming. He was from Canova, South Dakota.

Salter, Lt. Col. A. L.

Sampson, Lawrence
Lawrence was from South Dakota.

Sanders, Harm D.
Harm entered the United States Army in 1941. He was one of the original group ordered to Ft. Francis E. Warren, Wyoming. He was from Minnesota.

Sanders, Willard
Willard was from Glasgow, Kentucky.

Sapienza, Rocco
Rocco was from Illinois.

Harm Sanders

Scannel, Raymond

Schafer, Dr. W. B.

Scheiber, Frederick H.
Frederick entered the United States Army in 1941. He was one of the original group ordered to Ft. Francis E. Warren, Wyoming. He was from Ohio.

Schmitt, Joseph

Schulz, Harold F.
Harold entered the United States Army in 1941. He was one of the original group ordered to Ft. Francis E. Warren, Wyoming. He was from Howard, South Dakota.

Schwade, Capt. Leonard Jerome
—by Dr. Schwade's children, Fran Meyers, Sandy Schmidt, and Jim Schwade:

Leonard Schwade was born July 1, 1911 in Odessa, Russia. Leonard entered the United States Army July 15, 1942. He left for Europe on August 18, 1942, arriving in Europe on August 31, 1942. Captain Schwade served as a physician and surgeon with the 48th/128th Evacuation Hospital, specializing in proctology. He served in Tunisia, Sicily, Normandy, France, Rhineland, Ardennes, Central Europe, and Algeria. He was awarded the EAME ribbon with eight bronze stars and one arrowhead. Schwade was honorably discharged November 22, 1945.

Before WWII, Dr. Schwade was a resident at County Hospital, Milwaukee, Wisconsin. One of his fellow residents arranged a blind date for him with Esther Temkin Liebman. They went out on several dates, but then he left for West Virginia to work as a physician in a small town. He came back after a year, took her out again, and asked her to marry him. He then left his position in West Virginia, moved back to Milwaukee, and married Esther April 10, 1938. They were blessed with three children, a son, James (Jim), and two daughters, Sandra (Sandy), and Frances (Fran).

Dr. Schwade passed away February 10, 2001. His wife Esther, with daughters Sandy and Fran, and son Jim, answered the following questions that I asked about Dr. Schwade. How did the war change his way of looking at life? "Before the war, everyday life was rather ordinary and taken for granted by our dad. He was proud to be a doctor and took his work very seriously. When he went into the war, his life was literally put in constant danger for three years, and he was living in completely unfamiliar, unreliable, frightening circumstances . . . with no way to predict the outcome or the future. Therefore, when he returned to the U.S. in 1945, he found everyday ordinary life very satisfying. He did not need to be the center of attention or seek extra excitement. He lived an honest life, dedicated to his profession, family and friends. The mundane was now very much

Leonard Schwade

appreciated and gratifying."

What was the greatest lesson WWII experiences taught him? "Our father participated as a physician in WWII. He always believed in the cause and thought the war was worth fighting. After the war, he felt fortunate to return to a peaceful life in a country that believed in freedom. He was always grateful to have returned from his war experiences without injury, live peacefully with his family, and practice medicine."

What was his most vivid WWII memory? "Our dad would definitely say the most vivid and most difficult memory of WWII was the Invasion of Normandy! As part of the medical unit, the physicians and nurses followed the young soldiers onto the beaches. He would tell of some soldiers carrying much equipment and being hit as they ran onto the beach. He also remembered the many bodies floating in the water who did not reach the beach. The devastation, injuries and death of this invasion were always vivid in his memory. He always said the movie "Saving Private Ryan," did not begin to show how awful it was!"

What wounded soldiers stood out most vividly in his memory? "#1) Leonard's youngest brother, Laurence (Lorrie) Schwade had been shot, and dad went to Nancy, France to visit him in the hospital. The unit was using triage to treat the wounded. One of the doctors noticed Lorrie's dog tag and asked him if he knew Dr. Leonard Schwade. Lorrie said that was his brother . . . so they immediately moved him to another area and began treating him. Lorrie always thought that this saved his life. #2) Our dad talked about a very young soldier whose leg was mangled and was very scared. My dad and another doctor of higher rank disagreed on whether the leg needed to be amputated . . . my dad trying to save it. The higher ranked doctor decided to amputate the leg . . . leaving my dad always feeling so badly about this. #3) An officer came to see my dad with the complaint of rectal bleeding. As a proctologist, he found a piece of pipe, made a makeshift proctascope, and examined the officer. My dad then sent him back to the U.S.; the doctors there removed the malignancy . . . and the officer always credited my dad with saving his life. #4) A German soldier was wounded and came to my dad's unit. The soldier was scared and needed blood. My dad assured him they would take good care of him, and he gave him the transfusion. However, at the last minute my dad leaned down and whispered in the German's ear that he was getting blood from a Jewish soldier.

What was the most difficult part of his job? "The big picture: the horrors of war, the devastation, the young wounded soldiers, and the deaths were things no one could ever get used to. It was always difficult seeing so many young soldiers die or be debilitated. Our dad was a gentle man, who probably used his dedication, good nature, and good sense of humor to survive. 2) Adjusting to the sparse, difficult living conditions and living in a tent were never easy or pleasant. 3) It was difficult when he was hospitalized with malaria. 4) And, of course, the most difficult was being away from family, his wife Esther and daughter Francie, who was 2 years old when he left. During the entire three years he was away, we never spoke to him on the phone and we never saw him, until he returned in 1945. However, my mother and dad wrote letters to each other every day. My mother kept a very complete scrapbook of the war years and the things he sent."

What was the best part of his job? "I honestly think he would say there was no good part to being in this world war and seeing so many people wounded or dying. However, he was proud to be a physician where he could save lives. He took care of the wounded with great skill, gentleness and caring. He also made many close friends with the men and women in his unit. For many years he continued to correspond with his war buddies."

Self, Gladys B.

Gladys Self

Gladys was born March 9, 1911 in Oxford, Alabama. Gladys enlisted in the Army Nurse Corps on January 21, 1942 at Ft. McClellan, Alabama. She was commissioned a 2nd Lt and served in England, North Africa and Sicily with the 48th/128th Evacuation Hospital. After separating from the 128th in Sicily, she went on to serve with another evacuation hospital in Italy. Gladys was awarded the "Bronze Star" while serving on the European-African Middle Eastern Campaign.

On her return home trip after the war ended, she was aboard the ship S.S. Mariposa, where she (as a passenger) volunteered for duty and worked throughout the voyage on the ward. The work was especially appreciated as very few trained medical enlisted personnel were available for the care of a large number of seriously ill patients.

Transport Surgeon, Major Paul D. Garvin was quoted as saying, "Lt. Self's work was of the highest type and her cheerful performance of duty did much to raise the morale of the patients. She is worthy of the highest commendation and her services contributed greatly to the efficient functioning of the Medical Department." Major Gladys B. Self retired from the service April 30, 1961. Gladys died May 3, 1984. She never married.

Shanks, Hunter W.

Hunter entered the United States Army in 1941. He was one of the original group ordered to Ft. Francis E. Warren, Wyoming.

Sheridan, Vivian

Vivian was a nurse with the 48th/128th Evacuation Hospital.

Shiffler, Capt. Harry Kirby

Harry was an anesthetist with the unit. He was from Iowa. Harry passed away December 1, 1983.

Silva, Torivio

Torivio entered the United States Army in 1941. He was one of the original group ordered to Ft. Francis E. Warren, Wyoming.

Frank Simion

Silverberg, Maurice A.
Maurice entered the United States Army in 1941. He was one of the original group ordered to Ft. Francis E. Warren, Wyoming.

Simion, Frank A.
Frank entered the United States Army in 1941. He was one of the original group ordered to Ft. Francis E. Warren, Wyoming. He met and married Doris "Britt" Brittingham, a nurse from the unit.

Skiver, Herman I.
Herman entered the United States Army in 1941. He was one of the original group ordered to Ft. Francis E. Warren, Wyoming.

Smith, Carrie
Carrie was a nurse with the 48th/128th Evacuation Hospital. She was from Virginia.

Smith, Delmer I.
Delmer entered the United States Army in 1941. He was one of the original group ordered to Ft. Francis E. Warren, Wyoming. He was from Michigan.

Smith, Edward J.
Edward entered the United States Army in 1941. He was one of the original group ordered to Ft. Francis E. Warren, Wyoming.

Smith, George

Smith, Gilbert
Gilbert Smith was born September 10, 1919 in Haywarden, Iowa. His parents were Mable (Johnson) and Porter Smith. Gilbert attended school in Hudson, South Dakota. He entered the United States Army March 19, 1941 and was one of the original members of the 48th Surgical Hospital when it was activated in February 1942 at Ft. Francis E. Warren, Wyoming.

T/3 Smith was a surgical technician with the unit. He served in Algeria, Tunisia, Sicily, Normandy, Northern France, Central Europe and the Rhineland in Germany. When I asked "Gib" how the war changed his way of looking at life, he said it made him realize how precious life is and since the war he has looked on the bright side. When asked what the greatest lesson WWII experiences taught him, he said how lucky he felt to live in the USA. His most vivid memory of WWII was the landing at Utah Beach in Normandy. The horrors of war also remain in his memory, such as the young patient

Gilbert Smith

brought in with a bazooka shell sticking out the front side and out the backside of his abdominal area. They had to remove the shell, which was still armed. The shell miraculously missed all vital organs and the patient lived. The job that has haunted him the most is the enormous amount of amputations of arms and legs he assisted in surgery. After removal, the limbs were stacked outside the tent like cordwood. A burial detail would come by every morning to remove them for burial. His memory of Kasserine Pass in Africa is one of great stress and urgency. The Germans pushed through and we counterattacked headed out in open country where the 48th was located. A General approached the hospital unit and yelled that the German's had broken through and why were they still there? The General said they had 30 to 45 minutes to get packed and ready to leave and a space would be left in the convoy for them. The unit was told if they did not get all the patients loaded in time, that they were to have volunteers to remain behind with the critically wounded and they would be taken prisoners. "Gib" said that you would not believe how fast they loaded! No one was left behind. The best part of his job was being able to help the wounded infantrymen. "Gib" said he felt sorry for them and knew they hadn't seen an American woman in months. The nurses got an allotment for liquor and beer the first of the month. Those nurses that did not drink alcohol would give up their allotment. The enlisted men were not allowed to socialize with the nurses as the nurses outranked them; so careful planning resulted in a party that definitely cheered up the wounded infantrymen.

Speaking of booze . . . it was a known fact that several trucks had 5-gallon spare gas tanks in the front, one on each side. The spare gas turned out to be wine. "Gib" was honorably discharged from the army August 22, 1945. On his return home to Hudson, South Dakota, he married his high school sweetheart, Gladys (Wold) September 9, 1945. They have two children, a son, Gary and a daughter, Linda. Gladys passed away August 18, 1996.

Smith, John
John was from Oregon.

Snyder, Lt. Col. John M.
John was chief of surgical service with the unit. He was from Pennsylvania.

Solomon, Capt. David

Sorlie, Arnum L.
Arnum Sorlie was born April 14, 1919 in Hudson, South Dakota. He was a cousin to Oliver Sorlye also from Hudson. Arnum's job with the unit was to type all the patients names and personal information as they were

David Solomon (right)

brought in to the hospital. He served in Algeria, Tunisia, Sicily, Normandy, Northern France, Central Europe and the Rhineland in Germany. Arnum was awarded the "Normandy Medal" in 1999, for his part in the landing, which his wife, Fay accepted for him. Arnum passed away March 1, 1991.

Sorlye, Oliver A.
—by G. Jesse Flynn

Wednesday, January 9, 2002 about 3:30 p.m. I rented a car at the Omaha, Nebraska airport and headed north to South Dakota. I arrived at Oliver's house just after dark. I hadn't announced my arrival because he had no phone. Snow covered the vast cornfields and the moon was breaking through the clouds as I pulled in the drive. I saw no car, but a light showing through the kitchen window toward the rear of the house. I parked the car and I could see Oliver in the kitchen reading. He came out the door and asked me if I was lost. I yelled back and identified myself. Recogniz- ing my voice, Oliver fought back tears as he invited me in. As I expected, he was dressed in overalls and a sweater.

Oliver Sorlye (right)

He gave me a bear hug and dragged me into the kitchen. It was a room about 12 x 15 feet with a wood-burning cook stove with the door open for heat. The table where he had been seated contained a stack of magazines, and a rabbit-eared TV was in the opposite corner of the room with the national news playing. A neatly made army cot was on the far side of the kitchen. We sat down and chatted for forty-five minutes and then at my suggestion we departed to visit Bill Thorson, son of his recently deceased best friend and comrade in the 48th/128th and his family who lived about ten miles away. The roads were mostly unpaved, but well maintained. They were graded with a brownish stone. Bill lived in a house formerly occupied by his father. It was a two story brick of 1940's vintage surrounded by a clump of trees and several outbuildings and grain storage buildings. I had been to this house eighteen months before when Bill's father, Charlie, had died. Oliver and I got out of the car and were greeted by Bill's wife and three children. We went into the house and proceeded to review Charlie's photo albums and discuss the situation in Hudson, South Dakota in the early 1940's.

Oliver, Charlie and ten other young men answered the call to duty in 1942 on the same day. Oliver was born August 26, 1912 in Hudson, South Dakota. He was one of nine children. He entered the United States Army March 19, 1941 and was honorably discharged August 22, 1945. His duties in the army included truck/ambulance driver and overall maintenance of the medical unit. Oliver spent more than three years in Africa and Europe. The memories of the war still haunt him. He chokes up with the thought of his comrades lying dead in the snow in the winter of '44 at the Battle of the Bulge. "The Germans lined up a lot of medical men and shot them at Malmedy, Belgium," he says. He remembers carrying the dead, knee deep in mud to the morgue. "It was awful," he says. Oliver was awarded the Bronze Star in Germany, a medal of which he is very proud.

My favorite story recited to me by Oliver involving my dad was as follows: "It was a cold rainy night in Belgium and the shrapnel from our anti-aircraft guns had torn numerous holes in the tents. I had been patching holes since early in the morning and finished the last about 10:30 p.m. Your dad called me into his tent – thanked me for a good job and handed me a canteen. It was the best whisky I've ever tasted."

Oliver and his wife, Marie, never had children. Marie died July 18, 1985.

Spears, Lois A.
Lois was a nurse with the 48th/128th Evacuation Hospital.

Sramcik, Margaret
Margaret was a nurse with the 48th/128th Evacuation Hospital. She was from Cambridge, Ohio.

Standley, Hazel C.
Hazel was a nurse with the 48th/128th Evacuation Hospital.

Stanfill, Margaret B.
Margaret was a nurse with the 48th/128th Evacuation Hospital.

Margaret Stanfill

Stappenbeck, Dr. Richard

Steinmetz, John E.
John entered the United States Army in 1941. He was one of the original group ordered to Ft. Francis E. Warren, Wyoming. He was from Ohio.

Stephens, Frank E.

Stephenson, Russell
Russell was from Oklahoma.

Stevenson, Paul W.
Paul entered the United States Army in 1941. He was one of the original group ordered to Ft. Francis E. Warren, Wyoming. He was from Iowa.

Stone, James O.
James entered the United States Army in 1941. He was one of the original group ordered to Ft. Francis E. Warren, Wyoming. He was from Henderson, Kentucky.

Stratton, Harold H.
Harold entered the United States Army in 1941. He was one of the original group ordered to Ft. Francis E. Warren, Wyoming.

Straub, Paul R.
Paul entered the United States Army in 1941. He was one of the original group ordered to Ft. Francis E. Warren, Wyoming.

Strode, J. R.
J. R. was from Tompkinsville, Kentucky.

Stubbs, Howard W.
Howard entered the United States Army in 1941. He was one of the original group ordered to Ft. Francis E. Warren, Wyoming. He was from Iowa.

Sturdevant, Richard H.
Richard entered the United States Army in 1941. He was one of the original group ordered to Ft. Francis E. Warren, Wyoming.

Sullivan, Mary Ann
Mary Ann was the chief nurse with the 48th/128th Evacuation Hospital. She was from Maine.

Sundby, Karnes
Karnes was from Montana.

Surmeyer, Orville J.
Orville entered the United States Army in 1941. He was one of the original group ordered to Ft. Francis E. Warren, Wyoming.

Bruce Sutton

Sutton, Capt. Bruce B.
Bruce was a ward officer with the unit.

Sutton, Ralph E.
Ralph entered the United States Army in 1941 from Camp Robinson, Little Rock Arkansas. He was one of the original group ordered to Ft. Francis E. Warren, Wyoming. He served as a truck driver with the unit. Ralph was from Hopkinsville, Kentucky. He passed away in 1980.

Svec, James
James entered the United States Army in 1941. He was one of the original group ordered to Ft. Francis E. Warren, Wyoming. He was from Illinois.

Swan, Wesley
Wesley was from Colorado.

Swaney, Edith M.
Edith was a nurse with the 48th/128th Evacuation Hospital.

Swanson, Jack
Jack was from Iowa.

Swezey, John P.
John entered the United States Army in 1941. He was one of the original group ordered to Ft. Francis E. Warren, Wyoming. Surgery Technician-4th Swezey was a tentmate with George Willett. He was from Kansas.

Tall, Vernon

Tarr, Oliver W.
Oliver entered the United States Army in 1941. He was one of the original group ordered to Ft. Francis E. Warren, Wyoming. He was from Ohio.

Taylor, Edward

Taylor, Gerald C.
Gerald Taylor was born September 10, 1919 in Oregon, Missouri. Gerald entered the United States Army December 6, 1940 and served as NCO in charge of

Edward Taylor (left)

laboratory with the 48th/128th Evacuation Hospital. Tech. Sgt. Taylor was honorably discharged July 15, 1945. After landing on the beach at Arzew, Algeria on November 8, 1942, he and Jim Murphy, from Iowa, dug a foxhole large enough for two people. Before relaxing for the night they lined the foxhole with tent canvas as a barrier against the sand. They neglected, however, to stabilize the walls of sand. During the late evening hours, one of their members, reeling from too much stimulant from the bottle, decided to take a stroll through the camping area, thus walking too close to the foxhole causing the wall of sand to cave in on the occupants. Murphy, getting the worse of it arose with a vengeance and while spitting sand and glaring through sand-filled eyes described the culprit with language that would cause

Gerald Taylor

Satan to blush. Murphy then recognized the somewhat unsteady individual as one of their commissioned officers. This was surely the only time Murphy was privileged to be disrespectful to a superior officer.

Gerald soon learned that the local water was unsatisfactory for certain laboratory procedures and they had no means of distilling water. The problem was solved when a member of the laboratory crew suggested using rainwater, since it was raining every day. A square of canvas supported by four poles served as a collecting basin and the problem was solved. After a few weeks in Arzew they were transported to central Tunisia just outside Kasserine Pass.

When Rommel's African force was

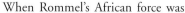

retreating northward in Tunisia, he took time out to punish the troop of GI's holding the Pass. Being outgunned and out armored, the forces retreated to the rear. Gerald and Jim Murphy along with several others volunteered to stay behind with the patients in the event of capture. This, thankfully, did not happen and they were evacuated to Northern Tunisia.

As a designated NCO in charge of the laboratory, he was fortunate to have a capable crew of Maurice Halverson, who came up with new ideas and kept them in good moral with his wit; Leon Weiss who seemed to speak the language at any location; Sammy Kutner who could spend an hour at a microscope to find one organism, and "Tex" Luedecke, who was quite proud of his home town which was Cat Springs, Texas.

Upon landing in Sicily they were trucked to a beautiful setting on the northwest coast of Sicily, with high cliffs overlooking the Tyrrhenian Sea and a short distance west of Palermo, the capital. Two things he remembered during the trip were the enormous number of small children lining the streets of the small villages and tomato paste drying on the roofs without protection from flies. His unit landed at Newport Wales on or about November 1, 1943. They were trucked to a location near Chipping Sadbury a short distance North of Bristol where they spent the next six months. London, Stratford of Avon, Stonehenge were among the many sights he was able to visit. They were housed on an estate with a large mansion (the "castle"), which was said to contain eighty rooms each with a fireplace.

On or about June 4, 1944 they were transported to an "unknown destination", which turned out to be Falmouth on the English Channel. On D-Day plus four, June 10, 1944, they anchored off Utah Beach. They were awakened the first morning with a blaring of air raid sirens. Since there were no foxholes aboard ship, the only recourse was a position face down and praying. Fortunately their ship was spared. Their stay at this location was a short one. After about a month they were on their way again passing through a countryside filled with dead cows, Germans, and bomb craters. They arrived in Southern Belgium and were trapped and rescued in the Battle of the Bulge.

Gerald met Mary Jane Pistorius at Kansas University in Lawrence, Kansas. They were married August 6, 1950 and had four children, two boys and two girls. Gerald and Mary Jane reside in Decatur, Georgia.

Taylor, Kathryn R.
Kathryn was a nurse with the 48th/128th Evacuation Hospital.

Taylor, R. T.
R. T. met and married Emily Nickerson, a nurse with the unit.

Tello, Dr. Rocko

Thoeny, Ralph H.
Ralph entered the United States Army in 1941. He was one of the original group ordered to Ft. Francis E. Warren, Wyoming. He was from Iowa.

Thomas, Leonard
Leonard worked in the head and spine ward alongside Jodie Harmon and Doris Brittingham.

Thompson, Julia D.
Julia was a nurse with the 48th/128th Evacuation Hospital.

Thorson, Charles
Charles "Charlie" Thorson was born March 28, 1918, on a farm in Lincoln County, South Dakota. He grew up and attended a country school in Highland Township. Charlie entered the United States Army March 19, 1941. He served with the 48th/128th in the European Theater. Corporal Thorson was a truck driver for the unit. Charlie married Anona Ulrickson Hall December 9, 1961. They made their home on a farm south of Canton, South Dakota.

Charlie Thorson

Charlie passed away June 5, 2001. He is survived by his wife Anona; a son, Bill Thorson; two stepsons, Robert Hall and Cameran Hall; two stepdaughters, Cathryn and Elizabeth and several grandchildren.

Tisler, Joseph

Tonzes, Berneice A.
Berneice was a nurse with the 48th/128th Evacuation Hospital.

Toschi, Aldo

Treece, Thomas J.
Thomas entered the United States Army in 1941. He was one of the original group ordered to Ft. Francis E. Warren, Wyoming.

Tropea, Jr., Capt. Frank
Frank was a thoracic surgeon with the unit.

Tyler, Eunice C.
Eunice was a nurse with the 48th/128th Evacuation Hospital.

Urbanski, Joseph L.
Joseph entered the United States Army in 1941. He was one of the original group ordered to Ft. Francis E. Warren, Wyoming.

Van Delinder, Scott
Scott entered the United States Army in 1941. He was one of the original group ordered to Ft. Francis E. Warren, Wyoming.

Van Woert, Dwight E.
Dwight Van Woert was born July 27, 1912 at Canistota, South Dakota. Dwight entered the service March 1941 and was honorably discharged

Dwight Van Woert and wife, Maxine

September 1945. Pfc. Van Woert served along side with his fellow comrades of the 48th/128th Evacuation Hospital in Algeria, Tunisia, Sicily, England, Belgium, Normandy and the Battle of the Bulge. He was awarded eight battle stars and one good conduct medal. His duties were helping out in the hospital wards and taking care of patients.

Dwight married Maxine McKillop, June 1, 1960. This was their second marriage due to the death of their spouses. Dwight and Maxine have known each other most of their lives. They grew up on farms close to each other and even dated each other before marrying others. They raised three children, two sons from her first marriage and a daughter from their marriage. Maxine spoke of the sadness and heartbreak they suffered at the loss of both sons, Dr. Dennis Ondrozeck, a professor of music for over twenty-two years with a doctorate in piano, and was the first American pianist to play concerts in East Germany after the wall came down. Dennis died at the young age of forty-nine. The other son, Donald Ondrozeck, was a Viet Nam Veteran who received a presidential citation for work above and beyond the call of duty. Donald also died at an early age of fifty.

Dwight now resides in a nursing home due to Parkinson's disease. They both enjoy spending time with their daughter, Donna and their three beautiful granddaughters.

Veres, Charles J.

Charles entered the United States Army in 1941. He was one of the original group ordered to Ft. Francis E. Warren, Wyoming. He was from Ohio.

Vogler, Vilma E.

Vilma or "Vogie" as she was called by her comrades during WW II, was born August 13, 1909 in Chippewa Falls, Wisconsin. She was one of nine children. Along with her brothers and sisters, she attended a one-room grade school for her first eight years of schooling.

When Vilma was eleven years old, her mother died of lung cancer at Christmas time. This and the death of her only sister in a car accident, at the same time of the year seventeen years later, made the Christmas season a sad time for her. Nursing became her lifetime career when she entered the three-year diploma program at Luther Hospital in Eau Claire, Wisconsin in the fall of 1927. She

Vilma Vogler

went to Ann Arbor, Michigan in the late 30's for additional training in her field. In 1939 she and a friend joined the Red Cross Army Nurse Corps for two years.

With the declaration of war in 1941, she began the long, arduous journey of her career as an army nurse in the 48th/128th Evacuation Hospital. Her war duty took her through the African campaign, and the wet, cold muddy Sicily campaign, the Normandy campaign and the Battle of the Bulge. Vilma carried an Army issue steel helmet, a gas mask, a 26-pound pack loaded with rations and canteens of water. Her job with the 128th Evac. was working with the chest and abdominal injury soldiers. Vilma served a total of forty-two months overseas, retiring with the rank of captain. She came home very weary and emotionally exhausted. She was rather silent about those awful years.

On separation from the military, she moved to Milwaukee and worked at a Veterans hospital. She continued to care for the men she had seen suffer so much and sacrifice their youth for their country. Vilma retired in 1969 at the age of sixty. Vilma died February 22, 2001. She never married.

Wagner, Robert L.

Robert entered the United States Army in 1941. He was one of the original group ordered to Ft. Francis E. Warren, Wyoming.

Wain, Albert E.

Albert entered the United States Army in 1941. He was one of the original group ordered to Ft. Francis E. Warren, Wyoming.

Wahl, Capt. Robert H.

Robert was a ward officer with the unit.

Waller, James A.

James entered the United States Army in 1941. He was one of the original group ordered to Ft. Francis E. Warren, Wyoming.

James Waller

Warner, Wilfred E.

Wilfred entered the United States Army in 1941. He was one of the original group ordered to Ft. Francis E. Warren, Wyoming.

Watson, William

William entered the United States Army in 1941 from Camp Robinson, Little Rock, Arkansas. He was one of the original group ordered to Ft. Francis E. Warren, Wyoming. He was from Hopkinsville, Kentucky.

Weathers, B. P.

Weaver, James A.

James entered the United States Army in 1941. He was one of the original group ordered to Ft. Francis E. Warren, Wyoming.

Weber, Clarence F.

Clarence entered the United States Army in 1941. He was one of the original group ordered to Ft. Francis E. Warren, Wyoming. He was from Bridgewater, South Dakota. Clarence passed away in 1980.

Weber, Leo D.

Leo entered the United States Army in 1941. He was one of the original group ordered to Ft. Francis E. Warren, Wyoming. He was from Minnesota.

Weinberger, Dr. Howard

Weisel, Dr. Wilson

Weiss, Leon

Wertz, Donald

West, Woodrow W.

Woodrow entered the United States Army in 1941. He was one of the original group ordered to Ft. Francis E. Warren, Wyoming.

Wheeler, Ruth E.
—by Patricia Douglas, her daughter

Ruth Wheeler was born in Lowell, Massachusetts February 28, 1920, the eldest daughter in a family of six children. Her mother passed away when she was 15, so the role of motherhood fell to her. This foreshadowed her lifelong profession as a registered nurse. She attended New Hampshire State Hospital School of Nursing in Concord, graduating August 1942 and enlisted in the Army a year later.

Ruth began active duty stateside and arrived at the 128th Evac unit in October 1944. She served as a surgical nurse/anesthetist and attained the rank of 1st Lieutenant. While stationed with the 128th she met her future husband, Corporal Joe Tom Douglas, a medic with the same unit. They were married in Beyreuth, Germany on July 18, 1945, with Sgt. Howard Bellrichard and Caroline Ducibella as attendants.

Following her discharge from the Army she joined Joe in Wewoka, Oklahoma, his hometown. It was quite an adjustment moving from the Boston area to a tiny town in Oklahoma. She was often teased for being a "damn Yankee." Still, she worked very hard to make a place for herself, and before long she was well regarded by neighbors and friends alike. She and Joe had two children—Michael, born in 1946, and Patricia, in 1952.

She was a magnificent seamstress, extremely artistic and creative. She worked for a local crafts store and created a line of doll clothes that she named "Petite Pat" for her daughter. In addition to sewing, Ruth worked as a public health nurse until 1959 when she took over as head nurse for a local nursing home. She was greatly loved by her many patients.

In 1961 she and Joe divorced. She moved with her children to Oklahoma City in mid-1962. There she continued to work in nursing homes for several more years before switching to private duty nursing which allowed her more flexibility and variety. She was a very hard worker and exceptionally dedicated to her work.

Though engaged for a short time, Ruth never remarried. She was active in her church and made sure that her children were, too. She was the first female inducted into the VFW chapter in Oklahoma City, an honor of which she was very proud.

Ruth passed away in her sleep July 13, 1978.

Through the friends I have been blessed to make at the 48th/128th reunions, my mother continues to live in my heart. She did not have an easy life but she lived with a fierce courage and a tenacious, determined sense of decency. I am humbled and honored to be her daughter.

Wheeler, Sarah P.

Sarah was a nurse with the 48th/128th Evacuation Hospital.

Wheeler, Capt. William H.

William was in charge of X-Ray with the unit. He passed away in 1979.

White, Ora
—by G. Jesse Flynn

Ora White was one of the three nurses of the 48th/128th that hailed from the Spencer County/Shelby County Kentucky area. I owe Ora thanks for the diary she kept, parts of which were made available to me. Born on April 9, 1906 in Spencer County, Ora's early years would prove to be difficult ones, suffering first the loss of her father in 1908 followed by her mother's death in 1916. No record exists of how the child Ora absorbed such loss but one can't help but wonder if it did indeed inspire her life's work in nursing. Following her mother's untimely death, Ora was taken in by an older sister and her family. Due to the upheavals of her young life, Ora's notes indicate her education was, on occasion, interrupted. The first mention of college attendance was recorded in 1929, followed by notation of receiving a "Teacher's Certificate" in 1930 after attending Kentucky Western State Teacher's College in Bowling Green, Kentucky. Ora taught in a rural Kentucky school before following her heart's desire and becoming a student of nursing at the Kentucky Baptist Hospital, Louisville, Kentucky in 1933. She was graduated in 1936 at 30 years of age.

While she briefly mentioned two gentleman friends during those years, she bluntly stated in her musings, "Always my friendship with men was not very lasting . . . they were not for me." Instead Ora set her

Ora White (right)

sights on learning all she could about the field of obstetrics and the care of premature, as well as, full term newborns.

Ora didn't dally long after war was declared December of 1941. Along with her longtime friend, Margaret Hornback, Ora White proudly joined the Armed Forces of the United States of America on January 15, 1942. She was sent to near by Fort Knox, Kentucky for training "for overseas duty in a field hospital." Ora spoke sadly of the hours she gave to the Obstetrical Ward at the Post hospital during the training period. It was heartbreaking to see the fathers bid the new baby and mother goodbye, many of them never to return." Lt. White's memories of the camaraderie on the troop train to New York, the group's general aversion to being hailed as "WAC" by New Yorkers ("This was most upsetting, since were of the opinion that we were a special group with an important mission to accomplish."), along with the heady, early morning departure of their ship, slipping past the Statue of Liberty, marked by "high spirits as if on holiday" are suddenly sobered by the realization that the convoy was turning north for the express purpose of eluding German submarines.

Ora departed the United States on August 6, 1942 with the 48th. She wasn't to return until September 3, 1945. She spent those three years exclusively with the 48th/128th. Upon arrival in Europe she was billeted with fellow Kentuckians, Hornback and Martin, as well as Kruzic. Ora's duty assignment with the 128th was Ward 22 where she supervised Pfc. Alvis Davis, T/5 Hoctor, T/5 McLaughlin and T/5 Wertz. Her official Military Record lists as Campaigns: "Algeria, Tunisian, Sicilian, Normandy, Central Europe, Northern France, Ardennes, Rhineland." Ora White participated in the totality of the 128th's service in WW II. And along the way she recorded she was always watching and alert for the treasured features of her beloved nephew, Tom. "On we went across France into Belgium and Germany as if racing with death. On our way we would see cattle and soldiers of every race lying in the fields dead. I kept looking for my oldest nephew, Tom . . ." Through it all she repeatedly underscored that her Christian faith in a loving and merciful God sustained her. Ora received the Bronze Star for her service in Normandy.

Upon her return to civilian life in Louisville, Kentucky, Ora continued to devote herself to maternal and newborn health with emphasis on the care of premature babies. In 1952 she received a B.S. from Indiana University in Nursing Education and later worked with the Maternal and Child Health Council as well as establishing prenatal classes in the late 50's.

Ora White was 90 years of age, being cared for by a niece, Mrs. Anna Clark, when she passed away in Kentucky June 16, 1996.

Whitman, James

James entered the United States Army in 1941 from Camp Robinson, Little Rock, Arkansas. He was one of the original group ordered to Ft. Francis E. Warren, Wyoming. He was from Henderson, Kentucky.

Wildman, James D.

James entered the United States Army in 1941. He was one of the original group ordered to Ft. Francis E. Warren, Wyoming.

Wiley, Col. Norman H.

Willett, George R.
—by G. Jesse Flynn

When I returned from my first 48th/128th reunion in 1998 at Sioux City, South Dakota, I was reviewing the roster of the known living members of the 48th/128th. There was the name George Willett, Louisville, Kentucky. The address was located about ten minutes from my office so I gave him a call and headed over to his nice white frame one story ranch house in south Louisville. George was born July 22,

1918 at Union County, Kentucky.

George and Lucille Laughary met one week before George went overseas at a basketball game on a blind date, got married one week after he returned three plus years later.

He entered the United States Army January 30, 1942 from Camp Robinson, Little Rock Arkansas. He was one of the original group ordered to Ft. Francis E. Warren, Wyoming. He was honorably discharged October 11, 1945.

George returned home on October 12,

George Willett

1945. On October 30, 1945, a Baptist preacher in the town of Madisonville, Kentucky tied the knot with Lucille and him. Two days later they returned to Louisville, Kentucky where they have made their home for over 57 years.

The Willett's have two children, one girl and one boy, five grandchildren, two girls and three boys. They also have one great-grandson.

George worked in the orthopedic ward with Dr. John H. Gordon. He remembers the long twelve-hour shifts working nonstop with only one nurse and two men taking care of forty bed-bound patients. He also worked with nurse, Eva Sacks caring for stomach wound patients.

George was highly praised by correspondent, Cy H. Peterman who was wounded in the Kasserine Pass battle and wrote the following story while in the care of the 48th:

"I marveled at the enlisted men doing the grubbiest of roles without promotion or much recognition, but just as devotedly as the doctors or nurses. They were the unsung Willetts of the medical forces."

"Willett! For me, there was no greater hero in that camp than Private George R. Willett, the kid from Russell, Kentucky. He did the work of two mules. He policed Post-Op Ward 7 with its double row of cots, made beds, served meals, built fires, and lugged water. He washed the dishes three times a day, emptied urinals and bedpans, and hung out blankets when they got full of sand. He fetched cans of fruit juice, blood plasma, hot coffee, and he ran a thousand errands a day. He summoned surgeons, nurses, or doctors, took the mail and brought it back, bathed sore backs when the nurses were swamped, or held a cup to a patient's lips. "Willie" was quite a man. And there were 270 others like him in that encampment on the hill."

Williams, Nell

Nell was a nurse with the 48th/128th Evacuation Hospital.

Willis, Kenneth E.
Ken was born November 27, 1916 in Forest Grove, Oregon. Having joined the United States Army on April 11, 1942, Ken served in the capacity of surgical technician or male nurse, and later he did secretarial work for the X-ray department. He was discharged August 1945.

Kenneth Willis

Ken said he didn't think much of General Patton. General Bradley was ok. Ernie Pyle was "tops" for his write-ups. Ernie remembered the privates. He went in on the third day of the "D" Day invasion in France. He also saw action in Sicily and Africa following General Rommel. Ken served for three years until receiving his Honorable Discharge on October 13, 1945.

His long time friendship with a neighbor girl, Roberta Mott, had grown through correspondence during the war years, and on August 11, 1946, Ken and Roberta were married. They had no children. He'd had enough of war and of hospitals, and he settled happily into farming in partnership with his father, an occupation at which he continued to earn his livelihood until his retirement in 1977.

Among his interests, Ken enjoyed both vegetable and flower gardening, fishing, reading, and traveling to visit his World War II buddies. Ken passed away November 14, 2001.

Willis, Luella
Luella was a nurse with the 48th/128th Evacuation Hospital.

Winzeler, Edwin C.
Edwin entered the United States Army in 1941. He was one of the original group ordered to Ft. Francis E. Warren, Wyoming.

Wood, Walter S.

Woodruff, Melvin S.
Melvin entered the United States Army in 1941. He was one of the original group ordered to Ft. Francis E. Warren, Wyoming. He was from Minnesota.

Woodyard, Marion M.
Marion entered the United States Army in 1941. He was one of the original group ordered to Ft. Francis E. Warren, Wyoming. He was from Iowa.

Zeichner, Edward

Zetterlund, Lawrence
Lawrence was from Duluth, Minnesota.

Zimmerman, Marieta
Marieta was a nurse with the 48th/128th Evacuation Hospital.

Zlataritz, Felix

Marieta Zimmerman

ACKNOWLEDGEMENTS

I hardly know how to begin acknowledging all the people who have been a part of this effort. The many homes I stayed in and families that made me welcome were beyond description. Martha Cameron (retired nurse corps) made me a room and office

away from home for my two visits in her beautiful high-rise condo overlooking Tampa Bay. Jodie and Mary Jo Harmon shared their ranch house in West Texas. Walt and Mayme Larson hosted Elaine and I for a long weekend and a pleasurable tour of the Minnesota countryside. I was twice a guest of Dr. Ed Rosenbaum and his wife, Davida in Portland, Oregon. Genevieve Thompson gave me the excuse to visit Western Washington State (which I found to my surprise was a desert). Margaret Reinier, Cedar Rapids, Iowa, Vaughn Fisher, Clarksburg, West Virginia, Dr. George Howe and his wife, Betty, Brandenton, Florida, George and Lucille Willett, Louisville, Kentucky, and all the South Dakota gang were immensely kind and helpful to me. The South Dakota gang more specifically was Marcus Duxbury, Oliver Sorlye, Gilbert Smith, Charles Thorsen, Bill Thorsen and their families.

Martha Cameron and Jesse Flynn.

Three special people were extraordinarily helpful in providing information, photos and artifacts from their loved ones who are no longer with us. Anna Clark of Mt. Washington, Kentucky is the niece of the late 1st Lt. Ora White. Sandy Schmidt of Milwaukee, Wisconsin, daughter of the late Dr. Leonard Schwade made available photos and the war diary of Dr. Schwade. Isabel Anthony, daughter of Dr. Frank Burton made a similar gesture.

A most fascinating find were the letters of mom's close friend and army nurse, the late Margaret Hornback. These were graciously provided by her niece, Marnie Terhune. They were stored in an old army locker in the Terhune home in Simpsonville, Kentucky. The trunk was stenciled with 1st Lt. John Flynn, Prentice Street, Waltham, Mass. It was gifted to me. Thank you Marnie!

My five-year obsession with this project has been made a pleasure with the help of long time secretary and friend, Rosemary Orr. Along with her typing and retyping of thousands of documents, she helped organize and host two reunions of the unit.

Rosemary Greenlee and Evelyn Monahan are hardworking noteworthy military authors and historians from Atlanta, Georgia who have guided me through much of the process of organization and interview. They assisted me with research and encouragement.

The Reverend Nick Rice, a good friend and spiritual advisor for almost twenty years, read a rough manuscript and gave me the title of the book. Nancy Henry, a professor at

Rosie Orr.

Jesse Flynn, Patrick Flynn, and Joey Dawson at Utah Beach, 1999.

University of New York at Binghampton, had input on organization and other constructive criticism. My business partners have allowed me to make our conference and training rooms military research centers. I have taken days and weeks of time that they have been kind enough not to mention.

My son, Patrick, daughter, Kathleen, and nephew, Joey Dawson, traveled with me through Normandy, France, Belgium and Germany. Kathleen is a professional photojournalist and helped arrange the photos for the book and shot the front cover.

My daughter-in-law, Kate, transcribed many of the interviews that I taped in my travels.

Patrick Flynn and Kathleen Flynn.

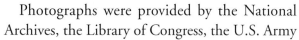

Various statistics and logistical military information was provided by the remarkable book written by Rick Atkinson entitled *Army at Dawn.* Atkinson took the American North African campaign and created a realistic, professional account of the green American Army entering a war two and a half years old. I also relied on various quotes from books written about WWII Army nurse experiences entitled *G.I. Nightingale* by Theresa Archard, *Helmets and Lipstick* by Ruth Haskell (a nurse in the 48th) and *Combat Nurse* by Roberta Tayhoe.

Photographs were provided by the National Archives, the Library of Congress, the U.S. Army

Kate and Patrick Flynn.

Signal Corps (WWII) and the Patton Museum of Cavalry and Armor.

My wife, Elaine, has encouraged me every step of the process. She has co-hosted two unit reunions and attended another with me as well as accompanying me in many of my travels. She has been immensely helpful in constructive criticism, proofreading and feedback. Elaine is my best friend, true partner and has a resolve that has supported my endeavors for over thirty years.

Elaine Flynn.

INDEX

(covering Chapters One through Eight)